*The
New Way
of the
Wilderness*

*Illustrated by Les Kouba*

# The
# New Way
# of the
# Wilderness

Calvin Rutstrum

The Macmillan Company

New York 1958

Second Printing 1960

Printed in the United States of America

Library of Congress Catalog Card Number: 58-5912

To Florence, My Better and More Orderly Half, Who Patiently Edited and Typed the Manuscript, and Who Accuses Me of Splitting Infinitives with More Dexterity Than I Split Wood, I Dedicate This Volume.

# *Foreword*

SINCE PRE-REVOLUTIONARY DAYS AMERICANS HAVE ANSWERED THE call of outdoor life. Such life challenges stamina, wits, and skill. It builds self-reliance, endurance, and lasting health, thus helping to keep our nation strong. No particular benefit or credit, however, accrues to those who merely follow a guide through the wilderness, relieved from all labor.

A majority of the previous works on this subject have come from the pens of writers whose experience has been short, professionally conducted sorties merely into the edge of wild country, in permanent camps and public camp grounds, augmented by what they have read of others who have had like limited experience. Theirs is not the "way of the wilderness." Their methods are of little value to the red-blooded man who feels the call of the wild, to enter an unmapped wilderness, with no outfit other than that carried on his back, in a canoe, on pack horse or on dog sled.

Calvin Rutstrum is a wilderness voyager who has spent much of his life in truly wild country, in fair weather and foul, in summer and winter. Rutstrum "savvies" the bush, and what he tells you in these pages will be a real help to those of you who plan to enter wild country for recreation or for other purposes. He points out in a practical manner the best ways to do things, the easiest way, the way to survive in emergencies, and the way to get real pleasures and benefits that such a life alone can bestow.

Many of us cannot afford the luxuries of all-inclusive outfits, of guides, cooks, and packers, or of modern camps on the fringe. To such this book will appeal, for all of us can assemble a modern little outfit, right but light, and some simple and wholesome grub. Beyond the jumping-off place there is no further expense. We can live there cheaper than at home.

I have been fortunate that my experience has been very like that of Rutstrum. Over a long life I have spent almost all my vacations, many of them long ones, in the wild, unspoiled country that I love.

My great thrill has been that of roaming alone through such lands, finding my way, doing my work, and in many cases wringing shelter and food from Nature.

In my youth I had the fortunate experience of spending nine months in a remote, almost unknown country in companionship of one of the last of our mountain men, and his ways started me right. Other companions have been real woods, plains, and mountain men, and Indians. And so I know that Rutstrum's ways are the ways of the real wilderness, the best, the safest, and the easiest.

It has often been said that you cannot learn such things from books. While experience is the best teacher, we should not neglect the wisdom of the ages laid down in good books. To the reader with a minimum of experience, such books can hasten ripeness of wilderness knowledge.

COL. TOWNSEND WHELEN

# Contents

# Contents

# 1

## The Wilderness Challenge

IN THE SUMMER OF 1927, LILLIAN ALLING, A YOUNG IMMIGRANT, homesick and compelled to perform menial tasks for a living in New York, made up her mind to go back to her homeland in Europe. Because she had no money for transportation, she decided to hike back to her native country. She tramped to Chicago, to Minneapolis, to Winnipeg, refusing all invitations to ride.

She was next seen on the Yukon Telegraph Trail in the northern part of British Columbia, a small pack on her back and a length of iron pipe in her hand for protection, heading toward Alaska. The provincial police at Hazelton prevented her from making a winter journey through the Canadian wilds, but they were able to detain her only until spring.

Starting out again, she hiked along the Telegraph Trail, over the wild mountain passes, finally reaching Dawson. There she worked as a cook, purchased and repaired an old boat, and in the spring of 1929 launched it into the waters of the Yukon River right behind the outgoing ice and reached a point east of the Seward Peninsula. There she abandoned the boat for overland travel, reaching Nome and later Bering Strait. She was last heard of bartering with the Eskimos for boat passage across the strait to Asia.

If you care to check the story, you will find it in the files of the provincial police in British Columbia.

To say that the courageous and almost incredible experience of Lillian Alling is within the bounds of anyone would be presumptuous. Few persons, either men or women, have the hardihood, let

1

alone the ability, to undertake such a journey. My purpose in mentioning it is to show that most of us could undertake a wilderness journey of some kind, and succeed, if we would but arouse our determination, lay our plan, and go ahead with it.

The actual risk that goes with a canoe journey in wilderness waters, a pack-horse trip into the mountains, or a trip by dog sled is no greater than that of participating in vigorous athletics. Bad rapids and many other hazards of the wilds are constant problems to the woodsman; but he treats them as problems to solve—not to fear. Experienced men are cautious; make no mistake about that. I have seen men long accustomed to the saddle walk and lead a horse along a narrow mountain trail; and I have helped old and experienced canoe men make portages around rapids that seemed no great risk to run. This is the common sense of experience and understanding.

There are those who assume the attitude that living and traveling in the wilderness are a simple process. Their only needs, they claim, are a single wool blanket, a jackknife, and a tin cup to take them through any wilderness in any season. The experienced woodsman screens out such persons quickly. Their actions give them away. They cut tent pegs six inches long when they should be twenty. They chop an ax into the ground or otherwise damage equipment. In crossing a river through fast water in a canoe, they get broadside of the current instead of tacking across with the sidewash. But the first three-day cold rain, sleet, or snow stampedes them back to their armchair adventures. Unfortunately, they are likely to become angered at the first suggestion you make for their safety as well as for your own. Thus, they never overcome their original error.

On the other hand, he who has little or no experience whatever, but who expresses a willingness to learn, scarcely ever fails to succeed. If he has any ability to do things with his hands, is of average intelligence and is open to suggestions, he learns amazingly fast. Such a person usually has something to contribute as a special skill or suggestion before the trip is over. This also applies to women. They possess an adaptation to this type of living which for some reason has been very much underrated. Indian women are as compatible with the wilderness as Indian men.

A casual interest in outdoor life is not enough for living or traveling in the wilderness. To know the best possible methods calls for work and a desire to learn. There are, for example, at least six canoe strokes one should master to travel competently in wilderness waters with a canoe. Work and knowledge are required to learn these strokes, but they can be mastered by anyone willing to expend some hours of effort.

Whether paddling a canoe, finding one's position, using an ax, building a fire, or performing any of the other tasks of wilderness life, there is a skilled, or improved, way to do all of them. An ax in the hands of a trained chopper is a fine instrument; in the hands of a novice who defies method it becomes a crude, hazardous implement. A suitable tent pitched correctly and in the proper place is a shelter and a comfortable home. A poorly designed tent improperly pitched in the wrong place is a hovel. The finest provisions badly cooked may bring illness instead of nourishment.

Most of the basic tasks of wilderness life can be learned before starting out on a journey into the wilds. Cooking can be learned in your own kitchen. Once you know how to cook substantial meals over a kitchen stove, all you need to learn is how to build and control a campfire. The same thing applies to all other tasks; they can be learned in advance, in part at least, and applied later when a journey is undertaken.

Need for a knowledge of living out-of-doors has been demonstrated many times in the past. Soldiers who were sent to the Aleutians, to Korea, and into tropic wilderness relied on their camping knowledge to live with some degree of comfort; and at times such knowledge was the factor which meant survival.

Some years ago, a Midwest Armistice Day blizzard caught a large number of sportsmen in the field. Many perished. Unfortunately, too many sportsmen concern themselves with bag limits rather than with the art of living out-of-doors.

A considerable part of the earth is still in a wild state. Many of us, sooner or later, will come in contact with some part of it; and the ability to travel in such areas can be a real source of enjoyment. Engineers, prospectors (professional and amateur), archaeologists, foresters, and other kindred groups find the ability to live in the wilderness essential to the success of their work.

In the wilderness a set of principles applies of which some are best described as calculated risks. The success of any such calculation must, of course, be based on knowledge and experience. Most of these risks are obvious. You do not run rapids or embark on a heavily running sea in a canoe without some apprenticeship.

Usually there is little to fear in the wilderness apart from your own mistakes. Carelessness with an ax or a knife, or going beyond your ability to calculate the risks, need be the only dangers in the average day of travel.

Wild animals will not molest you, notwithstanding the hundred and one stories to the contrary. An animal you have wounded can possibly become dangerous. If unknowingly you get between a mother bear and her cubs (a most unlikely happening), you may find her conduct unpredictable. Firearms for protection against wild animals are not necessary. There have been a few exceptions to this; for instance, where a polar bear has become mixed up with sled dogs, or where other bears have entered camps in the absence of the owners. But in the wilderness camp wherever you are personally present the creatures of the wild will keep clear of you. Wolves do not run in packs as commonly believed, although at times a mother and her family of grown pups will hunt together. As to their attacking human beings, after long research no authentic case has been found, and the subject has been broadly explored by the best men in the field. So, sleep serenely.

If you do not care to venture alone on your first trip without a guide, remember that the guide has a responsibility for your welfare that you cannot set aside. His knowledge of the trail is what you are seeking and paying for, and if you overrule his better judgment you are not getting the value and service for which you bargained. Therefore, abide by his decisions for your own welfare and safety. Give him all the manual assistance you can. It will pay dividends in congeniality and acquired skills.

The qualifications of guides, however, vary so greatly that the term covers everything from experienced men of the wilderness to incompetent individuals who are looking for a few weeks' work of any kind. Your choice of guide will be a very important one, and it should be based on responsible recommendation.

If your trip is your first wilderness venture of any consequence, alone or with companions, it will have far greater significance and prolonged pleasure if it is taken without a guide. It then becomes a test of an individual's maturity.

Each year a great many people enter the outdoors who have

guides that do just about everything for them. Guides are valuable and important members of a party, but when they are taken along to perform all of the tasks the true value of outdoor living is lost. Too objective an interest becomes a thing apart. A famous guide of the North described it as comparable to studying botany from an airplane. Most guides are willing instructors if their charges make some effort to learn. Sometimes an inexperienced person will evince a reluctance to do things connected with wilderness craft because he believes that he will fail. Many a success story is attributable to the fact that an individual of no unusual talents accomplished something simply by trying. You *can* live well outdoors. Make up your mind to that.

# 2

## *Carrying the Pack Afoot*

PERHAPS THE MOST INDEPENDENT TYPE OF TRAVEL IN THE WILDERNESS is to carry a back-pack afoot. It calls for a great deal of skill and scientific treatment of equipment. While this form of travel has special advantages for those on recreational trips, it also holds marked advantages for prospectors and for those engaged in scientific work, since it offers them a means of reaching remote areas inaccessible by any other method.

The close contact with the forest enjoyed on trips afoot is seldom possible by other means of travel. For many years I traveled on foot in various sections of Ontario, Canada, which later I traversed by canoe. The difference was always apparent. The deep recesses of the forest, the inland lakes, the small meandering streams, the great bogs from which led numerous game trails, the frequent sighting of wildlife—these were a lure that constantly afforded a surprising contrast to open waterfront travel by canoe.

When you travel on foot, carrying all your equipment on your back, you can make camp anywhere that water is available. When you reach the edge of a bog, for instance, where a small stream trickles down from high rocky country, a secluded camp can be pitched late in the afternoon. The time just before dusk can be devoted to observing the arrival and departure of large game and other wildlife. When night comes to these Silent Places, there is the advantage of a comfortable camp nearby.

When you travel with a pack, rivers must be crossed, and lakes too, where they cannot be successfully bypassed. In such instances, they must be rafted. Three simple ways of constructing a raft are:

nailing, using a small auger and doweling, and lashing. I prefer lashing.

Raft materials consist of any dry tree butts conveniently near the waterfront, and several green poles a few inches in diameter. Do not be too fussy about the shape of the dry wood that goes into your raft; the structural principle should be your greatest concern. A raft should be made quickly, and ought not to consume much more time than you would take to make a portage when canoeing. As long as the dry wood is sufficiently large for buoyancy, and will hold together, it will do.

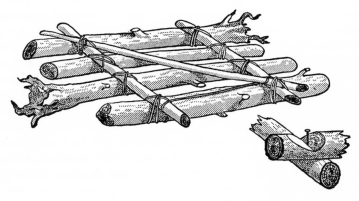

**Improvised Raft—Lashing and Nailing Methods**

Trim off any limbs and drag the dry butts down to the water-front. Lay them parallel, close to the water. Then take the green poles you have cut and lash them crosswise, saving one pole for the diagonal brace. This last is important. The failure of the average raft lies in the fact that no diagonal piece is used; hence it collapses like an old-fashioned grocery box. Lash this diagonal pole last. For this job, No. 5 sash cord is best; this cord will serve for your tent rope as well as for other uses. When the raft is complete, throw a pile of evergreen bows on it to keep your pack high and dry. If nails are used in the construction of the raft instead of lashing, the green poles should be notched. This will allow the use of smaller nails.

The paddling is done with a pole ten or more feet in length. This pole is used just as you use a paddle, except that you will be standing. The amount of resistance set up by the water against the slim pole will carry you across fast enough. If the return journey is over the same route, the pieces of the raft can be stowed along the bank or on the shore. In any event, remove the rope lashing. Where nails are used, these can be taken out and reused.

Very likely there will be times when you will reach a river and find that your best route is to go downstream. Rafting downstream is fascinating. Rapids may be run with the raft if it is well lashed and if the flow of water between the rocks permits safe passage. In some short portages the raft may be taken apart and portaged piece by piece; but if the portage is long a new raft should be made at the foot of the rapids. I have allowed empty rafts to go over falls or through bad rapids—sometimes with a line attached and sometimes without—with success. If the paddle pole is lashed to the raft before this is done, you can swim out to the raft in the quiet water below the rapids and salvage it, continuing downstream after the raft has been grounded and the pack loaded. The safest way not to lose both rope and raft is to take the raft apart, float the logs downstream, and then reassemble it. Of course, retrieving the various pieces will take time.

All items to be carried on back-pack trips will be treated under "Wilderness Camping and Equipment," "The Itemized List of Camping Equipment," "The Wilderness Food Budget," and "Wilderness Cooking."

Trips afoot with a camp outfit carried in a pack offer innumerable possibilities. I dislike using the word "vagabond," but wandering through the country with a light pack is about the most interesting life imaginable, and perhaps the healthiest.

Pack travel on foot may sound like tedious hiking. It is not necessary, however, to hike at all times; there are variations possible in this type of travel, as I have indicated in the use of a raft. Once I made a trip, taking advantage of more than a half-dozen types of transportation. I went by rail for several hundred miles, caught a ride with a small fishing boat through Lake Superior, tramped fifty miles to the Canadian border over a tote road, accidentally hooked up with some Indians traveling by canoe along the boundary, caught a bus at the western end of the Superior National Forest, took the Canadian National Railroad for another lap, hiked seventy miles along the same track, and there bumped into a mining party heading forty miles into the country by a boat of the old York type. I went along, helping them to transport some coal and drills. I thought I was a guest, and was glad to go along for the ride. To my utter surprise, when we reached the railroad a week later, I was handed a check for my services at five dollars per day and keep.

Wandering through a wilderness area is not aimless. You hit the target of adventure more often than you miss. Traveling afoot, with a pack that contains all your equipment for living outdoors, makes you the most independent person on earth. And the cost is remarkably low. I urge you to try it.

# 3

## Canoe Travel and Procedure

THE CANOE IS ONE OF THE MOST WONDERFUL OF ALL WATER CRAFT. If you have any criticism of the Indian, remember that he created the canoe and the snowshoe. Until the advent of the aluminum canoe, the white man's canoe was a bulky, heavy affair. A birch-bark canoe weighed only about half of the white man's wood, or wood-and-canvas, canoe. Only when the aluminum canoe was developed did the white man make a craft as good as or better than the birch-bark canoe. The aluminum canoe is very light and strong; and since it is such a wonderful craft it deserves your best care and treatment.

This does not mean that I do not on occasion remember with pleasant nostalgia the earlier wood-and-canvas canoe and that magnificent craft the Peterborough wood canoe. I have also used a birch-bark canoe made by my Indian friends at Mille Lacs Lake, some of the best canoe makers on this continent. But grim reality compels a choice. If I were to live on a lake or river and found that it was unnecessary to portage, I should certainly select the warmth of a wood, or wood-and-canvas, canoe.

I once carried a wood-and-canvas canoe by half-mile stages over a watershed for five and one-tenth miles, after the canoe had been absorbing water from a three-week journey. (A wood-and-canvas canoe can absorb from ten to fifteen pounds of water.) At each half-mile rest the bow of the canoe was leaned into the crotch of a tree, or between two trees close together, so that the canoe could be shouldered again without raising it from the ground. Some years later I went over the same portage with an aluminum canoe of the same size. I planned to rest when I felt weary. Then, suddenly I discovered that the weight was so small that I could keep going indefinitely, and thus carried it the whole five and one-tenth miles without setting it down. These are the realities that are too compelling to let sentiment rule. On the long journey the choice is inevitably the aluminum canoe.

Canoe nomenclature is interchangeable. When you refer to one part or another of the birch-bark, wood, wood-and-canvas, aluminum, or plastic canoe, you can use the same terms, with only additional reference to materials used in construction.

The so-called Fiberglas canoes have not gained prominence up to now, owing to the fact that they are far heavier than aluminum. Such canoes in fact are not made of pure Fiberglas but of a Fiberglas mat filled with a plastic. Because of the large amount of plastic resin used in these canoes they should be called "Fiberglas-plastic" canoes. If they were made like Fiberglas fishing rods, with closely packed filaments, bonded with little other material, they would be very strong. Both aluminum and Fiberglas canoes are supplied at each end either with air compartments or with chambers filled with Styrofoam, a light, very buoyant substance. These keep the canoe afloat in an upset. (Caution: Gas and oil will dissolve Styrofoam, and air chambers can leak—therefore, it is well to watch both.)

If an aluminum canoe upsets, unlike the wood-and-canvas model, it always rights itself. You can then get into it and paddle it ashore even though it is filled with water. You can also get under an inverted aluminum canoe and throw it free of the water. This is done by rolling the canoe over, bottom up, then grasping the center thwart with both hands and throwing the canoe up and over. You will be driven down into the water by the throw; but when you come up you can get into the canoe by drawing yourself over the gunwale while doing a flutter kick with your feet. (Caution: The wind may blow the canoe beyond your reach.)

In pulling a submerged canoe from the water over an upright one, bring the canoe up on its side, then turn it upside down across the upright canoe, and finally right side up as you slide it back into the water. This process is simple, and involves little risk of upsetting the upright canoe.

You should know the parts of the canoe so that you can talk intelligently to your guide or canoe partner. The front end is the bow, the back end the stern. We refer to the various parts as: stern seat, bow seat, stern deck, bow deck, stern thwart, bow thwart. (Thwarts are the cross braces.) The long strip of metal along the bottom center is the keel, and the rails along the top edge of the canoe are referred to as gunwales. Then there are ribs and the outer covering which is often referred to as the skin. The center brace or thwart is provided with an encasing brace on which are pads for carrying the canoe on your shoulders; it is called the yoke. At either end are the air or Styrofoam chambers, compartments providing buoyancy.

There are other terms which you should know for free discussion of your craft and its handling. If you hear someone say there is plenty of freeboard, it means that the distance from the gunwale, or top edge, of the canoe to the water is ample. It is measured in inches. There are six inches of freeboard, and so on. Of course, as you increase the load the freeboard gets less. Often you hear the expressions, "Trim your load" or "Load back of center." A canoe rides better if it is perfectly in balance from side to side, which is a trimmed load. However, a canoe also rides better in most instances if the weight is slightly to the back, so that the bow rides higher; thus you load back of center. But in loading back of center, see that the entire load is worked well away from the ends to the center rather than spread over the entire canoe. In short, keep the bow and stern as light as possible; then you can ride a heavier sea, since the bow and stern will not plunge so deeply.

In a heavy sea or in rapids, where an upset is likely to happen, you will be battered about and you will have to do the best you can. If you can manage to hang onto the canoe, which, with the wind and the waves, will be on its way to shore quicker than you can recover your wits and swimming position, that is your best bet. In rapids your chief worry is to keep from getting injured on the rocks; especially is this true of head injuries which may cause you to "black out" long enough to drown. There, too, stick with the canoe if you can, and use the canoe as a buffer, letting it take the bumps.

There is more to the recovery of an upset canoe in the wilderness than in settled country. In the wilderness, loss of equipment may mean serious exposure or hunger. Most equipment is usually so packed that an upset is serious. If equipment is properly packed and properly loaded in the canoe, nothing need be lost in the average rough-water upset.

Every packsack should have within it a waterproof bag; the most economical type I have found so far is the army clothes bag which fits the standard No. 2 Duluth Packsack perfectly. This is not just a matter of water resistance but of being absolutely waterproof.

In the event of an upset, if the weight is properly divided in the packs beforehand the packs will float. The one item likely to suffer damage in an upset is the camera; but if this is placed in a waterproof bag and tied to a thwart, it, too, should come out dry in bad water. A thin waterproof bag with a tie string should be carried in the pocket at all times for ready protection of the camera in case of rain. It is the one covering I use for my camera, but I take it off as soon as possible. Leather cases protect cameras but also prevent pictures—usually the best ones. This does not apply to dropfront-type leather camera cases.

In a canoe with proper depth, packs will stow under the thwarts. If they fit fairly snug, they will not come out in an upset. Since the buoyancy of wood-and-canvas—or, in an aluminum canoe, air or Styrofoam chambers—is all that keeps a canoe afloat in an upset, the packs, being lighter than water, increase the buoyancy of the canoe if they remain in the craft.

In discussions on safety so much stress is usually placed on upsets that one takes it for granted they are common. They are not common among experienced canoemen. It is not possible to avoid some risks in heavy water. There is a way to canoe in a heavy sea, and running rapids is part of the canoeman's art. You cannot always avoid risks. It must be stressed, however, that foolhardiness belongs to rank amateurs. There are times when you must cross a body of water where waves and wind make it a risk, but you should do so only when necessary. If ice is forming on a body of water, and to remain where you are might mean being trapped on an island or remote shore for an uncertain time with little or no food, the risk of crossing would be worth taking. You should, of course, run all rapids that it is safe to run. If you encounter a short stretch of bad rapids with a good portage trail around them, by all means choose the portage. If a riverbank allows tracking or lining a canoe along a lively rapid, again it would be only wise to track instead of paddle. See page 23.

## THE KNEELING POSITION

In a canoe the kneeling position is the most secure, since this lowers the center of gravity and gives you, the paddler, a better stance. The difficulty is the discomfort most people experience in this position. This is due largely to the fact that the position is incorrectly assumed. For some unaccountable reason certain manuals of instruction demand that the kneeling position be used at all times. This, of course, is a needless affectation.

The unalloyed pleasure of sitting on the seat of a canoe in calm or reasonably calm water while the canoe is slowly paddled along a strange and wild shore certainly cannot be contested on the grounds of improper procedure. On the other hand, in rapids or a heavy running sea it would be unwise not to assume the kneeling position, both for safety and for greater control-power in paddling.

To remove the seats and to substitute thwarts is basically bad practice. Desire for relief from kneeling is bound to come; and you will then have to sit on the thwart, where you are in a precarious position. Especially is this true when the thwart becomes slippery from use.

To assume the complete kneeling position, you should first sit on the seat and then kneel, but in such a way as to leave most of the body weight resting on the seat, the knees merely acting to steady your balance and give you good stance.

In the semi-kneeling position the same general principle applies, except that one leg is brought forward until your weight is distributed at three points: the greatest part on the seat, a part on one knee, and a part on your extended foot. For relief, you can alternate leg positions.

## CANOE STABILITY

An empty canoe at first seems a very tippy affair. The same feeling of insecurity is experienced during the first hours in a saddle. Experience brings confidence. On the other hand, a canoe loaded with several hundred pounds of camping equipment and provisions is very stable. When the load is low, the canoe usually gives the beginner a feeling of security. The fact is that, unless you make some awkward movement, a loaded canoe will ride a heavy sea with little risk.

The point to bear in mind is that a canoe will ride a heavy sea and ride well. When the canoe pitches, keep paddling and do not start "reaching for the lake." The impulse is to stop paddling. This is bad because it allows the canoe to travel at the same speed as the run of the sea. If the canoe does not travel faster than the run of the sea, steerage is lost, the canoe starts turning broadside to the waves, and the chances of swamping are high. Most upsets occur near shore, with the bow resting on land, offering support only at the keel, and none at the bilges.

## ON BEING WINDBOUND

Being windbound on an island or at the far side of a lake is like "cabin fever." It may make you very restless. Generally, being windbound is due more to the direction of the wind across one's path than to the height of the waves.

If you can travel with or against the wind, there usually is no need to be windbound. The plan in crossing at right angles to a heavy sea is to head into the wind and turn the bow a few degrees off the wind in the direction you wish to go; then, with very little effort at paddling, simply hold the canoe in this position without attempting to make any forward progress. If you watch the shore you will find that the wind is tacking along on one side of the canoe, moving it sidewise quite rapidly in the direction you wish to go.

Frequently, two or more canoes are used on an expedition or on trips where the group involves more than three people. The great advantage of two canoes lashed side by side with two poles for braces is much increased seaworthiness. I have run heavy seas with such an arrangement, where the water kept spilling into the canoes, but where frequent bailing was the only inconvenience. It is almost impossible to become windbound with two canoes lashed together in this manner. In addition, it is an ideal way to carry such cumbersome items as stoves, lumber, and other cabin paraphernalia.

The method of lashing is important. The canoes should be lashed about four feet apart at the bow, and about six at the stern. Otherwise, water will pile up between the canoes and spill in, or a bad backwash will occur and add to the bailing problem. The poles should be cut green. Dry poles might break and bring tragedy. Lash the poles to the thwarts, and do a good job. Paddling is done on the outside, but if an outboard motor is used on a bracket it must be placed on the side between the canoes, for easy control. Sailing goes well, too, with this double-canoe arrangement, with none of the usual risk in sailing one canoe. See illustration.

Running with the wind in a single canoe sets up more trouble than paddling against the wind. When the heavy tail wash is felt, there is an impulse to stop paddling and to rely on the thrust of the waves. But, as I have mentioned before, steering will not be easy unless the canoe is kept moving faster than the run of the sea. The

Sailing Two Canoes

simplest way to run with a heavy sea is to use a "sea anchor." The best type for a canoe is a cooking pail on the end of a rope.

The plan is to use the largest cooking pail on hand with a secure bail (arched wire handle). Tie a length of rope, from ten to twenty feet long, to the bail. The other end of the rope is fastened to the stern of your canoe. As you get under way in deep water, throw the pail into the water and let it drag behind. The pail will fill with water and sink, but the forward motion of the canoe will keep it just under the surface. Thus the stern of the canoe is held back while the bow runs out with the sea, the canoe keeping straight with the wind. If it is a tough sea, get down low in the canoe and slightly forward. This will lower the weight and, because the waves are most apt to wash into the stern, it will give you the added advantage of keeping the stern higher out of the water.

This use of a sea anchor should be arranged for in advance. The end of the rope fastened to the canoe must not be high on the canoe; it must be fastened low at the stern end of the keel. Since there is nothing there on some canoes to tie a rope to, the plan is to make a "bridle." Run the rope through the gunwales or stern seat, then come down on both sides of the canoe and tie the rope at the keel. The pull is then from the lowest part of the canoe, and tends to hold it upright rather than to tip it over, as might be the case if the rope were fastened high.

If heavy seas are expected, the pail to be used as a sea anchor should be set in the canoe, ready to be thrown overboard when needed. This plan should be followed even when in doubt, since heavy seas are met far from shore and not in the lee at the near shore. In an upset the pail will fall out of the canoe; and as the wind and the waves begin to carry off the canoe the sea anchor will hold it back, enabling you to catch up to the canoe by swimming. This is especially important with a light aluminum canoe.

The above bridle can, of course, be lashed while the canoe is afloat, the loop then tied at the seat and the bridle rope pulled around to the keel.

## WILDERNESS CANOE SAILING

Standard sailing gear for canoes is not practical on most wilderness travel because of its weight and bulk in portaging. If the water course is such that travel must be mostly by sail, then the gear will be worth its extra weight. For stretches of water where sailing can be used, a simple sail that I shall describe serves well.

Canadian freighting-canoes are equipped with a mast bar. Masts can be cut from saplings along the trail as needed. Where long distances are traveled with outboard motors in freighting, the gasoline load on the portages is made considerably less by the use of a sail.

Paddling-canoes, I find, are best sailed with a ground cloth or poncho mounted on two slender poles held in the hands. The poncho is best because the head opening becomes a window for a view ahead.

Using the poncho for sailing is simple. Two slim eight-foot poles are cut. Both feet of the bow paddler are extended forward to brace the lower ends of the poles. The sail is fastened between these two poles as a flag to a mast. The poles are then grasped about three feet above the lower ends and the sail is spread. The wind fills the sail with a deep pocket, and even with a fair wind it will be found that the bow begins to churn the water. The stern paddler steers with the paddle as a rudder. This type of sail is safe. When a heavy gust comes along, the poles are brought closer together, thus lessening the surface of sail spread to the wind. Surprise gusts of wind may even cause you to drop the sail to avoid upsetting.

### TOWING CANOES

Towing canoes with a launch or with an outboard-motor craft has been regarded as unsafe practice. For organized camps and for a pastime it should be avoided. It involves more risk than at first seems possible. However, in many commercial fields, such as freighting and transporting men and equipment, towing with an outboard motor is necessary.

Where towing of paddling-canoes is necessary for a special use, it is best to put all persons in the motorized canoe or launch, and tow the canoes containing the freight or equipment. Even better, if capacity will permit, you should carry persons and freight in the motorized craft and simply tow the empty canoes.

As described in the use of the sea anchor, the towing ropes must be attached at the keel by the use of a bridle. The rope forming this bridle is fastened at the gunwales or the seat ends, brought down to the keel and there tied, so that the pull is from the bottom of the canoe. The primary purpose of this, as I explained, is to avoid pulling the canoes over; but it also helps to bring the bow up over the water and prevents a down drag in towing.

If you have a long distance to travel down a river with few if any portages, let me suggest that you lash two canoes together; then make a floor of a number of slim poles, or lumber, and pitch your tent on the platform you have created. You can travel twenty-four hours a day in shifts. Cook with a Primus stove on rainy days. But look out for waterfalls. If you have to buck a wind, drop the tent, leaving the bottom fastened. If the wind is with you, such travel can be fun. You feel snug; and if you have the patience just to float, you will enjoy a feeling of calmness and serenity.

## WIND AND THE CANOE

Wind is an important factor in paddling a canoe. Let us suppose that you are alone in a canoe and that a wind is blowing. If the canoe was unloaded, and if you were seated in the stern, the wind would blow the bow end around until the stern headed into the wind. Then it would run with the sea, the bow going with the wind. You could, if you desired, now turn the canoe completely around without paddling a stroke by moving to the bow end of the canoe. The wind would simply take the stern end, which is now brought higher out of the water, and blow it around until the bow end headed into the wind. Though this is almost too simple to mention, it forms the basis of all canoeing, and should be thoroughly understood.

Now, if you were to move to the *waist,* or center, of the canoe, both bow and stern would be brought an equal distance out of the water; and the wind would simply carry the canoe along, most likely broadside, unless you used your paddle to right it.

It is plain to see that the wind should not prevent you from turning the canoe in any direction you choose, and that it should in no way interfere with your maneuvering. To paddle forward against the wind, the first move is to shift your present kneeling position at the center of the canoe to a point a few inches ahead of center until the canoe is blown around to face the wind. Now, by shifting your position again to a few inches back of center, and by allowing the bow to swing a few points off from the direct wind, the full stroke of the paddle can be used for the forward motion, while most of the steering will take care of itself.

With the advent of aluminum canoes, I often found it necessary to defend the behavior of this craft in the wind. After a number of years of working with boys and girls, I have no hesitation in saying that if a canoeist finds trouble with an aluminum canoe in the wind, then he has not learned the elementary factors of canoeing. He should not blame his canoe; he should work harder to master his craft.

The tendency of the wind to swing the highest end of the canoe in the direction in which the wind is blowing will be important in other instances. It will be just as important, for example, when there are both bow and stern paddlers as when there is one paddler. Taking advantage of the wind reduces the task of paddling considerably. As a final example, let us suppose that you are traveling with bow and stern paddlers in a canoe loaded with camp equipment and provisions. The direction is directly into the wind. To buck the wind you will need every ounce of your paddle stroke, and it would be foolish to waste some of your energy in steering if the wind can be made to help. The plan here is to load slightly back of center, so that the bow will come higher out of the water. When you turn a few degrees off the wind, the wind exerts a side thrust on the bow. Just as with the single paddler, all energy can be exerted on the paddles toward a forward motion so as to compensate for the side thrust on the bow. Where the angle is greater than ten degrees off the head wind, it is likely that both paddlers will have to paddle on the same side of the canoe to compensate for the heavier side thrust. Since nothing is lost in steering, the effect, of course, will be greater speed with the same energy.

## THE RAPIDS

On most canoe journeys rapids will be met. Earlier in my life I shot rapids that I now choose to portage or track—or at least pole. This may be the caution that comes with the years, but it seems quite proper to choose the safer method if there is a choice. Too often, however, you will encounter rapids that have to be run, unless a grueling portage over rough country is to be made.

Usually both men in a canoe study the rapids together. If you should upset, you can, so to speak, congenially divide the blame. When approaching rapids in strange country, it is well to tie your canoe to some mooring along the shore in the quiet water above. For this purpose use two fifty-foot tracking lines already attached to the bow and the stern of the canoe.

The common practice over the years has been to run the rapids at as high speed as possible in order to gain steerage on the turns. In recent years I have found that a powerful sculling draw stroke could maneuver a canoe in rapids with much less hazard than by the old steerage method. (See sculling draw in the list of canoe strokes.) This sculling draw enables you to maneuver a slowed-down canoe and thus avoid the heavier impact when an unforeseen rock lurks beneath the surface.

Rapids are water flowing over rocks on a downgrade. I know no better way to teach you about rapids than to make you walk and push a canoe through a shallow stretch where they are not violent enough to make you lose your footing. Walking through such mild rapids will reveal, quicker than any other way, how the white water is created. What you need to know is: Where are the rocks and where is the water which will best float the canoe? Such a trip will help to break down much of your nervousness and distrust. You will learn what sort of swirls have rocks close to the surface and where the water is deep. I learned more about rapids one summer by pushing a loaded canoe up several shallow stretches than in any other way. Later, you should run a canoe through rapids that will allow some footing in an upset, if such a stretch of water is at hand. It will not be dangerous. What you must learn is the difference between dangerous and safe waters.

Like all things calling for skill and some risk, you should use caution. By taking a canoe through shallow rapids, and by gradually working the craft in deeper waters, the time will come when your judgment will tell you the outside margin of safety. Skill will come too, and with it a calmer outlook. The types of strokes discussed at the close of this chapter will best show which are to be used in rough water and rapids.

## POLING A CANOE

Poling is part of the canoeman's art. Where swiftness of water prevents paddling, and where the water is shallow enough, poling should be used. The pole should be about twelve feet long, shod on the lower end with an iron cap or shoe fastened with two nails in holes provided in the shoe. This shoe holds the pole under water and prevents the pole from brooming and skidding on the rocks.

You will find the first hour of practice in poling a canoe very instructive; in fact, the first five minutes will give you some real surprises if you have not practiced standing up in a canoe. Practice in shallow water.

If the weather is mild, shallow rapids and shallow stretches of fast water are often traversed by walking in the water and pushing the canoe with its full load. In colder weather, or if the river bed is too rough for walking, poling is necessary. It is a matter of standing or kneeling in the canoe and pushing it upstream by snubbing the pole on the river bottom.

The shoe end of the pole is first dropped to the bottom. The canoe is forced ahead with a hand-over-hand thrust as though you were climbing the pole; this is then repeated. Much will be learned once the pole is in the water, since current and canoe will set up problems best solved by the trial-and-error method of gaining experience.

### TRACKING OR LINING THE CANOE

No matter where you are canoeing in the wilderness, you would do well at the very start to attach a pair of tracking lines, not less than fifty feet in length, to the bow and to the stern. In some waters, depending on the shore, you may have to use tracking lines one hundred feet or more in length. For most situations, however, the

Tracking or Lining the Canoe

fifty-foot lines will do. You will find these lines valuable as *painters* (lines for tying the canoe to a mooring while loading).

The idea is either to pull the loaded canoe upstream or to run it downstream with the tow ropes. The work becomes interesting when you discover that the canoe can be steered either away from or toward shore by pulling on one or the other tracking line.

In tracking upstream, if you pull harder on the stern line the bow will turn out into the stream, owing to the wash of the current on the near side. The reverse is true going downstream. The wash of the current on the forward side of the canoe keeps the craft from being drawn toward the shore. By pulling on one line and by letting out the other, the canoe can be steered around rocks or other obstacles at will. Your success or failure in tracking is a question of whether or not you can walk along the shore. Tracking is sometimes done with one person in the canoe paddling or poling while one or two persons on shore use the tracking lines.

The outboard motor has become an important factor in fast water. Running rapids downstream with the motor reversed may seem like a peculiar aspect of canoeing, but I have found it an interesting art to develop. In going upriver in a rapid or in fast water, the outboard motor has eliminated much poling and tracking, and has become a tremendous help in long-distance travel. Of course, there will be many sheared pins, except in those props where a clutch is used. There will also be broken props, but spares are not heavy equipment.

My method of running against fast water with a motor is to set it in a straight-forward position and with just enough speed to make reasonable progress against the current. Then paddles are used with the sculling draw stroke (see canoe strokes) for maneuvering. The bow and the stern paddler both take part in the steering operation. In running downstream in rapids the motor is fixed in a reversed position. This holds the canoe back. Then the canoe is maneuvered forward with paddles used with the sculling draw stroke.

## PORTAGING

Between bodies of water, around dangerous rapids, and around waterfalls the canoe and equipment must be carried. After long hours of paddling, a portage is usually welcome. It allows intimate contact with the forest and affords interesting diversion, despite the often arduous labor.

Here, as in other departments of canoeing, opinions differ as to method. Some like a yoke for carrying the canoe. The trouble, I have found, is that most commercial yokes are bad. They exert too much pressure on your neck or they have big pads that raise the canoe to an awkward height or they gouge your shoulders painfully.

Beginning the Canoe Portage

On the Berens River, Manitoba, I found a yoke made by a white trapper which had the first right to the name "yoke" of any I have seen. It was carved out of white spruce and was shaped like the early yokes used for carrying two buckets of water, except that it was broader and more form fitting. The principle was a hollowed-out section perfectly molded to the back, shoulders, and neck. The load pressure was spread over a large area of the shoulders and the back, making portaging a comparative pleasure. It was attached to the gunwales as a thwart, had a light felt padding, and it did not have the prisoning effect of most yokes.

Because paddles have to be carried over a portage, some travelers prefer to use them as a carrying yoke. The method is to lash the paddles lengthwise to the canoe and on the thwarts in such fashion that the blades will rest on your shoulders as you carry the canoe inverted over your head. The spacing of the paddles on the thwarts to fit your shoulders is important, and this is accomplished by using permanent cord loops on the thwart through which the paddles can be inserted. The paddles are then securely lashed with a tumpline. The advantage of using a tumpline (see description of the tumpline in a later chapter) is that the headstrap of the tumpline is used to take stress off the shoulders. In this way, part of the weight of the canoe rests on your head.

Cushioning for the paddles is made by using a wool shirt in a novel way. First, lay the shirt on the ground, back down. Starting with the shirt tail, roll the shirt to the shoulders. Place this roll on the back of your neck and over your shoulders. Take the sleeves and bring them forward, then under your arms, buttoning the cuffs of the sleeves to each other at your back. There the shirt will stay while you bring the canoe upside down on your shoulders for the carry.

## TWO-MAN CARRY

Two men can carry a canoe with considerable ease by lashing the paddle blades to the rear thwart, resting the handles on the center thwart. One man carries the canoe with the paddles resting on his shoulders; the other walks outside the canoe, resting the bow on one shoulder. In a heavy wind this is a good carry, because it prevents the canoe from being blown out of the carriers' control.

In both the one-man and the two-man carry, I have indicated that both blades and handles are lashed to the canoe. A few years ago I traveled with an Indian who lashed only the blades and allowed the handles to be free. He explained that this had two advantages: it allowed the paddles to be moved closer or farther apart, at will, for adjustment to the shoulders; and it was a safety measure in the event of a fall.

While the idea appealed to me, it had this disadvantage, I found, that if one man has to lift the canoe to his shoulders alone the paddles were rather unwieldy during the lift. As a compromise, I simply slip the blades under the spacing cord on the middle thwart, and the handles under a second spacing cord on one of the end thwarts. This allows sufficient adjustment without the paddles sliding too far along the thwart and becoming unwieldy. (The cord on the center thwart is described in the one-man carry. The cord on the end thwart is tied in the same way.)

A simple two-man carry for short portages and lift-overs is to rest the bow seat on the back of the neck of one carrier and the stern seat on the back of the neck of the other carrier.

Carrying anything as big as a canoe troubles many people. A 17-foot canvas canoe weighs from 80 to 85 pounds when new and not water soaked. In a packsack the same amount of weight would be no appreciable load. Yet, to tell someone to relax while portaging a canoe is like the dentist telling the small boy to relax whose tooth he is about to pull. But this relaxed mind, together with keeping a trim balance, is, after all, the secret of portaging a canoe. The various models of the 17-foot aluminum canoe weigh from 58 to 74 pounds.

Shouldering a canoe by picking it up out of the water single-handed or setting it down again in the water at the end of the portage gives some travelers a great sense of pride. But when assistance is available this is simply not good sense. Several years ago I came upon an Indian friend of mine at a portage on the Winnipeg River, and was interested to know if he had a better way of lashing a tumpline on a canoe for portaging. This man was outstanding as a guide in the Pointe du Bois Country. He made the lashing, then asked me to help him lift the canoe to his shoulders. This, and similar experiences, taught me the folly of showing off. Common sense is the best guide toward settling most questions of method.

If you are alone and have to pick up a canoe singlehanded from the water or on land, stand alongside the upright canoe midway from bow to stern, facing the canoe. Take hold of the near gunwale and roll the canoe away from you until it is on its side, or just far enough to rest the canoe at the center against your knee. Stoop over and reach for the far end of the yoke. Roll the canoe up onto your knee, balancing it carefully there. Now reach for the highest gunwale with your left hand and grasp it just a few inches ahead of the yoke. Then grasp the other gunwale with the right hand a few inches back of the yoke. Now, by a heave of the arms and a jackknife boost with your knee, toss the canoe to your shoulders. For a trim balance grasp both gunwales ahead of you.

There are many ways to raise a canoe to another man's shoulders.

One is to raise one end of the upside-down canoe, while the other person gets under; but this is sometimes hard on the canoe where it grates on rough ground. Simpler and easier, I think, is for two persons to raise the canoe as described for one man. Both stay near the center of the canoe, six feet apart, and work together. Then, as the canoe comes down from overhead, one of them backs into the yoke and is off over the portage. It is well for both packers to stay together on a long portage, so that one can give relief to the other, if desired. It is wise also on a long portage to carry the load part way and return for another load. The short interval of walking back empty-handed is a relief. Usually, however, one becomes toughened by days of portaging, and nothing seems to slow one down. At the start, it is good sense to take it easy.

## EMBARKING AND LANDING THE CANOE

The novice does most damage to a canoe in getting it in and out of the water. The best method for embarking and landing is very simple. The canoe is first placed right side up on the ground, with one person at each side of the center thwart. The canoe is then picked up by both persons at the center thwart, where it is balanced and carried stern first—not bow first—to the water. Here the stern is let down, and the canoe is fed hand-over-hand along the gunwales into the water. The bow paddler, standing upright, holds the bow of the canoe between his legs to steady it, while the stern paddler walks down the center of the canoe to the stern, supporting himself by holding onto the gunwales. The stern, now being heavier, raises the bow from the shore, so that the bow man can get in to push off.

You will not always be lucky enough to have a sandy beach or dirt shore that allows for such nicety of embarking. In the north, rocky shores predominate. There, parallel landing and embarking are often the practice. The two tracking lines, one fastened at the extreme bow and one to the stern seat, should be used for snubbing the canoe to such shores, especially on rivers. Never leave a canoe moored very long with an on-shore wind, or on a river of fast water. Grinding against the rocks will soon wear a hole in it.

Landing a canoe is simply the reverse procedure of embarking. Whether the shore allows parallel landing or not, once the occupants are out, the stern should be swung out into the water at right angles to the shore. In this position the bow can be lifted from the water by two men, one on each side, and brought up hand-over-hand along the gunwales, until the center thwart is reached. Here, the balance will allow the stern to come out of the water, and the canoe can then be carried to dry land, where it should be left right side up if portaging is to begin at once. At night, or for long periods on shore, a canoe should be turned upside down, well away from the shore, to prevent it from being blown into the lake and lost.

### CANOE KEELS

One night in northern Ontario I sat by a fire and listened for three hours to a pair of experienced canoemen argue about canoe keels. One was a keel man; the other considered keels a devilish invention. Both of their arguments had merit. A canoe with a standard deep keel is a far better canoe to ride a heavy sea than one without a keel. It is steadier. But in rapids, where sharp turns are necessary, a canoe without a keel is better.

The argument advanced by those who do not want keels is that a good canoeman can handle a canoe without a keel in a heavy sea anyway, and that in rapids there is a distinct advantage. But the keel man says he has little trouble in the rapids with at least a shoe keel; and in a straight chute in fast water he finds the keel an advantage in that it saves the canoe from the rocks. And so the argument goes.

My own experience has been that the shoe keel is a compromise between the two, where little of each virtue is lost and something gained. The shoe keel is a wide shallow strip of wood, or of metal on the aluminum canoe, which does not greatly reduce maneuverability in the rapids so long as the loading is kept to the center of the canoe and away from the ends. This shoe keel is a great protection to the canvas or aluminum covering when the craft slides over a bad rock, and in a heavy sea it lends part of the steadiness of a deep standard keel. The peace of mind gained from having that strip of wood or metal for protection as you bounce over a rock in the rapids outweighs other disadvantages. Shoe keels can be had on order. On a long trip they save the canoe from much abuse. Aluminum canoes are made with stamped and drawn parts and, because of the riveting construction, must come equipped with keels.

## MODERN CANOE DEVELOPMENT

At this writing, plastic canoes have been developed, along with veneer canoes bonded with plastic resins, not to mention canoes made of aluminum alloy and also of Dow metal. This last type, I believe, is made of magnesium. How the plastic canoes will hold up under sun, water, subzero temperatures, and hard usage only time will tell. They are very heavy.

After several years of testing canoes, I am won over completely to the aluminum alloy canoe. I have battered it against the rocks of rapids both by accident and with the deliberate aim of a laboratory experimenter, and it puts all other materials to shame. Granted that it is tinny and noisy, nevertheless 60 to 74 pounds in an 18-foot aluminum canoe compared to 90 or more pounds in a water-soaked canvas model spell the difference between expeditious travel and a sluggish, grueling journey. There is a heavier aluminum model, but the lighter canoe seems to take the bumps so well that the choice is preponderantly in favor of the lighter material. Air chambers, or chambers filled with Styrofoam, keep the aluminum canoe afloat when upset. Its best safety feature lies in the fact that it rights itself in an upset. In addition, it can be thrown almost free of the water by a single swimmer—a feat impossible with the canvas canoe. Thus, if equipment is packed to float, complete recovery in an upset can be made in deep water.

The canoes with almost straight gunwales and rapidly rising bow and stern that dot the parks and waterfronts are unsuited to wilderness work. Even the Guide's model, with its shallow depth of about 12 inches, does not allow quite enough freeboard, with a load of men and equipment, when used in heavy rapids and running seas. In wilderness travel one canoe must serve for all waters: shallow rapids, heavy seas; and it should ride high in quiet water. To accomplish all this, it should not be less than 17 feet in length. If it is shorter, it will not ride a heavy sea without danger of shipping water. It should have a depth of $13\frac{1}{2}$ inches if it is to have enough freeboard with a heavy load to allow for the list and the wash encountered in moving at a quarter-angle to heavy waves. In my experience I have found shallow depth in canoes for river work a mistake. The increased depth is a great help in the rough water of bad rapids. Furthermore, depth helps in the trough of waves on a lake. In any event, depth is a safety factor, and deep canoes carry far greater loads. The theory often expressed is that the waist needs little freeboard, and that it is at the bow and the stern where freeboard is needed. This is partly true, but it ceases to apply when all-around canoeing is required. In the fast water of rivers where the course is reasonably straight, shallow waists do not cause trouble. However, in all-around wilderness travel there is no room for special canoes.

The beam should be from 36 to 37 inches, and the bottom should be reasonably flat, not too sharply rounded. This combination of beam and bottom in a canoe is often exchanged for a rounder bottom with narrower beam by some who argue that this combination is faster. But in the shallow water of many streams, the last-mentioned combination will not carry a good load without dragging. In rapids it "reaches" down for the rocks more than the flatter bottom, which rides higher. The theory of round-bottom canoes is that the rounded shape conforms better to the sluiced and irregular water of rapids than the flatter bottom, thus giving more stability, and making for more speed. Where everything possible is to be gained by a wide range of adaptability, the round-bottom canoe offers little more than a slight technical advantage. Again, let me insist, when running rapids with a load, keep the load away from the bow and the stern.

One of the oldest theories of boat building is that a pointed bow "cuts" the water. A better theory is to widen the bow and the stern, thus increasing the buoyancy and reducing resistance. Narrow bows and sterns plunge deeper in a heavy sea, shipping water more readily.

An aluminum paddling-canoe is presently available in the 18-foot length, which is patterned after the Canadian Prospector model canvas canoe. Unfortunately, the manufacturers have not seen the merit of producing their 17-foot aluminum canoe on the same model. The 17-foot model, badly designed, is not as suited to wilderness travel; but in the 18-foot model we have the best canoe so far made in the United States that is suitable for wilderness travel. Because other firms making metal canoes are beginning to offer competitive models, we can expect an increasing availability of wilderness canoes.

The weight of the 18-foot aluminum lightweight model is 60 to

74 pounds, depending on the model, thus reaching a perfection in portability that leaves little to be desired. For short trips there is a 13-foot aluminum canoe weighing from 37 to 45 pounds—a canoe that has become the trapper's delight.

## FREIGHTING-CANOES

In Canadian waters, where canoes carry heavy loads for freighting, trapping, and other enterprises, there are many square-sterned canoes considerably larger than the paddling-canoes just mentioned. I shall describe them briefly for anyone interested in such special enterprises.

Until the development of aluminum canoes, the most popular canoe used in the North was the 18-foot wood-and-canvas model with a depth of 18 inches, beam of 46 inches, weight of 130 pounds, and a carrying capacity of 1,600 pounds. The 22-foot freighter has also been very popular; it has a beam of 62 inches, a depth of 24 inches, weighs 300 pounds, and has a capacity of 5,000 pounds.

Makers of aluminum canoes are now providing freighting-canoes considerably lighter than the wood-and-canvas models. This is a great boon on portages. A popular aluminum model now being made weighs 113 pounds, is 20 feet long, has a beam of 40½ inches, a depth of 14 inches, and a capacity of 1,600 pounds.

Freighting-canoes are usually portaged by several persons, although it is possible for a single individual to struggle over portages with them. The three-man carry, in which the gunwales rest on the shoulders of the portagers, two men on one side, one on the other, is unique. The theory of the three-man carry is that every man must carry his load, no leg of the tripod being dispensable. While this is theoretically true, the theory falls short in practice.

Freighting-canoes are used largely for special work such as mining operations, organized camps, and the fur trade, where heavy freight must be hauled. Two of the largest size mentioned, placed catamaran style or side by side, will carry almost any item of building material or machinery needed for an inaccessible camp. The freight is loaded across the two canoes by means of poles or planks. An outboard motor, or even two, can be used. (See the section on "Outboard Motors" which follows.)

## OUTBOARD MOTORS

Including portages, the average experienced canoe party will travel a hundred miles in five days using a paddle. By traveling in this manner, much more game will be seen. Physically the members of the party will gain priceless development. Freezing on the lakes and sweating on the portages is not the order of travel. A peace and serenity in keeping with the Silent Places will have sway, and the abominable smell of exhaust fumes will not obliterate the perfume of forest-scented air. Yet, since speed, and not a deeper understanding of Nature, is the order of the day, here are a few tips on canoe motors.

Except in the freighting-canoes, the bracket support for the motor is better than the square stern. The loss in efficiency is negligible, and steering is more convenient. However, you will find in using a motor with a canoe that by setting the steering arm rather tight and using the paddle for steering, greater steerage and motor efficiency may be had.

For canoe travel with a motor, keep in the 1- to 3-horsepower class. I use the 1-horsepower motor, set it in a straight-forward, fixed position, then guide the canoe with a paddle. Against fast water, I paddle to help the motor power.

Outboard motors should be carried in some kind of case that is grease-proof. This will keep you from smelling like an oil shed throughout the trip. I find that mixed gasoline and oil should be carried in single one-gallon cans and that the cans should be disposed of when empty. This will not apply where the trip is long enough to require a refill at some outpost. Extra shear pins and an extra prop should be included, along with the necessary tools for servicing the motor.

Once a motor is carried, there is a temptation to use it in all waters. This only increases the gas load and robs you of the quiet relief periods. Running with a heavy sea can be done with a paddle just as well as running with the current of a river. A sail, as already described, will save many gallons of gasoline.

Use only outboard motor oil for gas mixture, and mix well.

Drain the motor well when storing. Remove the spark plugs, shoot some oil into the cylinders, and revolve the prop to distribute the oil; then reinsert the spark plugs.

## CANOE STROKES

Canoe strokes have been the subject of discussion for many years, and have caused considerable confusion. Some are simply affectation, with little practical value. Fortunately, agreement has finally been reached on most names to be applied to certain strokes, so that such strokes as the *J*, Bow, Backwater, Sweep, Quarter-Sweep, Scull, Crossbow, Draw, and Underwater are now established nomenclature, and generally understood.

### The Pitch Stroke

Very early in my canoeing I developed a stroke which came as a natural movement to me. I shall call it the Pitch stroke, and that term accurately describes it. In simple theory, the paddle blade passes through the water, not at right angles to the canoe as in a simple paddling stroke, but at an angle somewhat similar to the pitch of a marine propeller, but less acute. The slight pitch of the paddle prevents the canoe from veering, thus maintaining a straight course.

The mark of a good canoeman is that his steering is not apparent. A poor canoeist either takes a stroke and then trails his paddle to

**The Pitch Stroke**

steer, or is continually using steering strokes at the expense of forward motion.

Perhaps the greatest nonsense in canoeing has been "straight elbow paddling" and its variations, which were supposed to be "good form." All that can be said about straight-elbow paddling is that it is novel, like goose-stepping. It may be form, but what good it possesses has escaped me entirely.

As to the use of the arms in paddling, little need be said except to mention a few simple fundamentals. In the kneeling position there is great latitude for paddling. Great sweep and long strokes are possible for maneuvering in rapid water. The question arises as to whether a short or a long stroke should be taken. You might just as well ask if long steps or short steps should be taken in walking. In the end, a natural gait is assumed, whether in walking, in snowshoeing, or in paddling a canoe.

As to the position of the arms, forget everything except this: When taking the stroke, do it in the most natural manner possible; then try pushing the upper hand forward much more than you have been doing, while the lower hand is used in the way that comes most natural to you. At the same time let your body bend forward comfortably on each stroke. Don't overdo it.

What happens once you get the feel of it is that your lower hand is being used partly as a fulcrum and partly to bring the paddle back in the stroke, while the upper hand acts to *pry* the paddle through the water. The force that you get on a paddle by using it as a sort of lever is tremendous. Overdo the prying operation for the first few times; then settle down to a steady rhythm that is comfortable to you, putting into practice the simple points mentioned. Do not pry your paddle against the gunwales. One point of advice is more important than all: Paddle as close to the canoe as possible without dragging the paddle against the canoe. Keep the lower hand close to the water but not in it.

### The J Stroke

Since the *J* stroke is used for early instruction, and has some advantage in a sharp emergency turn, it must be included.

In theory, the stroke is simply a Bow stroke with a pushover at the finish. It is often defended on the theory that there is no push-over at the finish, and that the paddle is whipped or knifed out

The J Stroke (First Part)

The J Stroke (Second Part)

of the water. Assuming that this is correct, the canoe, nevertheless, veers on the comeback operation of the stroke; and, though it is righted on the knifing movement, the canoe continues to take a sawtooth course—which is not good canoeing.

### The Quarter-Sweep

While paddling in the bow, if you place your paddle straight out in front along the bow and sweep it quickly around to a point at right angles to the canoe, you will find that the bow veers away from the side on which you are paddling. The same thing can be done at the stern. When both bow and stern paddlers make the stroke at the same time, the canoe can be rapidly turned in its own length. Once you have learned the Sculling Draw you will drop the Quarter-Sweep. (See *Sculling Draw*.)

**The Quarter-Sweep**

### The Full Sweep

The Full Sweep of 180 degrees is a valuable stroke in the stern and for the single paddler working near the waist, or middle, of the canoe. To complete this stroke, place the paddle as far forward as you can reach, then sweep out and back to the stern a full 180 degrees. The canoe will veer off in the opposite direction from the side where you are paddling.

### The Bow Stroke

A great mistake is usually made in considering the bow paddler of no more value than "horsepower" to keep the canoe going ahead.

**The Full Sweep**

The practice I have followed is to adopt the Pitch stroke in the bow as well as in the stern, but more modified in the bow. The Sculling Draw is also valuable here.

The Bow stroke in its simplest form, as commonly taught, is to

**The Bow Stroke**

dip the full blade into the water at right angles to the canoe and bring it back to a comfortable point, where the operation is repeated.

### The Backwater Stroke

This is simply the reverse of the forward stroke, used in backing up. The Pitch stroke should be applied here except, of course, in reverse; otherwise the canoe will not go straight back.

The Backwater Stroke

### The Draw Stroke

The best way to describe the Draw is: reach out a comfortable distance from the canoe, dip the blade full length, and pull the canoe toward the paddle.

### The Sculling Draw

This stroke is perhaps the most essential in canoeing and, except for the important Pitch stroke, it should demand most of your attention in its development. It is difficult to describe. Its big function is forcefully to draw either the bow or the stern to one side to

**The Draw Stroke**

avoid obstacles, make sharp turns, and thus give the control needed in a bad stretch of rapids or in the run of a heavy sea.

Any person with some canoe experience will know at once that the difficult problem in canoeing is not so much getting forward motion as getting a forceful turn or lateral motion. If you will look

**The Sculling Draw**

at the illustration of the Sculling Draw, you will observe that the paddle is drawn through the water like the Pitch stroke, but with a great deal more pitch. It is then drawn forward through the water with the pitch of the paddle reversed. This drawing of the paddle back and forth causes no forward motion because the forward stroke neutralizes the backward stroke. But it does very effectively pull the canoe to one side—the purpose of the stroke. More can be gained by a careful study of this illustration than by an involved description here. The route that the paddle takes through the water in executing this stroke has often been likened to the figure 8, or to an hourglass.

### The Diagonal Draw

This is an important stroke but the least understood. In theory the Diagonal Draw is simple. Instead of a straight paddle stroke, the paddle is started forward in the usual manner but away from the canoe, then brought back diagonally to the canoe. Or, the paddle can be started forward near the canoe and brought back diagonally away from the canoe. This applies to both the bow and the stern paddler. The success of the stroke depends upon perfect

**The Diagonal Draw**

coordination between the bow and the stern paddlers. Variations of this stroke will move the canoe in any direction desired.

### The Bow Rudder

The Bow Rudder is simply the process of using the paddle as a rudder ahead of the moving canoe. Strokes such as the Scull or the Sculling Draw perform this function much better.

The Bow Rudder

### The Underwater Stroke

The Underwater stroke calls for the greatest care and refinement of all strokes if it is to accomplish its end—that is, to move quietly upon wildlife. The least noise of the water in making this stroke defeats its purpose. Cover of some kind is necessary in nearing wildlife, for sight of the moving paddle will undo your chances as quickly as noise. Where wildlife may be expected along a stream or waterfront, the Underwater stroke is employed to great advantage.

Actually, the Underwater stroke is the Pitch stroke, except that the paddle is brought forward under rather than out of the water. Keep rotating the paddle knob in your hand on every stroke, and you will avoid disturbing the water. See illustration.

**The Underwater Stroke**

## CANOE PADDLES

Much discussion has developed from time to time regarding the shape of paddles, their weight, and other details, though most canoemen are in agreement as to their length. A good rule to follow is that a bow paddle should come just under your chin as you stand upright and rest the paddle on the ground before you. A stern paddle should come to your eyes. Some suggest the nose for the bow paddle. But I think you will like the chin and the eye measurements best.

In the order named, I like paddles made of: white ash, white spruce, and hard maple. There is a spring to ash that makes for some comfort in the stroke, and it is very strong. I always feel more secure with this wood than with any other. It has about the proper weight to slip into the water. Maple is good paddle wood, but it is stiffer than ash and more brittle. Spruce makes a light and strong paddle; but to be as strong as ash and maple the shaft must be very thick, whereas I like a shaft small enough to feel secure in my hands. Blade shape is not an important factor, though one that is much discussed.

In the event of a broken paddle in the wilderness, proceed as

follows to make another. Choose a tree having a diameter slightly
more than the width of the blade. Fell the tree. Cut off the branches.
Now find a large windfall on which to support your pole. Cut a
notch in the windfall with your ax. Rest the pole in the notch and
ram the small end of the pole into the ground. Make a number of
cuts with your ax along the butt end of the pole and then hew this
side flat. Turn the pole over and make a number of cuts in that
side and hew it flat. Thin the pole down to paddle thickness at the

**Measuring Paddle Length**

blade part and to handle thickness at the opposite end. Then cut
in on both sides of the handle, using the broken paddle for measurement. Allow enough width on the handle for the knob. If you are
skilled with your ax, you will have done most of the work with no
other tool. Finish the paddle with your "crooked" knife, if you have
one (see *Knives* under "Wilderness Camping and Equipment"), or
finish with your hunting knife.

The secret of successful workmanship lies largely in the fact that
the wood is being held as if in a vise while you work on it. It is a
mistake to cut a length of pole equal to your paddle and attempt
hewing it. You need both hands for your ax, and you need both
hands to use your hunting knife as a drawknife.

It is difficult to find a piece of wood that is seasoned on the stump and that is not decayed, except, perhaps, cedar and ash. For an emergency paddle it is best to start with a green pole, even though it is heavy. For easiest working you may resort to pine, but this will not make a very strong paddle.

To carry a spare paddle is good policy, especially where bad rapids must be run. Keep it within reach of the stern paddler at all times, since the loss of his paddle involves the greatest risk.

## CANOE PARTS

*Bow.* The bow is the front end of the canoe and is usually the same shape as the stern. It should be full and buoyant, not narrow. Arrangement of seats distinguishes the bow from the stern. The bow seat is farthest from the end of the canoe. For square stern see pages 31, 32 and 44.

*Bow Seat.* This is the forward seat, and the one that is farthest from the end of the canoe. It should never be dropped low, or it will cramp the legs and not allow room for the kneeling position described earlier. Raise it to the gunwales if necessary.

*Stern.* This is the back end of the canoe. It, too, should be formed like the bow—full and buoyant. Some sterns are shaped square for outboard motors. If this type is used, be sure that the square part of the stern does not run below the water line. This will impede both backward and forward motion when the canoe is used with a paddle.

*Stern Seat.* The stern seat is quickly identified by its position nearest the end of the canoe.

*Keel.* The keel is a strip of hardwood or, in aluminum canoes, metal placed along the center of the bottom of the canoe from end to end for protection. (See above for discussion of Keels.) There are standard deep keels and shoe keels. The standard keel is narrow and extends out from the bottom about an inch. The shoe keel is a flat wide strip about one-half inch in thickness, less on aluminum canoes. Bilge keels are usually shoe keel strips spaced along the bottom of freight canoes to protect the canoes from rocks. They must always be parallel with the regular keel—simple in theory but somewhat involved in adaptation.

*Thwarts.* These are strips made of the particular material of which the canoe is constructed, running from gunwale to gunwale

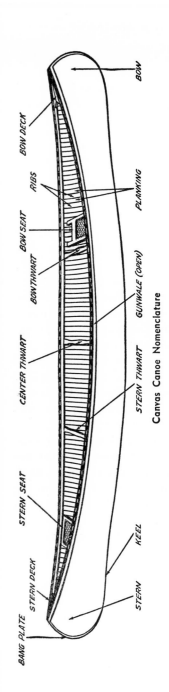

BOW

BOW DECK

RIBS

PLANKING

BOW SEAT

BOW THWART

GUNWALE (OPEN)

CENTER THWART

STERN THWART

STERN SEAT

KEEL

STERN DECK

BANG PLATE

STERN

Canvas Canoe Nomenclature

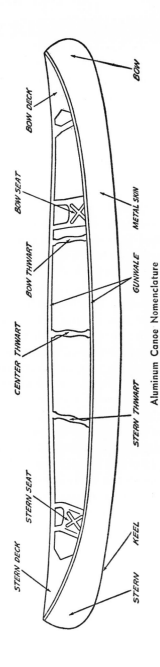

BOW

BOW DECK

BOW SEAT

BOW THWART

METAL SKIN

GUNWALE

CENTER THWART

STERN THWART

STERN SEAT

STERN DECK

KEEL

STERN

Aluminum Canoe Nomenclature

as braces to keep the canoe in shape. Most canoes have three. The center thwart on aluminum canoes acts as an additional support for the carrying yoke. On wood and canvas canoes the thwart is removed and the yoke substituted, which serves as a support for the canoe as well as a means for carrying.

*Gunwales* (currently pronounced "gun'nels"). These are the upper rails of the canoe. Most canoes now have open gunwales. In other words, the ends of the ribs are not sealed off with a molding but are left exposed so that water and dirt may drain from the bilges and not lodge under the gunwales to rot them. Aluminum canoes have openings in the top rails (gunwales).

*Yoke.* A type of thwart fitted with shoulder pads for portaging the canoe. Paddles are sometimes laid across the regular thwart and used for carrying the canoe.

*Ribs.* These are the cross supports on the inside of a canoe, running from gunwale to gunwale across the planking; in aluminum canoes they are riveted to the outer shell. There are also half-ribs in some canoes for reinforcing the floor, but these are not considered good construction. They save the bottom of the canoe and keep it from getting rounded, though they are apt to cause the bilge to become deformed where they terminate. Ribs are closely spaced in freighting and in heavy-duty canoes. In paddling-canoes they are widely spaced for lightness. In aluminum canoes they are very widely spaced because the metal of the canoe shell lends it strength.

*Bang Plate.* This is the metal strip running along the far edge of the bow and the stern from keel to deck. It does just what the name implies: guards the canoe if it bangs against an object. Bang plates are usually made of brass on canvas canoes. On aluminum canoes the manufacturers now supply a channel-like bang plate to fit over the regular bow for rocky country.

*Decks.* There are decks fore and aft, but most canoes have very small ones for bracing. They are the wedge-shaped panels inserted at the bow and at the stern of the gunwales.

*Planking.* This is the canoe covering of wood over the ribs under the canvas. Some canoes have no canvas where this planking forms the watertight shell. On aluminum canoes there is only the sheet-metal shell over the ribs.

*Bilge.* This is the part of the canoe under water, running from the keel to the part having the sharpest curvature.

*Freeboard.* This is not a canoe part but is the distance from the top of the gunwale to the water line. It varies with the load carried.

*Painter.* This is the rope used to tie a canoe to a mooring. In wilderness travel the usual short painter is removed and two tracking lines are attached to the bow and to the stern. These tracking lines are about fifty feet long for normal work, longer for high banks and where the distance from the canoe to the bank is greater. A one-fourth-inch sash cord, if new, is about right. Old rope should be heavier.

*Beam.* This is not a part of the canoe but the distance from gunwale to gunwale at the waist, or middle, of the canoe. It should be $36\frac{1}{2}$ to 37 inches on a 17- or 18-foot canoe for all-around wilderness travel.

*Depth.* This is the distance at the waist, or middle, of the canoe from floor level to gunwale level. It should be about $13\frac{1}{2}$ inches in a 17- or 18-foot canoe to ride out most waters.

*Buoyancy Chambers.* Aluminum and Fiberglas-plastic canoes are made with watertight compartments or Styrofoam compartments to make the canoes buoyant when upset.

## REPAIRING CANOES

In repairing a canoe, the common mistake is to put a patch over the canvas. This spoils the looks of the canoe after it has been patched a few times. For an ordinary hole in the canvas, dry the spot first by putting the canoe a safe distance from the campfire, or heat a stone and apply it to the spot to evaporate the moisture. Then take your knife or a flat stick and loosen the canvas for about an inch around the hole. Apply Duco cement, amberoid, or some other quick-drying waterproof cement to the underside of the loosened canvas and to a thin piece of closely woven fabric. Insert the fabric under the canvas and smooth it out. Apply cement liberally to the hole and let it dry. This will do for the trail. When you reach home, fill the hole with plastic-resin glue and wood flour to a height slightly above paint level; let it dry; sand off level. Then paint the whole canoe. Very likely it will need painting after a good trip; if not, touch up the spot with paint that matches the rest of the canoe.

For emergency patches, where no waterproof cement is available, the hole can be filled with any pitch or gum you can find on cone-bearing trees. However, mix this pitch with a small amount of fat or lard. Do not get too much fat in it. Try a small amount and heat the two together. There is a simpler method. Dry the hole and apply a piece of warmed adhesive tape. When it is cool, rub the tape with a candle. Your repair job will probably last to the end of the trip. Rubber electrician's tape is also good.

A bad crash may call for some skill in repairing the damage. If both planking and ribs are smashed, with a gaping hole in the canvas, find a camp spot nearby, if possible, and settle down for a careful job on the canoe. Dry the entire broken area and remove any part that is loose. (For emergency repair carry some copper wire, a few nails, a pair of pointed cutting pliers, waterproof cement, some tightly woven fabric, and an awl.) I carry a small can of plastic-resin glue with me; and if time permits I lay over in camp for a day to allow the glue to set.

If you can buy from the Hudson's Bay Company what the Indians call a "crooked" knife, mentioned elsewhere in this volume, the splicing job on the wood will be much easier. If you have plastic-resin glue with you, and time to wait for it to set, the broken pieces can usually be put back and glued in place, no matter how small they are. If you do not have plastic-resin with you, it is best to get rid of the broken parts and replace them with new pieces from the forest. These may have to be steamed, bent, and dried. Do such steaming with hot wet cloths. For the new replacement pieces, use whatever wood is handy; but cedar, spruce, and other canoe-making woods are best. If you are to glue the job, split the pieces from dry wood. Work them out with an ax first, then split the pieces with your hunting knife, using a small club for a mallet. Do this job carefully. It takes time, but it will prove that you are a self-sustaining camper and will give you a feeling of confidence. Dress each piece down to match the piece you take out, but allow enough for a splice. Splice the ends in the canoe, then sew them together with copper wire, or just glue them. You will need to loosen the canvas somewhat to get at the paneling for the sewing or glueing. Make holes with the awl and draw the wire tight. If the pieces are glued, weight them with rocks until they are dry.

When the wood part is repaired, fit a piece of fabric under the canvas with cement, as in the small repair, and smooth it out. Then scrape away the paint on all sides of the tear, down to the canvas;

put another fabric patch on the outside and allow it to dry. Duco cement dries very quickly. Amberoid is also good.

In an emergency, where no materials but those in the forest are available, a temporary repair can be made with birch bark and thin flat strips of wood inserted between the canvas and the paneling, sewed in with strands of spruce roots, then gummed with a mixture of pitch and fat (six parts pitch to one part fat).

Concerning repair of aluminum canoes, we can dispose of the final and major repair simply by stating that when circumstances permit a punctured aluminum canoe should be welded. Repairs in the wilderness, however, can be made in various ways, several of them quite satisfactory. An aluminum compound is made which will temporarily serve as a repair. It is easily daubed in the hole and should be allowed to dry for an hour or so.

Frequently, when an aluminum canoe is punctured, the hole is very small. By placing the canoe in the sand, the metal can be pounded into position by a small bag of sand, and then pressed further into place with a blunt piece of wood. This usually leaves a fine-line crack at most. A piece of chewing gum heated and run over this fine crack on the inside of the canoe generally suffices; but if a piece of cloth is coated with the gum and then pressed on the spot, the repair is stronger. A mixture of resin from trees and fat will also do (six parts resin to one part fat).

## CANOE TRAVEL ON ICE

With the advent of the aluminum canoe, a form of travel developed in the North which heretofore was almost impossible. It is travel over ice during the spring breakup, and during those periods when the ice is unsafe for ordinary foot travel, by using an aluminum canoe much in the manner that a youngster uses a "kiddie car" or boy's wagon, with one foot in the vehicle and the other on the ground to propel it.

The method is to stand in the canoe with one foot, while the other, on the ice, is used to push the canoe along. The weight must be so disposed as to leave no doubt that if the outside foot breaks through the ice the preponderance of weight will be on the foot inside the canoe. Both hands are placed on the gunwales, and the canoe slides along on the ice.

Do not use the above method where the ice is extremely doubtful and the footing is insecure. In that case, straddle the narrow part of the canoe, with your hands securely on the gunwales, and both feet outside pushing. Breakthroughs will be frequent, but with waterproof footwear this is negligible.

Travel will be from ice to water and from water to ice, sometimes over islands of ice and sometimes over shore jams. The approach is

**Travel from Ice to Water and Water to Ice by Canoe**

to run the canoe bow first into the water halfway off the ice. This permits you to walk to the water area of the canoe and draw it off with a paddle. On reaching ice, run the canoe halfway onto the ice where you can then walk to the ice area beneath the canoe and draw it up by hand.

The first time you see this done you will think it is a great risk. Strangely, however, it has become a common form of travel since the aluminum canoe came into use; and isolation on an island in a cabin during early spring and late fall has been eliminated. In addition, such travel has become a great boon in cases of illness or accident during off-travel seasons.

A canoe travels well on the ice or on heavily crusted snow and ice. It does not, however, travel well on soft snow. I once thought I could use an aluminum canoe as a canoe and also as a toboggan, to be drawn by dogs. It didn't work. The drag was unbelievable.

When walking across a sheet of ice, always carry a long slim pole. The pole straddling the opening provides a safe way to recover from a breakthrough.

# 4

## *Pack-Horse Methods*

UNLESS YOU LIVE IN PACK-HORSE COUNTRY, YOU ARE NOT LIKELY TO have the equipment, nor is it practical to attempt to accumulate the gear, and certainly not the horses, needed for a pack-horse trip. The best plan is to write to some agency in the territory where you intend to take the trip and ask them to suggest a good out-fitter. Make your reservation well in advance.

There is not much chance to "rent" a pack train, because any self-respecting, horse-respecting wrangler won't entrust his outfit to you no matter how convincing you are. It would be like trying to "rent" a dog team in the North. No dog driver would turn over his dogs to a stranger, and even if he were so indifferent to his animals they would probably go on a sit-down strike.

When you put in your reservation, there are a great many things that an outfitter will want to know. Who will make up your party? Will there be women? Will children be included? Do you intend yourselves to do part of the camp work, or will you want extra help? Do you want luxury material—from camp chairs to folding cots and house-size tents—or are you interested in traveling light, with the bare essentials of good camping? There will be a big differ-ence in the cost, depending on what you want. A big outfit means many horses and a great deal of gear; and this in turn will neces-sitate a well-stuffed pocketbook on your part.

For an average trip each member will of course need a horse to ride. One pack horse will usually accommodate the food and equip-ment for two people, although this can vary one way or the other, depending on what you want to carry. One pack horse per person is bordering on the luxury class, while one pack horse for three is in the go-light category. I suggest that you plan on one pack horse for two if your budget will permit. Thus, you will have three horses to each two people as an average train.

Do not expect the riding gait to be anything but a walk. The trip from beginning to end will be a slow, winding trek over steep trails, down slopes, through forest aisles, and over rough terrain where the trail is scarcely visible and where the horses are left slowly to pick their way.

Do not continually jerk the reins or give boisterous directions to your horse. He will appreciate a pleasant tone of voice whenever you feel like talking to him. Western horses are not directed by oral command but are trained to respond to neck rein. With a rather slack rein held in your left hand, simply ease the rein in the direction you wish to go; the horse will take the gentle cue as the rein touches one side of his neck, and turn. Kindness and understanding are necessary in handling animals. Relax. Enjoy the peace and quiet that the forest and desert will offer, and your horse will do the same.

Keep your personal items together in a small canvas bag, so that you will know where to look for anything you need, and won't have to ask the wrangler for each item. You will no doubt splurge on new clothing, but you had better try out your riding boots at home before you start, until you get used to them. They are not always kind to strangers. Blue jeans of the Western type, sufficiently close fitting so that they will not creep and slide, are perhaps the best, and also look best in pictures. Because there will be a change in the temperature from the low country to the high, take both cotton and wool shirts, with a mackinaw for evenings. A pommel slicker is absolutely essential for rain. You will buy that ten-gallon hat in any case, though I suggest that some felt castoff will do just as well. Wool socks for all seasons are my choice.

A good cold-weather down sleeping bag and an air mattress are musts. In warm weather you can pull just a corner of the sleeping bag across you. But there is a good chance you will be completely inside the bag before the first owl whoops it up in the nearest pine. If you are wise you will take along light wool underwear and, in place of wearing pajamas, change to a dry suit before going to bed. Because you will need to swap from night to night, you will have a suit of underwear that has been washed in a mountain stream drying across a saddle pack most of the time.

There is no really satisfactory solution to keeping dry while riding a horse. The pommel slicker is so constructed that it will drape down around your legs; but the need for splitting the garment both front and back, and fitting it around the saddle, leaves openings the rain can penetrate. It is, however, a tolerable solution. Rain pants and a rainproof upper garment are another. But the pants are slippery and give a feeling of instability, and the condensation within such garments is heavy. Where showers and fair weather alternate at short intervals, taking off and putting on the pants and upper garments becomes a nuisance.

One caution should be given in the use of the pommel slicker; you should put it on after mounting, especially if the horse is shy. The flapping of the slicker against the horse when you have one foot in the stirrup can be hazardous. Even when you are donning the slicker in the saddle, it is well to have the mount under full control with one hand as you put the other through a sleeve. A good practice is to acquaint the horse with the slicker by gently waving it near his head at first, then slowly tossing it around him at intervals. He then recognizes it as something of which he does not have to be afraid.

If you are not supplied with tents by your outfitter, consult the section on tents in Chapter 8. The modified *A* tent is the best for the pack outfit.

When you load the panniers (wood, rawhide, fiber box, or basket-like carriers slung on either side of the pack horse), do not put fragile items near the outside, because they will bang against every obstacle on the trail. A pack on a horse is not as safe a cache as a pack in a canoe or even on a dog sled. Every step that a horse takes jolts your cherished possessions. Cream, for instance, will turn to butter if there is any play in your container; but because you will be carrying canned or powdered milk this is not as important as it used to be. I am not trying to be facetious. When you go on a pack-horse trip remember that your entire outfit, including your food, is going to be subjected to such a strenuous bouncing and banging despite the slow pace, that fragile articles will be reduced to junk if they are not well protected. Pancake flour left in the package instead of being placed in a food bag may lend a dusty rose hue to everything in the pannier. If your horse should decide that his pack itches and that a good roll on the ground would help, well . . .

Your wrangler will probably show you the many tricks necessary to protect your outfit. The daily packing may seem like all work and no play, and after breaking camp every day for ten days you may wonder if it is worth it. The solution is to get into a good spot about the second night—far enough from the sound of an automobile to make you feel you have reached a remote area. Then set up a good camp and explore in every direction you wish within a day's ride. You will have no more packing or tent pitching for as many days as you want to stay. When saddle blisters begin to itch, and no longer are a constant painful reminder, it will be time to take off again for another base camp. If you suggest this base-camp idea to your wrangler, he will admire your good sense and will be happy with his own lot. Don't make a "rat race" out of your wilderness trip. This is the tendency of the tenderfoot.

One of the best features of a pack-horse trip is its physical activity. Riding a horse may in theory seem like passive gymnastics, but a day in the saddle will send you to your sleeping bag convinced that sleep is a wonderful thing. As for your waistline, forget about it, and eat to your stomach's content. No one ever got fat on a pack-horse trip. Your food can be chosen from Chapter 11, "The Wilderness Food Budget," because it will be largely the same for the northern forest and lake sections as it is for the mountains and the desert.

Some wranglers insist on hauling along that immensely heavy item called the Dutch oven. It is simply an oversized iron pot with legs and an iron cover. Every time I pack a Dutch oven I am convinced it should be given its own horse. But despite its crushing weight, it is not only the most traditional, but also the most wonderful apparatus for cooking conceived by Man. Meals of every description can be made in it, along with delicious bread and venison roasts that call the angels to mess. So, like the ten-gallon hat, take one along. If you want a substitute that will do a good job of baking and roasting, take an aluminum reflector oven. You will be happy enough with its results, but it does not have the traditional association of the Dutch oven. When you pack the Dutch oven, place it on top of the middle of the pack, well balanced. What am I saying? There isn't any other place where you could possibly carry it.

How is it used? First, you burn a fire to coals. Set the oven on the coals and put whatever you are going to prepare into it. Then place the cover on and shovel hot coals on the cover. You will soon

Dutch Oven
(Sixteen Quart Size)

get to know how much of the coals you will want under the oven and how much on the cover, depending on what you are making. The legs keep the bottom of the oven off the coals; otherwise the food would burn, unless the coals are much reduced.

## THE RIDING SADDLE

Wholesome controversy is ever present concerning the various methods employed on pack-horse trips, but the part which always seems to take top billing is the argument as to the best choice of saddle, and what position to assume in the saddle. Should you slump into the dished cantle, as though you were sitting in a chair, or should you assume an erect position, resting on your thighs and crotch, your spine upright without stiffness, chest up and waist rather supple?

In the first method it will be argued that on a long pack-horse trip you do nothing but amble at a slow walk, and you can afford to sit back and enjoy the scenery. The built-up saddle, sloping toward the fork and dished out at the cantle, allows little else than a slumped seat. This puts the rider about one foot back of the fulcrum in the horse's movement. The farther back, the harder the ride, the greater the bumps, and the weaker your position if the horse makes a sudden movement.

But you say you want to slump back and enjoy the scenery. The question is, Will you? If you are not with the horse in his movements, but bobbing about in reverse of every movement, unprepared whenever the terrain takes a sudden dip or rise, you will not be the relaxed rider that you want to be.

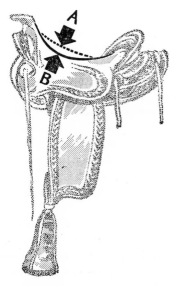

Showing Effect of Built-Up Saddle

As a child, sitting on a teeter-totter, you probably found out that the easiest place to stay on was at the point where the teeter-totter was balanced across the sawhorse. In the same way, there is a place on your mount where the teeter-totter of your horse will afford you the best position. You sometimes hear this called the fulcrum. You will find it up near the withers, and not back on the loins where you have slumped in the built-up saddle.

The first thing to do is to get a saddle that is not built up toward the fork and not dished at the cantle. It is not easy to find. When I first started riding in the West, this type of saddle was common. It was styled on the Mexican tree, and why the built-up saddle has crowded it off the stage I shall never understand. However, saddles so constructed are available, and your outfitter will supply one for you if you insist upon it.

Once you get forward toward the withers, your legs will grip the narrow part of your mount. Sit so that your weight pressure is between your legs and at your crotch. You will know when this has been achieved by assuming a position which will allow an imaginary vertical line to be drawn from your eye to your knee to your toe. *Vertical,* remember. You will be what is sometimes called "tall in the saddle."

Now, no one ever got a good grip on a horse by knee pressure alone. Therefore, instead of trying to secure your position by a knee grip, take a grip hold with your legs. You will not have to be told what part of your legs to use because you will do it instinctively. You will want to apply pressure instantly when the need arises; you will probably relax your grip when you do not need it, but it will be there without effort when you do. Balance is not enough, although you can rely on balance most of the time if your legs can take hold instantly. This can be done only when your legs are close to the sides of the horse. Thus you have a firm stance at all times, no matter what notions your horse takes, which may be many in strange country.

If you have any doubt as to whether your horse prefers this position better than the slump in the saddle, note how he begins to move when you get off his loins and over his withers. You will find that he moves easier, and that his movements are far less restricted. Now you are a mobile part of your mount, with every movement of your body geared to his.

## PACKING THE HORSE

This part of the trip might well be entitled, "Notes on a tender theme," since any method I suggest will probably start up a host of horse packers ready for an argument. May I relieve the tension by saying that of the two general methods, each is loaded with more faults than a glassy-eyed bronc. Don't let the problem worry you. Neither solution is ever satisfactory.

During my early days of horse packing, we made two panniers by drying cowhides on wooden boxes, breaking out the boxes, and then varnishing the panniers. At that time, in some sections of the country, we called these panniers "kyacks"—not to be confused with the word "kayak," a hunting craft used by the Eskimos.

Our packsaddle consisted of a small sawbuck (tree) mounted on two flat boards which rested on the padded back of the horse, and

**Packsaddle and Pack Outfit**
**(Ground Packing Method)**

held there with a harness gear having two cinches, a breast and breeching strap. A waterproof packcloth and about forty feet of half-inch rope completed the outfit.

The panniers, hung by straps to the sawbuck, which was padded underneath with a straw-filled bag, held all the items which might be of the hard variety or which might get broken. Tents, blankets,

**The Modern Fiber Pannier**

sleeping bags, tarps, and so on were piled on top and covered with the packcloth; the whole was then lashed with a single diamond hitch. Clothes usually were stuffed into the panniers as buffers for the more fragile items.

This style of packing is still in use today, but fancy pack trees of metal and leather have been invented to replace in large part the wooden sawbuck type. The principle, however, is the same.

The second method is the one used by the packer who thinks the first too much of a chore. Though he uses the same pack tree and rigging, he will have no part in throwing pack hitches of the conventional variety. Moreover, he will tell you that all the packing should be done on the ground and not on the horse. His argument is almost too strong to be contested.

In any type of horse packing, the load must be trimmed for perfect balance. It is not always easy to get perfect balance when using the first method. In the second, two packcloths are laid on the ground. Bedding, tents, and clothes are then laid on the packcloths. Hard items and food are rolled into the center of the soft items. Finally, the packcloths are brought up and around as a wrap to form a dustproof and rainproof bundle, lashed with a rope. Two such bundles of equal weight are then hung on the pack tree. Some packers do not even bother to lash the packs to the packsaddle, considering that if a horse should buck or fall the packs would become disengaged, and could be easily retrieved.

Such packs, pressing into the sides of the horse, do not seem like a kindly arrangement. Of course, panniers are really no relief, except that less of the load goes into them, with the rest of the pack resting over the saddle area.

Personally, I have no serious objection to either method; and it cannot be denied that there is much to be said for the second method, when the horse is standing, tied to a tree, harnessed with the pack rigging, while the actual packing of equipment goes on nearby. This is especially true with a pack animal that has no intention of cooperating with you in the first place. In this instance the horse is no problem. When the moment comes to hook the packs on the saddle tree, one pack on each side, it will not matter if the horse is uncooperative. He is trapped between two persons and receives a pack whichever side he moves. Obviously, both packs go on at once, to facilitate balance.

A certain amount of skill goes into the making of the two pack bundles to be hooked onto each side of the packsaddle. For example, they can be tied with a curve in the bundle, and in that way hooked high on the saddle tree, so as to throw a part of the weight over and just back of the withers. They can be tied flat to keep them from pitching back and forth; and if you do a good job of arranging the duffle, with the soft part against the horse, you will see the merit of this pack.

The packing will probably be determined by the man in charge of your outfit. It is a good idea not to question his method, as he will have learned through practice which way works best for him. If he is a considerate man, he will apply methods that bring the greatest comfort to his horses; he will also consider the roughness of the terrain.

## PACK HITCHES

If you adopt the first method of packing, you are now ready to throw one of the many hitches. To name a few, there are: the *Single Diamond, Double Diamond, Squaw, Bucking hitch, Lone Packer, Miner's hitch, Square hitch,* and so on, each proclaimed by its adherents as the best.

The flattening effect of the *Diamond* has done much to make it popular. Curiously, among lone travelers, such as prospectors, it is not much used because of the belief that two men are needed to throw it. I do not agree with this, since a *Jam* hitch on the cinch hook will hold the rope from back slack, and thus the Diamond can be completed by one person. Any forward pull on the rope tightens the cinch and jams the rope automatically.

The method for throwing the Diamond hitch is as follows: Tie one end of the rope firmly to the ring of the cinch. Now, while standing on the near side of the horse, throw the cinch over the horse and keep the rope in the center of the pack. Reach under the horse and pick up the hook end of the cinch. Place a jam knot on the hook. This is a simple knot made by going once around the shank of the hook and through the jaw, so that the loose end of the rope is jammed between the hook and the tight part of the rope. Bring the loose end to the top of the pack. There slip it under the standing rope, which is now over the pack, and pull out a small

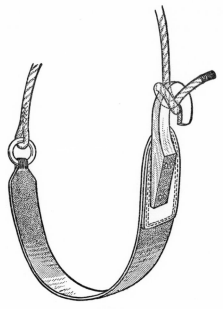

Jam Hitch

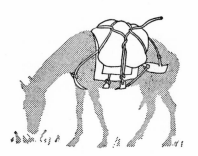

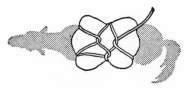

**Single Diamond Hitch (Two Views)**

loop toward the head side of the pack. Take this loop and go under the standing rope once more with the loop. Now walk round to the off side of the animal. Take the loose or running rope and bring it backward around the pack, then forward, then up to the loop just mentioned. Slip it through this loop. Now walk around to the near side of the animal and bring the loose rope forward around the pack, then down and back, and up to the top of the pack again. There slip it under the standing rope. Now you are ready to tighten the hitch. To tighten, take up the slack on the cinch and pull it taut. Then walk around to the off side again and take up all the slack. Finally, take the loose end of the rope and pull hard toward the tail of the horse, placing your foot against the pack to brace yourself. It will form a diamond on the top of the pack and flatten the load—the admirable part of this hitch. This last pull also tightens the whole hitch. Once it is tight, secure the loose end, and you are ready.

Around the campfire, it would be well to have your guide teach you a few simple knots and hitches for handling horses and outfit. Of course, you will want to learn the Diamond hitch. There are a few others, however, which might enrich your experience and make you a more useful member of the trip.

A simple knot is the *Bowline*. This knot will not slip, and for

**Bowline Knot
(Improved Version)**

that reason can be used around a horse's neck. Do not make the mistake of tying a running Bowline which becomes a slipknot—a sure way of choking a horse. (See illustration of simple Bowline knot.)

One of the most ingenious combinations of knots is the creation of a rope halter. First, tie a rope around the horse's neck with a Bowline knot. Bring the long end around the horse's muzzle to form the common Clove hitch; then reach under the bottom loop of the Clove hitch, pull the top loop of the Clove hitch through this bottom loop and draw it up over the horse's ears to the top of his head. You will now have an excellent halter. You can, of course, simply make the tie around the horse's neck, as described, and then put a simple loop around his muzzle; but you will not have as good a halter.

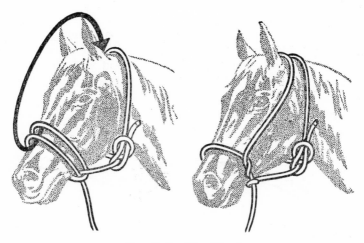

Rope Halter (Two Views)

When you lead a horse by a halter or a bridle, or even by a rope around his neck, do not face him and start pulling. Simply pick up the rope, turn away from the horse, and walk off. He will follow.

For many years we used to sit around the campfire, or in bunkhouses and cabins, tying knots for practice and entertainment, but more often for practical needs. We made halters, or "whipped" the ends of rope to prevent unlaying. Then along came a series of waterproof glues, plastic resins, and other commercial compounds.

All that was required was to dip the end of the rope in one of them and it was sealed for the life of the rope. After these came the stay-open loop, a smooth end for a pack-horse rope, and other aids to utility. Thus the old knots and the splicing process of kind memory threaten to go the way of other fine traditions. Yet, these knots and splices are still in wide use, and necessary on occasion. But now we seldom "whip" the end of a rope; instead, we simply dip it in some plastic resin or in any good modern waterproof glue.

In the making of such equipment as rope halters and lariats, knots frequently need to be "locked," or permanently tied. They can be locked by the application of plastic resins or waterproof glue; but where resiliency is required plastic resins which "set soft" should be used. Any firm making plastic-resin glues can supply various kinds, hard and soft. Fabric material and fabric straps can now be converted to the "feel" of leather by the simple rubbing in of soft plastic resins. This same "feel" in part can be accomplished in rope and cotton strap or fabric by the simple method of heating pure beeswax and soaking the rope or strap in the hot melted liquid. Considerable strength and durability is gained by the beeswax process, which has been in use for centuries. If ends are to be sealed, they must be dipped in glue or resin first, since the wax would prevent sealing.

All ropes should not be so treated, except perhaps the sealing at the ends, because certain knots, such as the taut-line hitch and those based on a friction principle, will not hold on a waxed rope. Various splices should be treated with plastic-resin glue to lock them and to prevent them from brooming under friction. If rope ends are whipped by the old methods, they, along with fixed knots, should also be dipped in glue or resin to lock them and to prevent the whipped ends from fraying.

Your horses must be shod for mountain travel or they will soon go lame. Extra shoes and shoeing equipment will be needed on an extended trip. Your riding saddle will be of the cowboy type because you will want to use the horn for dragging wood into camp or for pulling a horse out of a bog. For steep mountain travel the double-rig cinch of the riding saddle works best. It is less likely to slip. Hobbles will be needed. These are "cuffs" for the horse's front feet, with a short piece of chain between, worn to make his capture easy if he should run away. They should be made wide to prevent chafing. The most convenient bridle is one improvised from a halter. A snap is attached to either side of the halter at the position of the bit. Then, instead of using the bridle, merely place the bit in the horse's mouth and snap it in place. At night leave the halter on, but unsnap and remove the bit.

# 5

# Winter Travel by Dog Team and Hand Toboggan (Winter Camping)

THE IDEA THAT CAMPING IN WINTER IS AN ORDEAL THAT ONLY THE tough and those insensible to pain can endure may be disregarded. Camping in winter is an orderly procedure in which you can enjoy activity comparable to any other active winter sports, with the full assurance that you will be able to sleep in warmth and comfort after the day's work. You have the additional assurance that good, substantial meals can be had.

Foolhardy notions, such as the idea that you can sleep in a sleeping bag rolled out anywhere on the snow without a fire and have perfect comfort at forty below zero, or that you can roll up in a single wool blanket and sleep before an open fire at such a temperature, must be discarded. You will have to have the ability to camp in rain, sleet, snow, and subzero temperatures; but I shall offer you a set of principles that will enable you to do so in safety and comfort.

Mild-weather camping often becomes bad-weather camping owing to climatic uncertainties. In the North, ice can go out of the lakes and rivers at any time over a period that covers more than a month. While such a wide range usually does not occur when the ice forms in the fall, winter can arrive in dead earnest even though the water is still quite warm. Canoe country can thus become an area of free travel in open water while eighteen inches of snow lies on the ground.

The Eskimo's ability to withstand the cold and to propagate his kind under almost untenable conditions is no longer a mystery. The Eskimo, apparently, is not endowed with any special quality of resistance to cold that the rest of mankind does not possess. The Eskimo's seeming advantage over other races in withstanding cold now appears to be a matter of metabolism based on a meat diet. Tests have proved that an Eskimo and a white man living under the same circumstances with a diet largely of meat can resist the cold equally well—although the matter of temperament may be an insufficiently tested factor. It is wise, therefore, on a winter trip to keep to a heavy meat diet, and to go on this diet for some months in advance of the trip.

It is true that you cannot risk making the same mistakes in sub-zero temperatures in the wilderness that you might make in mild weather, for there is a greater chance of fatality. In any weather the careful camper makes less mistakes than the careless or inexperienced one; the careful camper, trained to make winter journeys, does not make the average mistakes. If he does, tragedy may ensue. But this need for care applies to almost any walk of life; it is not necessary in winter wilderness travel to apprehend more than the usual risk or danger.

The safety principles under which you travel in winter are not so different from those you employ in summer, but they are altered to fit the season. You can travel alone in summer, and if you should have an accident you can remain where you are until a search party finds you. If you have a companion, he can make you as comfortable as possible before leaving to summon help if it is needed. In sub-zero temperatures you can travel alone or with a companion, but you face an altered set of circumstances. If you are alone, and if you have an accident or an illness of a serious nature, you may not be able to maintain a camp, gather wood, prepare meals, or otherwise help yourself. If the odds are too much against you, by the following June the porcupines will probably be gnawing your bones. With a companion you multiply your chances of survival by an almost safe ratio. If your case is serious, your companion has a choice of two things: to stay with you and maintain a camp, or to provide the best conditions he can with ready shelter, fuel, food, bedding, and so on, until he summons help. If you cannot maintain yourself under these conditions, your plight is almost that of the lone traveler.

Your best plan is to have three persons in the party. This will mean a companion for yourself and in addition a driver for the dogs. The third member will probably be the owner of the dogs, since it is impractical to own your own dog team. This solution will work in most cases. If you are the victim of illness or accident, you will have one person to remain with you while the other summons help—usually a plane flown in to take you out. Or, if your condition and the nature of the ground allows, you can be hauled out on sled or toboggan.

It is possible, on occasion, to set up your trip on the theory that if you do not return within a certain time a plane will be dispatched to reconnoiter for your safety. This can be very expensive, and also sets a deadline for your trip which a hundred and one unforeseen circumstances, none serious, could make it impossible for you to meet. If, for instance, you decide to extend your trip, owing to good hunting, it will be difficult if not impossible to continue it.

Thus, we have the application of a sound principle which should be the theme of all camping procedure as in all departments of planned living. This does not imply that lone travel and calculated risks, sometimes high, should not be taken. I like the challenge that goes with solitary travel. But we are dealing with factors of reasonable security, and such security should be available at all times except when circumstances demand great risks.

If you are to go by toboggan, it should not be the toboggan used for recreational sliding. It should be one designed strictly for wilderness travel. The one I use is made at Peterborough, Ontario, and is ideal. It has a long, high rise in front to mount the drifts; it is narrow for ease of travel but wide enough for all camp equipment, including the stove. It is nine feet long, tapers from front to back to reduce edge friction and snow-loading, and is made of maple. The curve is supported by varnished rawhide, and the toboggan has a pivot ring for attaching the drawing harness. Such a toboggan is small enough to be drawn by hand. It is also large enough for dogs, and if your outfit is well planned and light it can be pulled by three dogs of average size. Two large dogs could probably pull it, but you would have to help them over the rough places, which is not bad practice in any case.

Your shelter ought to be a double tent, although a single tent will serve. The double tent has an air space between the inside tent and outside tent. This provides a moderately dead-air space of about two and one-half inches for insulation. While double-wall tents are used in the wilderness for winter camping, they are not as practical as the *A* tent shown in the section on tents on page 114. The reason is that pitching a wall tent is cumbersome in cold weather when speed is important. The *A* tent with both end flaps cut all the way to the peak, and guy ropes holding out the walls to form a modified dome, is the most practical tent for most purposes.

Pitching a tent in the snow is no problem once you know how to do it. The difficulty arises from the fact that stakes cannot be driven into the frozen ground. Shovel away the snow with a snowshoe, leaving a depth of about six inches for ground insulation. Then tie the tent down to poles laid along the lower edge of the tent over the sod cloth. These poles should be longer than the tent so that the protruding ends of the poles can be weighted down with logs or covered with evergreen boughs and snow. Once the tent is thus staked down, it is easily drawn up either to trees or to poles.

For cold-weather camping where no stove is used, an open-front and lean-to type of tent with a log fire is the best combination. A backlog wall must be built to reflect the heat into the tent and to carry away the smoke. (See illustration, page 111.) A tent like the "all-weather" model is the one needed here. A camp of this type does not measure up to one where a closed tent and a stove are used; but the need for extremely light weight or an emergency might require it. In building the backlog, rest two slim poles at an angle in two crotched stick supports. Cut the logs and pile them against the poles, one on top of another. The slope will keep them in place. Large logs are not necessary. Five-inch logs are ample for a one-night stand, but they must be of green wood. With the reflecting surfaces of the tent, the backlog combination makes a practical and livable arrangement.

A tent for all-around wilderness travel and weather should not have a sewed-in floor cloth; preferably this should be a heavily waterproofed, good-grade muslin ground cloth which can be removed. Strips of the same material as the tent, twelve inches wide and waterproofed, should be sewed all around the lower edge of the tent to serve as a sod cloth. In summer camping this sod cloth will be brought inside the tent and the ground cloth placed over it to seal out insects. In winter the sod cloth is turned toward the outside of the tent and covered with snow to make a perfect seal and to hold the tent down without stakes as described on page 70.

In the arctic, one of the best tents for the prairie or for the ice pack is of a pyramid type with four aluminum legs, one at each corner, a short distance out from the corner. The tent is tied to the poles by tapes and left rolled up on the poles when not in use,

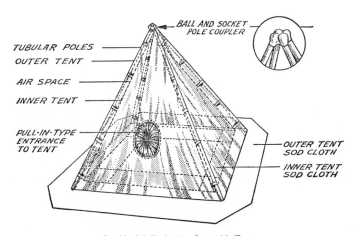

TUBULAR POLES
OUTER TENT
AIR SPACE
INNER TENT
PULL-IN-TYPE ENTRANCE TO TENT
BALL AND SOCKET POLE COUPLER
OUTER TENT SOD CLOTH
INNER TENT SOD CLOTH

**Double-Wall Arctic Pyramid Tent**

since the sled is long enough to carry it. The tent is set up very much as you would set up a camera tripod, except that of course it has four instead of three legs. (See illustration.)

The pyramid-type tent is usually equipped with a sewed-in floor to facilitate pitching. It can, however, be had with a sod cloth and separate floor cloth, which is my choice.

The pyramid tent is quickly set up, and all needed belongings are then carried inside, where they are placed around the edge of the floor to keep the tent from being blown over. Then a second tent is slipped over the top from the outside, very much as a woman drops a dress over her head. The corner poles keep the outside tent a little away from the inside, forming a dead-air space for insulation. On the lower edge of the outside tent is a surrounding flap similar to the sod cloth on tents with removable floors. The sled or any article not needed inside is set on the sod cloth; or the tent can be weighted down with snow or pieces of ice.

The tent is ventilated to accommodate a Primus stove for heating, cooking, and for drying clothes and sleeping bags, since in cold regions condensation is the big problem—and not primarily discomfort from low temperatures.

**Collapsible Primus Stove**

It is possible that the Primus stove may be rendered obsolete by new developments in military heating equipment. An amazing gravity unit, burning practically everything, is now being put into use. This is the unit I now use in the North because it can be adapted for travel in treeless areas, where there is no wood or arctic heather for fuel, to burn gasoline or kerosene. The complement unit is any small sheet-metal stove. The best, I find, is a small airtight stove, which costs about five dollars and can be left behind in the wilderness at the end of the trip. I shall shortly describe the oil-burning adapter, but first let us consider wood fuel.

The basic airtight unit is vented by means of a three-inch pipe. Instead of passing the pipe through the roof (always a spark hazard), I find it best to pass the pipe through one end of the tent. A metal safety thimble is first inserted into the tent to receive the pipe. Outside the tent, the pipe is fastened to a pole or tree with a wrap of copper wire which is pliable and which can be used over and over again. A small $T$ pipe at the end of the stack eliminates snow clogging. A second $T$ on the pipe near the stove forms the back draft and is the real secret for keeping an all-night wood fire going without having it run wild or go out. A cap made from a can, and placed over the back-draft opening when starting a fire, allows the draft to draw through the normal channel. At night the cap is removed and the draft comes through the $T$. (See illustration.) There is also a regular damper.

In the arctic there is little or no wood; therefore it is almost essential to use gasoline or kerosene. The unit I have mentioned, as adopted by the ski troopers of the army, is a simple gravity burner device set in the top opening of the wood stove. The oil drips between the two plates which form the burner. Around the edges of these plates is an air space. The whole affair weighs only a couple

**Tent Stove Showing Use of Back-Draft Principle for All-Night Fire
(Convertible A Tent)**

of pounds. The secret is that the draft of the stove draws the air around the burner in such a way that it requires no pumped air pressure, yet gets the same results. When the damper in the chimney is opened, forming a draft, it sounds like a flame burning under a forced draft; but the noise can be almost eliminated by partly closing the damper, and it need not disturb the sleepers in the tent. This gravity unit was publicly demonstrated at the St. Paul Winter Carnival, and the general description given here is not restricted material. However, the reader should get the details from the Quartermaster Department of the Army rather than from me, for reasons which are obvious. Write to Quartermaster Department of the Army, Pentagon Building, Washington, D.C.

It is clear that using gasoline or kerosene for fuel in this manner makes it possible to keep an all-night fire going without any worry about air pressure petering out, or the other troubles with filters, valves, generators, and so on. All in all, it is the most adaptable heating equipment yet discovered for arctic travel. An added feature is that the stove can burn solid fuels and fuel oils in the same stove and at the same time. This means that the greenest of woods, heather, bones, manure, peat, or any other semi-inflammable material can be burned in conjunction with fuel oils, thus conserving oil. In addition, this unit will burn old crankcase oil, rancid lard mixed with a little gasoline, seal oil, caribou or other fats broken down with the fuel oil by heat, and in solution. Almost anything you can muster in the arctic that will burn is efficient. Nothing goes to waste. If it cannot be eaten it can be burned. All is vented through the three-inch pipe.

You will need a down sleeping bag of the cold-weather type. An all-wool blanket sheet on the inside eliminates body contact with the clammy cotton fabrics often used in lining the bag. Use snaps on your sleeping bag. If the bag is fitted with a zipper, rip the zipper out and replace it with snaps before you start out on a trip. The snaps can be spaced to your liking, as close together or as far apart as desired and practicable. Zippers, which often jam, are clumsy and dangerous, and in the event of a fire breaking out in the tent they may trap you inside your sleeping bag. With snaps you can virtually explode out of your sleeping bag, which may be necessary in case of a fire. A fire hazard is not likely to exist if the back-draft procedure already explained is followed. There is a hazard in the open fire arranged with the reflector tent. Materials can be made fire resistant with commercial fire-proofing compounds.

Caribou and reindeer sleeping bags, used by the natives, are still made available to outsiders in some localities. These usually consist of double bags, with the fur on the inside of the inner bag, and on the outside of the outer bag. If these caribou sleeping bags are native-tanned, they shed badly and have a strong odor owing to only partial tanning. I think you will find that double down bags are more satisfactory.

Dog food is the important factor and problem when dogs are used for transportation. Trappers in the Canadian wilds usually work with two good-sized dogs when they cover their trap lines. A larger team is not practical from the standpoint of feeding. Cereal, fish, moose meat, deer, caribou, and dog pemmican are the standard rations. Soybean flour, because of its fat and protein, has recently been developed into a good dog food when mixed with ground cereals, or with meat and fish. A combination of fish, meat, cereal and fat is, of course, the best all-around diet. Dog pemmican consists mainly of dried rough meat, entrails, and so on, which have been pounded and mixed with fat. Commercial dog foods are good if supplemented with fat, cooked oatmeal, meat, or fish.

Normally, dogs and a sled will be hired along with their driver. If a trip is contemplated by dog sled (sledge) into some particular part of the country, arrangements should be made a long time in advance. The inducement to the dog drivers must also be made attractive enough to have them forego their usual occupations of trapping, freighting, and so on, in favor of greater or at least equal earnings.

In wooded areas dogs are usually harnessed in single or in double file. In some parts of the continent, where ice and snow are so rough that it is every dog for himself, they are harnessed fanwise on individual traces, to which a toggle is fastened. The toggles are looped on a bridle to the sled. When harnessed in this fashion, the dogs can be released from the sled in one quick and simple operation, allowing them to scramble out individually from some hazardous opening in the drift ice, with only a trace and a toggle ring dangling from their harness. (See illustration.)

Both sledges and toboggans are used with dog teams. Sledge runners in the far reaches of the North are iced for smooth going. For this purpose a thick mixture of bog humus and water, making a smooth mud, is troweled on the runner and allowed to freeze. A carpenter's plane is then employed to level off the mud, after which the mudded runner is iced. This is done with a fur mitt and water, and calls for some skill. Polar-bear fur is used for this type of mitt. Extra mud is carried for possible repairs, although oatmeal mush can be substituted.

Strange as it may seem, runners and even entire sleds have been made of the flesh of animals, shaped and frozen. In an extreme food shortage, the dogs and finally the sled were eaten.

Dog drivers should accompany their own teams. Dogs, like human beings, are creatures of temperament, and work best for the person who is accustomed to feeding and caring for them. A change of drivers is likely to bring about a "slow-down strike." As a rule, seven

**Author's Adjustable Sled-Dog Harness**

to ten dogs make up a team for heavy freighting, and the load is seldom more than five hundred to eight hundred pounds.

Sledges or komatiks, used in the North where the snow is hard or for traveling on ice, are most often replaced with toboggans in

**Toboggan Showing Upstands**

the soft snow of forest travel. The fact that toboggans are not built up like sledges, with upstands, and so on, is not an inconvenience in controlling them, because poles lashed to the sides of the load are brought to a convenient height as upstands so that the driver may support the load over uneven ground.

The method for lashing a load is as follows: Trim the load evenly and see to it that the load does not extend beyond the sides of the toboggan. Cover the entire load with a sailcloth tarpaulin to keep out drifting snow. Usually, this is first laid on the sled or toboggan; the load is then placed on the tarpaulin and the tarpaulin is brought up over the load.

Take one end of the lash rope and tie it to the front end of the toboggan side ropes; if on a sledge, to the front crossbar. Bring the rope across the load at an angle, skipping a part of the side rope on the opposite side; or, if on a sledge, skip the front crossbar and loop it through the second crossbar. Continue this back and forth lashing to every other crossbar until the rear of the sledge or toboggan is reached; then go forward, back and forth, the same way, taking in the positions skipped. This forms diamond shapes across the load. When the front is reached, fasten the rope end to the crossbar or to the side rope. When poles, lashed to the load of a toboggan, are used as upstands or supports, make loops around the poles as you come to them during the lashing of the load.

Now and then, as you travel through a wilderness section of the North, you will come upon one or more Indians pulling a toboggan. Not to have to feed and care for dogs is its own compensation. One man can haul his own weight on a toboggan, and two men can haul several hundred pounds. It is grueling labor, however, in deep snow.

The best method to haul a toboggan is to use a rather long, double trace rope tied low on the toboggan, so that an upward but not too abrupt pull will cause the toboggan to climb up and over the drifts. Three men usually make the best team for pulling the average eight-foot toboggan, two pulling and one pushing. The load is balanced over rough places by using poles lashed to the side of the load as described. Positions of the men can be interchanged occasionally for relief.

The two persons hauling walk between the traces. The front hauler has a breast strap attached to the main traces. The second hauler has a breast strap attached to shorter traces which, in turn, are attached to the main traces. This strap is either brought across the chest or held at the waist. The position of the strap is also alternated for relief. The reason the second man has secondary traces is

**Indian Pulling Narrow-Type Toboggan**

that when the lead man begins to pull, the main traces stretch out at a low level inconvenient for the second man, when pulling at shoulder level. When travel is over uneven ground, the secondary traces also take care of differences in ground elevation.

The toboggan used by the Indian in the North has a high arched curve for the snow lead. In addition, it is tapered. Some Hudson's Bay Posts sell the curved front separately, for splicing to the running bottom. Indian toboggans usually are made quite narrow and long, sometimes tapered from ten inches at the front sliding surface to six inches at the heel. Because a trail broken with a pair of snowshoes is not wide, the narrower the toboggan, the less resistance there will be. The same general principles for pulling a toboggan in wooded areas can be applied to sledges pulled by hand in arctic regions where the sledge is more adaptable.

If a wide variety of snowshoes could be carried from which to choose a particular pattern as need arose, the snowshoe problem would be solved. Bear Paws (oval shaped, tailless snowshoes) would

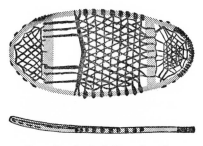

"Bear Paws"—Bush-Type Snowshoe

be the choice for moving about in heavy brush. The Pickerel (long, narrow snowshoes sharply turned up at the toe) would be chosen for open, lake areas and for mountain travel above the tree line. The large hunting-type snowshoe of several patterns would be the one used for trailing big game over deep snow—and so on, through the whole gamut of snowshoe patterns. But with the choice generally narrowed down to one type to do all jobs, the best all-around

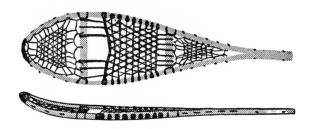

Michigan-Pattern Snowshoe

choice with the least sacrifice is a snowshoe which is 13 inches x 48 inches, is slightly turned up at the toe, and has a tail. This type of snowshoe has various names, since different Indian tribes and manufacturers have given it their own names. The American make of this basic pattern has a rounded toe, whereas the Canadian snowshoe has a pointed toe.

The traditional wood and rawhide snowshoe is already being threatened by the recent development of a snowshoe now on the market, made with a magnesium frame and mesh created from strands of fine steel cable covered with plastic. The shape and dimensions are patterned after the wood and rawhide snowshoes.

On average snows the 13-inch x 48-inch snowshoe will support a person weighing 170 pounds. The size of the snowshoes should vary with your weight. A 150-pound person will take a shoe 12 inches x 46 inches; a 100-pound person, a shoe 11 inches x 40 inches. Women use the same snowshoes as men.

Factory-made snowshoes, often condemned by traditionalists, are, on the contrary, good shoes. They are made of cowhide. A crusty snow will wear the webbing of snowshoes fast where it wraps the frame. Snowshoes can be made to last much longer by wrapping the webbing of the frame with additional hide, or even with strips of cloth. When you buy a pair of snowshoes, be sure that the weight of the snowshoe behind the foot is sufficient for you to lift the front properly; otherwise the toe will dig in and have a tendency to "dive."

Snowshoe hitches are as varied as snowshoes. The common one among both Indians and whites in the North is the squaw hitch made with lampwicking, sold by the yard in most stores handling outdoor equipment. (See illustration.) I do not like these lamp-wicking hitches because they offer little rigidity in maneuvering the

Lampwicking Snowshoe Squaw Hitch

snowshoes. Most commercial hitches are also unsatisfactory. The one I have designed for my own use (see illustration) is made of leather, the back part stiffened with varnish. All leather is removed at the sole to prevent snow balling under the foot. The toe is inserted, and the heel then lowered into the stiffened rear portion. No ties or lashings are used, the toe piece and the friction at the heel holding the foot. To free yourself, the snowshoes are kicked off like a low rubber—a great safety measure in the event of a break through the ice.

**Safety Snowshoe Harness (Author's Own Pattern)**

Over the years winter clothing has been the subject of much scientific investigation. Even today it is a serious problem, and our Armed Forces are continually testing cold-weather and survival methods. The big problem is condensation. Moisture which forms in the layers of clothing builds up frost and gets heavier with each passing day. When exploration parties first tackled the long stretches of the arctic and the antarctic, they were so intent upon saving fuel that after the evening meal was cooked the fire was put out and the men crawled into sleeping bags that were stiff with frost before morning. Clothes never dried out. It was almost impossible for the men to get their footwear on in the morning, and they died from the loss of insulation in their clothes and sleeping equipment due to the increasing moisture.

The next development proved a salvation. It was found that by using more dogs to haul extra fuel, and by keeping a fire going in the Primus stoves all night, life became bearable. Clothes were dried in the peaks of the tents, and sleeping bags were opened for every drying period.

The secret of winter travel is to wear as little clothing as possible during any physical activity so as to lessen excessive perspiration. To accomplish this a routine procedure must be followed. When I start out, I wear an alpaca pile parka. I also wear a pair of alpaca pile short pants that come to my knees. I do not put these under my woolen pants, as proposed by some arctic explorers; I buy them in a larger size and slip them over my outer wool pants. The moment I feel circulation developing, after a mile or two, I remove the short pile pants and tuck them into the ropes of the sled or toboggan. Up to this point I have worn a buckskin sash or belt round my parka. This belt now comes off and the parka is worn loose; it is also loosened at the neck as much as possible. Before I begin to feel full warmth surging through my body, and risk perspiring, I remove the pile parka and tuck that into the ropes of the sled.

Now, if the temperature is subzero, my combination of active-travel garments consists of two-piece wool or synthetic wool underwear; one pair of heavy all-wool socks and two pairs of duffel socks; wool pants; a light wool overshirt; moosehide moccasins or mukluks (moosehide for the soles, hair-seal or canvas for the uppers); a thin poplin parka windbreaker with fur-trimmed hood; a knit cap that covers my ears and is equipped with a sewed-in visor to keep the fur trim of the hood out of my eyes; and finally, soft, smoke-tanned moosehide mittens with duffel liners and fur-trimmed knit wristlets. If there is a biting wind I continue wearing the fur-trimmed hood; if not, the hood is dropped and only the knit cap is worn. The fur hood trim on the windbreaker parka buttons on as described elsewhere, so that it can be removed when the windbreaker is worn over the alpaca pile parka. Any short stop for tea or coffee (called a "mug up") requires the immediate donning of the pile parka and short pile pants.

A popular notion is that wolverine fur remains frost free. This is not wholly accurate. It is true that the frost brushes off more easily, but the fur is too coarse. I do not like it for comfortable hood trim. Wolf is softer, but not so resistant to clinging frost; nevertheless it works out well. My outside parka is made from a good grade of heavy pile, with wolf fur trim on the hood. I like pile better than fur for the main garment because animal skins lack sufficient porousness and, like any nonventilating material, readily condense moisture. Unlike skins, pile ventilates—a most important function in cold-weather clothing. On a living animal the skin and fur are a very efficient covering, owing to the fact that they serve a complex heat-retaining function. When they are reduced to a cured skin, this function is largely lost. Alpaca and camel piles are very soft and warm. However, any good grade is satisfactory. Piles are now made from synthetic materials—nylon, Orlon, Dacron, and so on, and their quick-drying quality is a point in their favor.

For thawing weather I replace the mukluks with a pair of four-buckle, wool-top overshoes, not the all-rubber kind. These are worn over duffel socks only, and not over other footwear. Thus, their size is kept small and they are not clumsy. There is a thin film of rubber between the wool fabrics of these overshoes which makes them waterproof as well as warm. On occasion, for short periods of thaw, I like to use sealskin mukluks, perhaps the lightest waterproof winter footwear known. However, they require considerable attention and must be changed every few days because of a bacteria problem they present, which only periods of non-use and thorough drying will retard.

Pants are of soft wool Mackinaw cloth with a knitted anklet to go into the overshoes when these are worn, and also into moccasins which are sometimes worn in wooded areas. In extreme temperatures, or when a heavy wind is blowing, a pair of thin poplin windbreaker pants are worn over the wool pants. Mukluks, of course, come up over the pants to the knees. The reason for having the tops of seal is to make them stiff enough to stay up, although in canvas-topped mukluks the drawstring at the top, when drawn loosely around the leg, works well. Or, the canvas tops can be stiffened by dipping them in beeswax.

Mittens are of the short gauntlet type, of soft two-year-old Indian-tanned moosehide, with duffel liners. Some travelers object to gauntlets. I was one of these objectors at first, thinking that this type of mitten allowed snow to get in at the gauntlet opening. It would, except that I have provided tapered knit cuffs on my parka, and the sleeve fits into the gauntlet like a cork in a bottle, the sleeve flaring over the edge of the gauntlet. Since these mittens are worn with a cord around my neck, they hang at my side where I can take a hand out when necessary and put it back without having to hold the mitten with the other hand—an important consideration

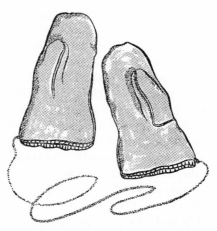

Moosehide Mittens with Duffel Liners

in very cold weather. There is a slight convenience in the use of short mittens without gauntlets when working with an ax and otherwise performing winter tasks. If you prefer the short mitten, I suggest you wear it with an army-type wristlet that covers the wrist and hand except for the fingertips. And if you will sew a band of wolf fur around the top edge of the wristlet, this fur trim will close the mitten opening when your hand is placed inside.

Before going to bed, I change my underwear and hang the garments which I have taken off in the ceiling of the tent. The next evening I put them on dry; and so on, until the end of the trip. You might do your laundry when you reach an outpost, but you do not wash underwear on the winter trail. Some of the synthetic materials now used for underwear dry very fast, but, even then, not quickly enough. At fifty below zero a week is required to dry a cotton handkerchief. Inside, even with a stove, the process is too slow for the trail. Perspiration should be kept at a minimum. In the clear, cold, snow-covered North, dirt is almost nonexistent.

Much of the clothing used by the natives of the Far North is made of caribou, and is not to be considered unsatisfactory. Yet the natives, in the warmer temperatures, used to suffer greatly with only fur and skin clothing, and it was a boon to them when the white man introduced them to more satisfactory materials. Only the traditionalist will refuse to use both the white man's clothing and the native's fur garments in the solution of his clothing difficulties.

Caribou and other hides tanned by the natives and made into clothes usually have an offensive odor. If time and circumstances permit, it is better to have the hides tanned commercially and have the natives make the garments. Their understanding of suitable patterns is good, but you will find poor workers among natives as well as among urban craftsmen. If suitable patterns can be obtained, the best solution is to have the garments made by a first-class fur house in the city. This may not sound very romantic, and will be doubted by those who cling to tradition, but you will like the garments.

Mention was made earlier of synthetic fabrics for underwear. These are undergoing extensive research at present. They are also being used in sleeping bags to replace down. My own tests have been going on for several years, but it will be some time before a conclusive report can be given. However, this material has a big point in its favor: its drying quality. Any gain over condensation, and toward its removal on the trail, is a victory. One trouble with these items is that the static electricity built up through friction draws lint to them from outer clothes and furs. This is difficult if not impossible to wash off; but since it is only a matter of looks, it is of little importance, of course, on the trail.

The old "fish net" type of underwear keeps bobbing up from time to time. At present it is being given a big sales push under new names. The general idea is that by wearing other clothing over such underwear, dead-air spaces are created between the garments, thus solving the problem of insulation. Various types of this underwear have come out with large perforations or voids in the fabric. The principle is the same. For those who do not like wool next to their skin, here is a possible solution. It has its shortcomings, the chief one being that when excessive perspiration takes place in subzero temperatures, the clammy feeling of cotton produces the effect of a cold sweat. When this garment remains dry during inactivity, such as ice fishing, it does quite well. Actually, the ribbed weave of wool garments produces the air-space insulation of the thermo-cotton type to a certain extent. What thermo-garment makers should do is to experiment with their principle in wool and synthetic fibers.

So far as the ladies are concerned, one general suggestion applies: *Wear largely what men wear.* There are a few exceptions.

Pants should be cut to your measurements and buttoned at the side, never zipped. You can risk zippers, if you like, in mild-weather camping; but with the ice, numb fingers, rough use, and the effect of cold metal, you had better stick to buttons of as large a size as possible in keeping with the garment. Even these will, on occasion, be hard to button; but at least you cannot come to grief.

The long red-wool underwear mainly designed for the skier has an elastic under the foot. For subzero travel in the wilderness, either get men's or boys' underwear, or remove this elastic and sew on knit cuffs. The tension of the elastic under the foot will cut down the circulation and increase the chance of freezing. Get two-piece underwear, with the upper garment slightly larger and looser.

If you insist on wearing a brassière, wear it as loose as possible to avoid loss of circulation. Your chest should be covered with some soft wool material to ward off the cold. Be persuaded to leave the "three-way stretch" item in the duffel bag or at home. By the time a woman gets through trussing herself up with all the stranglers of circulation, she has three strikes on her with Jack Frost even though she may gain a point in admiration from John Doe. Freedom of body action hasn't been mentioned here, but it is another reason for avoiding tight garments.

Women, as a rule, do not object to wearing men's clothes until they come to the hat. Here they seem to protest. I have bought for my better half Scotch caps, visor caps, knitted toques, stocking caps, even an expensive seal headpiece. Despite this, when she drops the hood of her parka there on the back of her head is an austere little dab of yarn that resembles a small tea cozy. A short hair style will be best for the type of headgear practical for the wilderness.

As to looking attractive, remember that your clothes will look picturesque and have their own beauty if their pattern fits the wilderness. Nothing looks more absurd than to see tailoring for "smartness" rather than for utility in the wilderness. The best tailoring, I believe, that has ever gone into an outdoor garment is that done by top seamstress Eskimo women. In such garments it is impossible to assume a position where the clothes will bind. The beauty of these garments is their artful adaptability and functional design.

# 6

## Go-Light Auto Camping

### (With Concluding Notes on Planes and Commercial Carriers)

THERE ARE PERTINENT REASONS WHY THE SUBJECT OF AUTOMOBILE camping should be included in an up-to-date book on the wilderness. The automobile provides a ready means of reaching the wilderness areas, and roads are being cut deep into some wilderness regions, permitting a large number of people the advantage of camping along the way and enjoying side trips into the wilderness from a fixed camp. The Alcan Highway is a good example.

The problem of reaching the take-off point in the wilderness is such an important part of any expedition that I have been compelled to give considerable thought to the transportation of equipment and the members of the party, along with the preparation of meals and sleeping en route. One of the difficulties of a station wagon is that the load has to be removed from the sleeping area every night. What to do with it presents a problem. The front-seat area is too small. Covering the load with a canvas tarp is not satisfactory, and pitching a tent for the same purpose poses an extra job.

A logical solution is to tow a small trailer, and to leave the sleeping area in the station wagon free for air mattresses and sleeping bags. The objection to this is that the trailer is always a care, and a nuisance every time you park. Furthermore there is no safeguard from theft for its valuable contents unless trap doors are put on the trailer.

There is a commercially manufactured, patented, light trailer unit that permits the unfolding of beds on hinged mounts. A tent-like canopy then unfolds over the entire sleeping- and living-quarter area.

I have excluded from this chapter travel with house trailers; and I might mention here that while trailer camps are to be found at some remote points they are to a great extent simply camp sites, and the conveniences of toilets, running water, electricity, and so on are not to be had. Small trailers will fare better than house trailers in the wilderness.

The ordinary car or station wagon poses other problems. It has such limited clearance underneath the chassis that the back roads into the wilderness areas will cause the frame to hang up when the weather gets bad, mudholes often bringing the car to a dead stop. Jacking up one wheel at a time and building up underneath, only to have the same thing happen over and over again, can be very dampening to your enthusiasm.

My own solution to the problem came when I was first introduced to the "Carryall" type of vehicle. The Carryall resembles a station wagon in that it has windows all around, and three seat sections, two of which can be removed, leaving a comfortable space for sleeping. In fact, this area contains space enough to cook and eat in during rough weather. The roof is so high that there is more than ample headroom when you are seated, and in packing and in making beds you can walk around almost upright. The chassis is a truck chassis, not a car chassis, which gives liberal clearance on bad roads, and allows for the rough usage a truck is subjected to. The Carryall should be equipped with snow tires for year-round driving. With these, the holes in a wilderness road generally present no problem.

Most trucks nowadays are no longer the rough-riding vehicles they once were, but fast, smooth-traveling units with the speed and mobility of cars, and with the comfort desired for long travel. Some are provided with four-wheel drives, but not always in a suitable body design. However, in traveling over rough country, the four-wheel drive will have to be selected even at the expense of an impractical body design for camping.

Truck seats, contrary to general belief, are designed for the riding comfort of occupational drivers who spend long days in them. They are well adapted for continuous driving. Such seat comfort is a part of the Carryall construction.

The distinct advantage in the Carryall is that the top is high enough to allow the loading of the entire floor area with wilderness equipment to bed level, with ample height left for sleeping quarters. Two rectangular plywood panels can be fitted, side by side, over the load on box supports, and air mattresses and sleeping bags can be arranged on top of them. Thus the beds can always remain made, and require no unpacking for the night. This makes it possible for one person to drive while the other sleeps, if round-the-clock travel is an advantage.

In the morning or at a stop for a meal, if it is raining, one of the long panels can be moved over onto the other to form a seat or couch. The gasoline stove is set up, and the food is cooked and eaten in the Carryall, with only a slight rearrangement of equipment necessary. Little time need be lost. There is no packing and unpacking. Travel becomes very simple, comfortable, and expedient. Personally, after forty thousand miles of this sort of travel, I have come to the conclusion that the Carryall is the ideal unit for travel to the wilderness, or for go-light auto camping.

There are those who for conventional reasons prefer a car or a station wagon. It is possible to pack your equipment in shallow containers on the floor of a station wagon and to use plywood panels beneath the sleeping bags, as in the Carryall. You will of course find yourself very close to the ceiling. This poses no problem when you are lying down, but it is extremely inconvenient for dressing or for undressing.

With a car the camp equipment will have to be carried in the trunk compartment and in the rear seat, if it is unoccupied. Roof carriers are also to be had. If a canoe or boat is carried, you will have to store your duffel in it and carry it right side up, with a canvas cover stretched tightly over it for protection against rain and dust.

A small trailer, as previously mentioned, can be towed behind. Here, however, let me make a plea for light auto camping. There is no more reason for taking a mountain of freight on an automobile camping trip than on a wilderness canoe journey. In either case the problems of packing and unpacking, load weight, and difficulties caused by weather, are just as vexatious.

It is possible to carry all the camping equipment you need, along with food, in the trunk of a car. In a station wagon it should be possible to store all items not needed at night in the driver's seat, if some discretion is used in selecting the outfit. If you will turn to the chapter "Wilderness Camping and Equipment," and select the same equipment for automobile camping as for wilderness camping, with the exception of certain items to be named, you will find travel much more pleasant, and less wearing, without the excess baggage usually carried across our land every year. With well chosen equipment you will be able to make side trips by canoe or other means into the wilderness. Unnecessary baggage will restrict you to auto roads.

The type of tent pitched in the wilderness does not lend itself to auto camping. The most satisfactory tent for this purpose is the "umbrella" tent, so well known that it needs no description. In addition to the tent, you will need a two-burner folding gasoline stove with a surface oven, and a gasoline lantern, a unit of about three hundred candle power, which will light up a whole camp area at night. An extension cord from the car battery will also supply light.

Carry full-length air mattresses and sleeping bags, whether you use a tent or sleep in the station wagon. Leave out folding chairs, folding tables, the folding stand for the stove, and all the cumbersome items that inhibit freedom of movement. At camp grounds you will usually find tables and benches on which to place the stove, cook, eat, and so on. If there are no tables, place the gas stove on the floor of the trunk compartment, or even on the ground. If you have to eat on a tarp spread on the ground, that's part of the pleasure of camping. There is one possible exception to the items mentioned. When using a tent, light folding aluminum cots will make rainy-day procedure easier and can be substituted for air mattresses, if this is a consideration.

While the portable icebox or "cooler" is a convenient unit in auto camping, where economy of space and greater portability are needed get one of the soft insulated, waterproof ice satchels sold at any sporting goods store. Dry ice and other patented refrigerants can be substituted for ice. Of course, there are also the mechanical refrigerating and air-conditioning units available as car equipment if you care to indulge yourself to that extent.

However, do not take so much food that you have to keep packing and refrigerating it. Why fill your car with groceries when there are a hundred grocery stores and trading posts along the way? All you need to carry is enough for a meal or two, until you reach the next store. These points seem academic, and almost unworthy of mention, but nearly every camper along the way has enough groceries to grubstake himself for half a season. Needless equipment and provisions cause confusion and inconvenience. "Do your book-keeping on your thumbnail," said Thoreau. Keep life simple and happily functional.

**Soft Insulated Waterproof Ice Satchel**

If you travel on the Alcan Highway you will be required by law to have two spare wheels instead of one. Carry the necessary tools for your car; above all, take a bumper jack, preferably the hydraulic type. You will probably have to jack up a wheel from the bumper if you get into the mud off a side road, and the under-chassis jack will be of no avail. A set of triple blocks (pulleys) and three hundred feet of three-eighths-inch rope, known as a block and tackle, will get you out of almost any bad place unassisted.

Be sure to carry a tire pump. Air is free and healthful in the wilderness, but you will not find it compressed in a tank for tires when you want it. You can use the pump on your air mattresses, but don't inflate them too much or they will be ruined.

Carry maps of every region you intend to cover, including some of the wilderness maps you may need for side trips. Don't let the wildness of the country disturb you. Don't search always for a tidy conventional campground. If you have to haul your camp equipment on your back from the car to a lake or river, by all means find the energy and initiative to do so. You will have more fun if you do.

Sometimes such unconventional camping areas have no water, or you may be skeptical about the purity of the existing supply. A good policy is to carry a supply of water in your car. The best receptacle is a five-gallon army surplus water can. It has a porcelain lining, and is of a shape for convenient storage.

Extra gasoline should also be carried in army surplus gas cans, since filling stations may be far apart in some wilderness areas. Don't forget white gas for stove and lantern.

And, last of all, be sure to get acquainted with a canoe, if you have not already done so. Carrying a boat on a car or hauling it behind can be troublesome in traveling through a wild region. You will probably find that in most places you cannot launch it because you will have to carry it to the edge of the water. An eighteen-foot aluminum canoe, weighing sixty to seventy-four pounds, can be carried with ease by one person for long distances; it can also be easily lifted on the carrying rack of a car, and it will allow you to take side trips that a boat will not.

If you are concerned about the capacity of a canoe, bear in mind that it takes 2,100 pounds to sink an eighteen-foot, aluminum canoe; therefore your few hundred pounds won't matter. Once you have learned to handle this craft, wilderness travel will open up new living. An aluminum canoe is so light that when you place it upside down on the top carriers, you can tie packsacks and other items inside it without any concern about the weight. This gives you much more space in your car. The motor needed, if you use one, is much smaller too. A one, or one and a half, horsepower motor is ample. Your motor should not exceed three horsepower. However, with a canoe you can dispense with the motor entirely. Twenty miles a day with a paddle is not strenuous going, and there is a much greater opportunity of seeing wildlife if you use a paddle.

The chapters on camping and equipment in this volume will list the needed items and describe camping procedure. The exceptions have already been noted. Camping is basic in principle no matter where it is done. Personal equipment and clothing will be the same, with possibly the addition of extra items that are, of course, a matter of preference. The chapters on food also apply to auto camping. But fresh foods, where available, should be bought to replace the concentrated variety.

The plane widely used in the wilderness has also become an important means of getting to and from wilderness areas. There are some wilderness regions where plane travel is restricted, such as the Superior National Forest, the Quetiquo Provincial Park, and others, although planes are permitted to reach stations at their perimeter. Anyone planning to use a plane in the wilderness should become familiar with the restrictions in such areas.

While wilderness maps show commercial passenger-plane routes to various outposts, it is obvious that a consistent schedule may not be maintained. Commercial flights must carry a full pay load, and are often sustained only by pay loads from mining operations or from the fur trade. Therefore in planning passage on such commercial planes, it is well to make arrangements, far in advance, to be included on one of the informally scheduled flights. Planes can be chartered, but this is an expensive procedure: about $0.75 per mile. Where such charters are made, the cost per mile includes the return mileage too, making your actual cost for being flown to an outpost or into an area $1.50 per mile if you do not return on the flight.

Pilots are not always willing to carry canoes because of wind hazards, but many do, and this should be ascertained ahead of time. Dogs and dog sleds or toboggans can be carried by plane without any greater inconvenience than an occasional plane-sick dog.

Load limit is always to be considered when using planes. This is determined by the size of the craft, the extent and condition of the field or water area for take-off, and whether or not there already is a heavy load. Your skill as a go-light camper will be revealed when you plan your outfit for plane travel. If you trim your load drastically, you will not be caught at the last minute with a pilot's refusal to carry your outfit.

The focus of travel has become so centered on the automobile that we overlook the fact that trains and boats can carry us to a great many wilderness areas not accessible by car. This is especially important in getting away from heavy tourist travel. In Canada the railroads offer a liberal service on their local trains, permitting you to get off with your equipment anywhere along the line, perhaps at some waterfront or other point a long way from any station. Your imagination will suggest great possibilities in such service. If your trip into the wilderness ends at a point back on the railroad, the local train can be flagged for a stop. If possible, however, your trip should begin and end at a regular flag stop.

The advantage of reaching wilderness areas inaccessible to cars is also possible on boats, small and large, making scheduled trips. This applies to the seacoasts, but it is also significant where there are large fresh-water lakes and rivers, such as Lake Winnipeg or the Yukon River. Though the automobile can be used to reach the nearest point of departure by train or boat, this usually involves a parking problem. It is more expedient, as a rule, to use commercial carriers for the whole distance traveled.

While a car can go wherever a commercial bus can go, there is an advantage in traveling by bus to a take-off point in the wilderness because it eliminates the risk of leaving your car at some isolated spot where it might be a temptation to looters.

The average person has developed almost a phobia for clinging to his car. If this attachment can be put aside for travel by train, plane, or boat, a new world of interest will be discovered.

# 7

✳
✳ ✳
✳ ✳ ✳
✳ ✳ ✳ ✳

# *Where Am I?*

FINDING HIS WAY THROUGH EXTENSIVE AREAS OF WILD COUNTRY HAS always been a difficult problem for the outdoor man. Enough information has now been gathered to prove that the ability to find your way is not instinctive. It is important that we understand and recognize this, if freedom of travel in wilderness areas is to be gained.

A number of universities have made a study of this problem. Wilderness guides, seamen, and others—all of whom laid claim to a special sense of direction—were brought in for experiment. A cloudy day was chosen, with no wind blowing, and a level piece of ground picked out, far from any noise. Thus the participants had no heat from the sun, no wind direction, no familiarity with the contour of the ground, and no noise to provide them with clues.

On the day selected an enormous white cloth target was set up on the ground at the horizon. The participants were asked to study the target for positions, and were then blindfolded. Cotton was also placed in their ears as an additional precaution. They were asked to walk toward the target, one at a time.

The results were startling. *All walked in a circle!* Some made the circle to the right, some to the left. Finally, they were asked to declare their positions; then the blindfolds were removed. Their surprise was so great that some of them insisted a trick had been played on them. Repeated tests brought the same results. Man, it was clearly established, has no instinctive sense of direction. When tests were made to determine whether the direction in which they turned was due to a slight difference in the length of their legs, it was found that some participants turned toward their shortest leg, others toward their longest. It became obvious that Man must have clues in order to travel in a straight line.

Some of these clues have already been mentioned. The wind on one side of your face can direct a course. The sun on one part of your body can do the same. The contour of the ground is another clue. The sun and stars are the best guides of all, and form the most important components of navigation. These, and many more, are the clues which competent men of the wilderness observe and follow, often, apparently, without being aware of them.

"Man has no sense of direction."

What the efficient wilderness traveler requires is, first, a good magnetic compass and a working knowledge of how to use it. A good type is a cruiser's model, since it is large enough to allow the reading of individual degrees. There are reasons for this close reading of degrees. One is the modern method of compass reading to be described; another is the need to distinguish between True North and the pointing of the compass needle.

Here I must inject a warning about the pointing of the compass needle, before explaining how to use the compass in finding True North. The problem is so serious that the government has issued a pamphlet stating that most books on the subject, which otherwise contain reliable information, are incorrect in the matter of compass pointing.

I shall try to give a simple, direct explanation. There is a magnetic field running through the earth with one pole in northern Canada and another in the open sea near Antarctica. (Do not confuse these with the North and South Poles, because they are a long way off from the magnetic poles.)

What actually happens to your compass needle is that it lines up with this magnetic field. Now let us consider how the needle points. Technically it doesn't point. It parallels the field. But let us assume that it does point, and you will understand why there is so much confusion about it. If, for example, you were on Prince of Wales Island in northern Canada, the needle would point down, roughly toward the center of the earth. If you were in the South Pacific Ocean at latitude 68 south and longitude 144 east, your compass needle would point overhead toward the sky. Fantastic, yes; but as you travel over the world you will find compass-needle pointings parallel to the earth which are almost as erratic. In some places, say in northeastern Canada, your compass needle will point west;

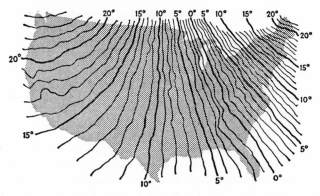

**U.S. Chart Showing How the Compass Needle Lines Up with the Magnetic Field**

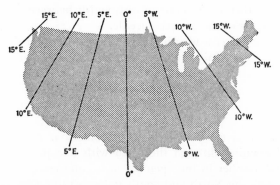

**What the U.S. Chart Would Look Like If We Accepted the Common Error That the Compass Needle Points to the Magnetic Pole**

in northwestern Canada it can point east, and in some sections of Canada it will have an unstable southerly pointing.

Thus it is plain that we cannot concern ourselves with the action of the compass in some selected provincial area only. Means of travel are shrinking the world so rapidly that all wilderness areas are now more accessible, and many of them have difficult compass problems.

How then are we going to find True North in all instances of compass pointings (variations)? For ordinary use we don't have to worry too much about it if we consult government maps now available, which show the difference between the direction the needle is pointing and True North. Usually, this compass variation, or needle pointing, is set off in a legend at the lower corner of a map. See sample legend of lake section showing such variations. This legend is a miniature of the whole map. We find our position on this map. At that point we read our compass variation

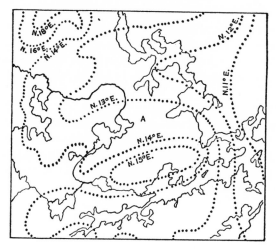

Sample Legend of Lake Section Showing Compass Variations (needle pointings)

(needle pointing). For example, let us assume that we are in British Columbia or in the state of Washington. There the legend will show the needle pointing roughly 20 degrees east of True North. True North, then, must be 20 degrees west of where the compass needle is pointing. We would call this "compass declination (variation) 20 degrees east." If we were in Quebec or in New York, the needle would point roughly 15 degrees west of True North. True North, then, must be 15 degrees east of where the needle is pointing. We call this "compass declination (variation) 15 degrees west." See illustrations, pages 98 and 100.

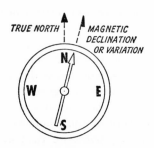

Compass Declination (Variation)

In the sample legend you will observe that the magnetic lines run in almost every direction. If your position happens to be somewhere between the lines, take the compass variation from the two nearest lines and average them. Each line is numbered, showing compass variation.

The difference in a particular area between True North and where the needle points can also be learned from the North Star (Polaris). To be most accurate the observation should be made when the star at the end of the handle of the Dipper (Ursa Major) is almost directly above or almost directly below the North Star. At such times the North Star will be close to True North. (See illustration.)

Failure to make the allowance between True North and where the compass needle is pointing is the cause of much difficulty in finding your way through the wilderness. The common mistake is to consider that True North is where the needle is pointing, or that the error is negligible. This becomes practically and mathematically unsound because one degree of difference between the compass-needle pointing and True North will throw the route off one foot in every sixty (to be exact 57.29 feet). A variation of from five to ten degrees' difference would cause you to miss your objective entirely. If you traveled a fraction over two miles you would find yourself one-fifth of a mile off on your reckoning.

The modern method of reading a compass is to use the degree numbers for naming the directions rather than the lettered compass points. There are 360 degrees around the dial of a compass. Every degree is a direction. *NE* (Northeast), for example, is at the same position on the compass dial that 45 degrees is. *S* (South) is at 180 degrees, *SW* (Southwest) is at 225 degrees, and *N* (North) at 360 degrees. These, or any variation in between these numbers, give an exact direction by number. The common term to describe these degree-number directions is "azimuth." If we were to take a direction in which to go, say 45 degrees, we should indicate our route as "azimuth 45," or simply "45." It is simpler and more accurate.

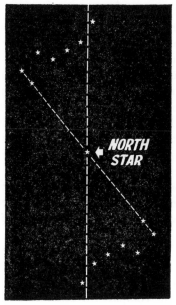

**North Star Is True North When the Big Dipper Is in These Positions**

Mineral areas will sometimes deflect the compass needle. This happens less often than is commonly thought. It is not easy for some people to orient a particular area with a compass direction, and when it seems "off" they become apprehensive and think that the compass is being deflected by minerals. Strong magnetic devices, such as outboard motors, axes, and knives, will deflect the compass needle if they are in too close proximity to it. The most overlooked item is the steel belt buckle near which the user often places the compass when making a reading. Get a buckle made of brass.

While a compass is a valuable instrument, it is not what might be considered a precise instrument. Where really accurate bearings must be taken, they are determined from celestial bodies; all good bearings are thus established.

The revolving dial compass is probably the simplest for the layman. This is no more than a common needle compass except that the dial is fastened to the needle and revolves with it instead of being stationary.

The cruiser's type of compass is the same as any stationary dial compass in general appearance, except that the East and West readings have been reversed or transposed, and the azimuth scale 1 through 360 is also reversed. This, as I shall show, has an advantage over a regular compass.

On your compass cover you will find a pointer. It may be a straight line, an arrow, a sight, or other device; whatever it is, it will enable you to point your direction of travel. This is usually called a lubber's line. Using the cruiser's compass you proceed as follows. (*Note, however, that the directions given in the following example are magnetic compass directions and not True North directions.*)

Suppose that you want to go west. Turn yourself and your compass until the "North" end of your compass needle comes to rest on *W* (West). Now, walk in the direction in which the lubber line or other device on the compass cover is pointing. It will point west. If you want to go south, bring yourself and the dial around until the "North" end of your needle rests on *S* (South). The lubber line on your cover will be pointing south. If you want to go northeast, turn yourself and the compass till the needle is at *NE,* and so on, around the compass. If you use the Azimuth System, which is simply all the directions by number from 1 to 360, then bring the compass around until the "North" end of your needle points on the azimuth (compass number direction) where you want to go: 45 would be Northeast, 180 would be South, and so on, with all the variations in between 1 and 360. This will amaze you the first time you do it.

When you begin to think about this procedure, you may become confused. "Why reverse everything?" you may ask. You will see why if you take the regular compass with a needle and try to do the same thing with the lubber line. If you want to go west, and you bring the lubber line or pointer on your compass cover around until the "North" end of the needle comes to rest on *W* (West), the lubber line will point east—the wrong way. "North" in quotation marks in the above explanation simply designates a particular end of the needle, usually colored black. This end is sometimes marked *N* (North).

The common notion that a traveler need only reverse his compass direction to get back to the point of beginning is correct in theory. In practice it becomes involved because any route through the wilderness is bound to deviate from a straight course. The deviation encountered owing to every contour, lake shore, river bend, swamp, or other obstruction increasing and decreasing in complexity is difficult to compute, so that a reverse compass direction from that of departure would only throw the traveler into another area somewhat parallel to, but remote from, his line of departure.

Certain compass gadgets to be inserted in the stock of a gun are sold on this departure-and-return idea, the makers claiming that if the gun is pointed in the direction of departure, and the instrument is then set in accord with that direction, the gun will inversely point the direction back to the starting place. But it must be recognized that a compass needle cannot point back to something. In fact, a compass needle does not point to anything in particular. As previously stated, it simply lines up with the earth's magnetic field. The implication that a magnetic compass setting or some compass gadget can be made to point back to a parked car, a farmhouse, or some other point of departure is grossly misleading.

The success of wilderness travel becomes one of base lines or coordinates.

Let us say, for example, that you venture five miles from your camp into unknown territory. Your wandering to the right and to the left of your intended route, because of rough country, plus the usual accumulation of compass error, will necessitate your taking a different direction back to camp from the one you used in leaving camp. Unless the contour demands that you take the same roundabout course back to camp, you will not try to retrace your steps, because this would only involve you in greater error concerning the direction of camp.

The most logical prospect for your return route to camp will be your best estimate of the compass direction back to camp. This probably will not be along the route you took when you left camp, unless you retrace your route by some definite series of guide marks. Actually, your course might, in most instances, be regarded as a "short cut." But the short cut will have to be, not a compass direction back to the exact point of your camp but to some base line. This base line can be quite general: a river, a road, a railroad track, a mountain pass, a valley, or a celestial line of position if you are a surveyor or navigator—anything that will form an intersection to your line of travel, from which you can find your camp. There is a great danger that you will arrive at a point near your camp and still be confused. Naturally, you will want to reach this shore line or base line exactly where your camp is; but, as already mentioned, you are more likely to strike the lake shore above or below your camp. Now, is your camp to the right of where you are or to the left?

To make absolutely certain of which side you will be on, you should strongly favor a point either too far to the right or too far to the left of your general return direction as you head back to camp. (See illustration.)

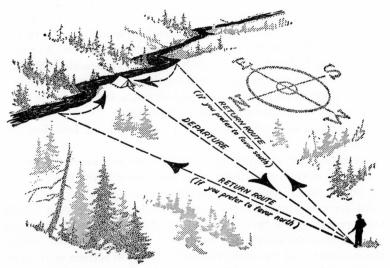

"... favor a point either too far to the right or too far to the left ..."

When you strike the shore line or base line, whichever it happens to be, you will know that, since you favored a point either above or below your camp, whichever you chose, it will now only be necessary to follow the shore or base line back to your camp.

If no landmark exists, as might occur on the arctic prairie or in the desert, it is well to establish one on some high point by erecting a rock pile or planting a flag.

There is another way of establishing your location before you leave camp. Assume that you are camped on the shore of a large lake. While you are at your camp, observe two distant points on the lake, or two distant landmarks that you can identify on your map. These may be islands, bays, prominent points—whatever will give you two compass directions. Now, draw lines across your map that will pass through each of these points in the directions indicated by your compass. Your camp is located where these lines cross. (See illustration.)

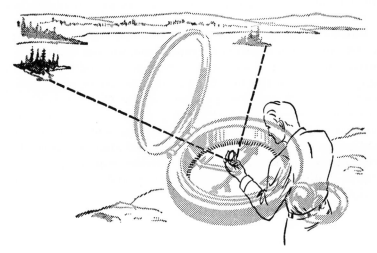

Two Compass Points Fix a Position

You can see that it would be impossible for you to have the same two compass directions extend to the same two points without being where your camp is. So, if later you reach this lake area or general terrain and see your distant landmarks but not your camp, proceed in the same manner as above and draw two more lines across your map through these landmarks in the directions now indicated by your compass. Where the two lines cross is where you are. From this point it will be an easy matter for you to determine the position of your camp in relation to where you now are. (See preceding illustration.)

Sometimes the location of a camp or other wilderness spot must be determined from a single point such as a distant island, hilltop, mountain peak, or other conspicuous landmark that can be identified on your map. Take a sight with your compass from your camp to the distant point mentioned above and draw a line on your map through this point and continue it through your camp location. Your camp will be on this line. If later you see your distant point but not your camp, draw another compass line in the same manner across your map through the distant point. You are now on this line. Compare your lines. Your exact position will not be fixed, but you will have two lines of position to help you return to camp: the line on which your camp is located and your present line of position.

Where extremely accurate triangulation for position is desired, say on exploration and scientific expeditions, you can resort to more precise equipment: a sextant, a transit, or a theodolite. But the simple elements of this subject and a compass are enough for most wilderness travel, and give great satisfaction. This does not imply that you should accept an elementary approach to the subject of position finding in the wilderness. The large number of research and scientific parties who are traveling in the wilderness now, along with an equally great number of prospectors, explorers, and other groups, justifies more than an elementary study of this position-finding problem.

A report from several recently returned expeditions shows that the weakest link in the chain of wilderness knowledge is the inability to know the various aspects of celestial navigation and position finding. The scope of their plans was hampered because of this shortcoming. And in my recent travels in the Far North, I was told by geological technicians in Canada that great wealth for prospectors lies away from the routes of travel, waiting for those who have the necessary ability to determine their positions accurately at all times and to locate with instruments the exact position of their findings.

It has been impossible, of course, to undertake the treatment of the technical aspects of position finding in this volume. However, those seriously interested in pursuing this subject may write to me, enclosing a self-addressed stamped envelope. The knowledge needed for free travel in remote wilderness areas of the world ought to include the following, or free movement will be restricted:

Astrocompass (Solar Compass) for Unstable Magnetic Areas

Use of the solar compass in all areas where the magnetic compass is of little or no value, such as the arctic regions.

Use of the polarized Phund sky compass when celestial bodies are not visible and where the magnetic compass is of little or no value.

Use of the gyrocompass and a knowledge of how to make its required periodic corrections for flights over areas where the magnetic compass is of little or no value.

Use of a sextant or a theodolite for making astronomical observations for latitude and longitude. The sextant or the theodolite will also provide a means of getting the time of day, the day of the year, triangulation angles for position finding, angles for measuring geographical elevations, and numerous other uses.

If a sextant or a theodolite is used in the arctic regions for navigation (position finding), a knowledge of grid navigation will be required.

A set of aneroid barometers, calibrated for elevations, should be carried on those expeditions where sextant altitudes are to be corrected barometrically, and elevations determined.

Such instruments of course require study; but they are fascinating and, contrary to general belief, well within the comprehension of the intelligent layman. If I had not succeeded as a layman in comprehending these subjects, my travels would have been seriously restricted, and so I offer them advisedly. Sweden has included what is called "Orienteering" in her public school system, requiring every child to know at least the elementary phases of the subject of position finding. We could gain much by a similar program.

# 8

# *Wilderness Camping and Equipment*

EACH ITEM OF CAMPING EQUIPMENT SHOULD BE JUDGED BY ITS weight, by its adaptability to a wide range of weather, and for its practical use. Above all it must not retard mobility. In our earlier discussion of a canoe suitable for wilderness travel it was pointed out that one canoe had to serve for all kinds of water. This applies to every unit of camp equipment. Because your equipment is limited, it must be so carefully planned that it will meet not only daily requirements but every contingency also.

Extensive shopping will be necessary to get what is practical, and some items will have to be custom-made if they are to have the quality suitable for long wilderness journeys. A good supply of catalogues by mail from firms well established in the field of outfitting expeditions will be a great help.

There is a strong urge to buy so-called "gadgets" in camping. Camping ability can often be measured by your expertness in screening out these novelties. It is well to ask yourself: "Shall I use this item every day of the trip? Shall I be continually handicapped without it?" If the answer is "No," leave the item behind.

Many campers, even those who camp periodically, have a tendency to disregard the possibility of sudden changes in temperature and the onset of rough weather. The sunny-day start of a trip somehow dispels thought of any possible change. Weather can alter from good to bad within the hour. If the possibility of bad weather is always kept in mind, and if you have the proper equipment and ability, then such weather becomes no more than a diversion to increase the scope of your wilderness experience.

Too many stories of wilderness travel, especially fiction, tend to dramatize the hazards of weather, and show their characters undergoing great suffering and surviving heroically. Weather in the wilderness can be an adventure, but it is not the continual violent experience generally depicted. Such tales create a false impression and lead the reader to believe he cannot undertake a wilderness journey without a continual battle with the elements.

## THE TENT

No standard tent that I have yet been able to find satisfies all conditions of extended wilderness travel and provides a practical and comfortable shelter for every change of weather. A tent to answer every need must provide protection for full cooking operations in rain over an open fire, sheltering fire, cook, and equipment; it must also protect from rain and wind during meals. Any cell type of tent which cannot be converted to form its own large canopy will not satisfy these requirements.

A tent should permit the drying out of clothes and of camp equipment during rain by an open fire. This condition excludes any tent that does not have a large lean-to or reflector adaptation. A tent should also reflect the heat of an open fire in cold weather, and allow for an all-night fire arranged with a backlog assembly. This again excludes any tent which does not have a large lean-to or reflector adaptation.

A tent must keep out insects. Almost any tent will do this when it is closed with proper mosquito netting and a floor covering. But if the occupants are compelled to shut themselves into a non-convertible cell type of tent with a netted opening, life can become monotonously confining during severe infestations of insects and long periods of rain. The only solution is convertibility to a large canopied area with netting on several open sides for ventilation, light, and view.

A tent must permit freedom of movement so that wood can be cut under dry cover and other camp tasks performed during prolonged rains. This shortcoming is the objection to nearly all but a few types of tents. The tent must be quickly convertible to meet sudden changes in wind and driving rain and still allow a certain amount of camp activity even during such squalls. It must allow ample space for storing equipment at night without having to pack it around the bed in crowded confusion, and it must be light and compact enough not to occupy much space in the packed equipment.

These requirements in tent construction are not personal preferences but the demands imposed on any of us living under wilderness conditions. Sudden changes in temperature, overlapping seasons, insects, intense heat, rain, snow, hail, and sleet set the pattern for practical wilderness tents. Seasons are not uniform. Even at the latitude of 48 degrees, approximately the United States and Canadian boundary, snow has been known to fall in every month of the year, though only in flurries during June, July, and August. This gives some hint of the possible extremes in temperature. Routine travel can also bring about this change, for example, from desert heat to mountain snow.

Obviously, such conditions eliminate all tents which are not readily convertible, and especially the common cloth-cell pattern which is simply a room with a flap opening. The only possible exception is the tent commonly used in the arctic or in subzero weather where a single-cell and double-walled pyramid type is used with a Primus stove or other heating unit. Even here, where conditions are strictly for winter travel, the seasons overlap, and it may be well to have the kind of tent that is quickly convertible to provide a canopy.

## THE ALL-WEATHER TENT

### (Reflector Type)

I found that one solution to the all-weather tent problem was to design and develop a tent on the reflector principle. The idea of the reflector type of tent was conceived hundreds of years ago and used extensively by the Hudson's Bay Company and others in the fur trade. However, to make this tent practical for all-weather use, I had to redesign it and add the needed features. In doing so, I made the base of the tent rectangular, 7 feet long by 6 feet wide, and added the feature of a convertible canopy, which will be described, to create an additional tent area 6 feet by 7 feet. The tent was constructed so that the open front of the tent proper was 6 feet high and the back 2 feet high, to give the correct reflecting angle of 60 degrees, the same as that of a properly constructed

reflector oven. So far, this might be described as simply a shed-like tent with the entire front open to the fire—the old original design, but changed to give it more practical dimensions and a better reflecting angle.

My next step was to stitch a canopy to the top front edge of the tent, extending this canopy forward 7 feet. Then two wings, each extending 7 feet, were similarly stitched to each side edge of the tent, to work in the same way as a door swings on its hinges.

If it rained, but there was no wind, the canopy was drawn out and tied to poles or trees; the cooking fire was then built under the canopy. If a wind blew up along with the rain, one of the wings was tied into place on the rainy side. Either tying-tapes or snaps can be used to join the wings to the top side edge of the canopy, where an overlap 6 inches wide on the canopy seals the joint and makes it leakproof. The lower edge of the wing is staked to the ground. (See illustration.)

If the wind blew from the opposite side, the other wing was tied into place. If the weather was squally, both wings were used. This left the front open; but if rain blew in, the canopy was dropped to an angle sufficient to shut out the rain. The wings and the canopy gave a large free area in which to move about. (See illustration.)

If the weather became very cold, a big fire with a backlog was needed. The canopy was then untied at the front fastenings, drawn back over the roof of the tent, and there stretched taut, a few inches above the roof, to serve as a fly. This served to keep snow off the main roof and eliminated the possibility of snow drip through the fabric of the tent—a common problem with the single-roof, reflector type of tent used before an open fire. (See illustration.) The side wings were now drawn out at an angle. The angle of the wings from the fire became the same as that of the roof, but vertical instead of horizontal. Heat was now reflected from three sides at a perfect angle of incidence. There was some reflection from the ground, too, because crosscurrents were cut off by the side wings.

To loaf or eat a meal on a cold wet day, while remaining warm, dry, and comfortable, not only makes outdoor living possible, but also adds a feeling of triumph over the elements.

One additional application of the all-weather tent should perhaps be mentioned here; and that is its adaptability to the desert. Nothing is more oppressive than the heat of the sun in the cell type of tent with the single opening. The canopy feature of the reflector type of tent at once offers the shade, ventilation, and freedom needed. In sandstorms this tent is pitched with its back to the prevailing wind, with the wings and canopy regulated to give relief from the blowing sand.

## THE CONVERTIBLE A TENT

While my final development of the all-weather tent provided comfort and convertibility for many campers, some found it too difficult to pitch. Tents which require only a single suspension rope at the peak are a tempting choice because of the easy pitching factor; but they allow no convertibility, and fall into the single-cell class often referred to by men of the wilderness as the "doghouse" variety.

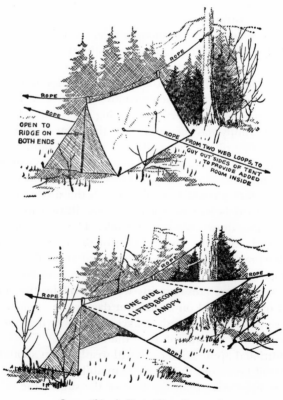

Convertible A Tent (Two Features)

My solution to simple pitching and at the same time gaining some of the advantages of the all-weather tent was to redesign a second tent—the old traditional *A* pattern. According to many leading explorers, this *A*-tent principle is close to the top of the list in efficiency, especially for wind resistance. It seemed the best basic principle on which to experiment.

My first alteration was to stitch an adequate number of loops (parrels) to the walls so that ropes could be attached to belly out the walls and overcome a bad feature common to the *A* tent—the tendency of the walls to sag inward. Two such loops on each side wall of the average-size tent are ample. (See illustration, page 114 for position of these loops.)

Up to this point, even with the walls corrected, I had little more than a single-cell tent with no convertible features. In its non-convertible form it was, however, suitable for arctic travel with a Primus stove, or with a camp stove when burning wood in a timbered area. But for all-season camping it still lacked the convertibility needed.

My next step proved to be the solution to my all-weather requirements. In its standard form the *A* tent opens at one end, with the flap opening made only three-fourths of the way to the peak of the tent. I cut this flap opening all the way to the peak not only at the regular tent opening but at both ends, and reconstructed the flaps to overlap about 6 inches. Tying-tapes sewed to the overlapping flaps form a good seal against the weather when the tent is kept closed and used in its simplest form as an ordinary *A* tent. The convertible features can now be applied.

To create a canopy from this improved version of the *A* tent, untie the flaps at both ends. Then untie half the tent from the ground stakes. Now this entire half of the tent can be raised to form a canopy as shown in the illustration on page 114.

Two methods of applying mosquito netting solve the problem of guarding against insects. Netting at both ends of the tent, sewed to the sides in the same way as the flaps and tied with tapes, will provide cross ventilation when the tent is pitched in its simplest *A* form. When half the tent is raised to form a canopy, and when this entire canopied area is generously draped with mosquito netting, it will create a sheltered living space during prolonged rains and allow complete relief from insects during the preparation and eating of meals and the performance of other diversions or camp tasks.

Obviously, the adaptable feature of the canopy principle of this tent is that if half the tent is pitched as a canopy on the windy wet side it can readily be staked back to the ground and the other half on the lee side raised to form the canopy.

One feature of the all-weather tent, however, was lacking—application of the lean-to, open-front feature with an open fire during low temperatures. This problem was solved as a matter of necessity at one time on a wilderness trip when the temperature dropped quite low late in the day. I pitched the tent on its side and used

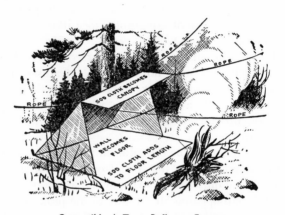

Convertible A Tent, Reflector Feature

one wall for the floor, leaving the open ground area of the tent exposed to the fire. This created a very satisfactory reflector lean-to shelter that made for good sleeping comfort. (See illustration.)

A third tent to consider if the expedition is largely to be on the arctic sea ice is the arctic pyramid tent developed by various explorers. It has been mentioned in the chapter on winter travel.

While both the all-weather tent and the convertible A tent have been used under a wide range of weather conditions, it must be pointed out that the selection of any tent should be made with special attention to distinguishing features, and that tent chosen which seems most suitable for your particular type of country and season. For example, the double arctic pyramid tent or the convertible A tent would be the best selection for camping on the sea ice and arctic prairie, where oil fuel must be used. If year-round camping in a forest area is to be done, the convertible A or the all-weather type should be chosen. This last choice would depend on whether or not a stove was to be used. If a stove is to be used, then the convertible *A* tent would be better. If no stove is to be used, the all-weather tent would be the best choice. Where the expedition includes desert travel, the choice will again be between the all-weather and the convertible *A,* perhaps in favor of the latter, owing to its larger shade area and advantage in resisting the wind. These are the fine distinctions to remember when considering the various types of tents.

While the common wall tent has not been considered here for general camping owing to its lack of convertibility, it must be mentioned in relation to the permanent camp. Here it has an important place in the housing of large groups engaged in surveying, logging, and mining operations, and for sheltering organized youth-camp groups. In summer these tents should be supplied with a canvas fly (a canopy that will form a double roof). In winter the tents should be double to provide an insulating dead-air space for warmth and economy of fuel. The walls can be either 6 feet high, for good headroom, or 4 feet high, and then pitched on top of a 2-foot high crib made of poles that are eventually banked with snow. The same furnishings should be provided in the building of such permanent tent camps as would obtain if the shelters were cabins. In short, they should have stoves, bunks, tables, seats, food boxes, gas or kerosene mantle lamps, and other necessary equipment. These must either be hauled or flown in. Bunks, tables, and seats roughly made in the forest also serve well. If possible, permanent wall tents should have floors; otherwise the ground becomes muddy during rains. Or in winter, when the tents are heated, and during dry summer periods, every step raises a cloud of dust. Permanent tent camps, unless guarded, are frequently ravaged by bears.

Most tents are wrinkled and out of shape when they are pitched. The reason is that the base will not form a perfect rectangle without special measurement. A sewed-in floor cloth makes an excellent guide, but it is an obstacle to much utility camping. A plan I have used for years in pitching a tent assures a perfect rectangle with little effort. Stake down the two rear corners of the tent. Grasp the two front corners and draw them taut to form the apex of a triangle with the two rear corners. This apex is the center line of your tent. Half the width of the tent to either side of this apex will determine exactly the side lines of your tent. One side of the tent is now drawn over to a side line and staked; when the other side is drawn to the opposite side line you will have a smoothly pitched tent. (For additional information on pitching tents for winter use, see the chapter "Winter Travel by Dog Team and Hand Toboggan.")

Plastics as tent fabrics have proved unsatisfactory. Even the best materials developed many tiny pinholes after only ordinary use. Their worst drawback is that they allow condensation to take place, wetting rather than protecting the occupants. This is especially true at temperatures of 50 degrees Fahrenheit, or colder.

The best tent fabric available on local markets is still Egyptian cotton made into what is commercially called balloon cloth, sometimes erroneously referred to as balloon silk. This material is also used for lightweight sails, from which it has derived the more common name of sailcloth or sail silk. Domestic cotton sailcloth is less expensive. Sailcloth is slightly heavier than some of the tightly woven percales, but stronger and light enough for most outfits. Special, very fine, tent fabrics which are extremely lightweight, very closely woven, mildew and rot proof, and immune to certain destructive insects are available. Tents for hiking trips and mountain climbing should be of very light material. For an inexpensive tent use unbleached muslin.

Any of the fabrics described shed rain well when waterproofed. For many years I waterproofed my tents each season to make sure they would resist the next year's rains. However, while experimenting with this problem, I found that by taking along a bar of beeswax on a trip, my tent could be kept waterproof. After the tent had been subjected to heavy rains and had lost some of its waterproof quality, I would wait until it was bone dry and well pitched, and then rub a cake of beeswax over the entire tent with a long ironing motion. The surface fibers would pick up enough wax to keep the tent water-repellent. When the hot sun hit the tent the wax was absorbed by the fibers.

A solution of one pound of beeswax to one gallon of turpentine painted on the pitched tent is another effective waterproofing. Gasoline may be used in place of turpentine, but turpentine is better because it leaves a valuable substance in the fibers and is less of a fire hazard. Paraffin can also be substituted for beeswax; but, though it is cheaper, it does not impart the preservative value of beeswax to the tent. Melt the wax, stir it into the turpentine, paint the solution on the stretched tent, and let it dry for several days during hot weather.

When pitching a tent, cut the tent stakes long, not under eighteen inches. Poles suitable for tents are abundant in an evergreen country. Cut all the poles you need for the entire job and carry them to an open spot near the tent where they can be dressed down for length and where the stakes can be cut from them. It is awkward, and bad camping, to get a tent half up and then have to search for more poles and stakes.

Some writers warn against pitching a tent under trees because of the danger of falling branches in a high wind. Most branches broken loose by the wind will be carried away from the tree and be more of a danger to your tent if it is pitched in the open. The important thing is first to check for dead standing trees and fell them before the tent is pitched. Trees are on occasion struck by lightning, but the bolt passes along the tree to the ground. The risk of being in the open or among trees is about even. Whenever possible I attach tent ropes to trees, and in my lifetime I have seen no great hazard in lightning while camping that would not prevail elsewhere.

Your tent site should slope gently toward the front for drainage. Make your bed with the head higher than the foot. Trenching along the edge of the tent is desirable but not essential when air mattresses are used. On the solid rock terrain of the North it is, of course, impossible to trench. One of the most useful tools for trenching, and one which will serve many other uses in camp (see "Wilderness Cooking"), is a small diamond-shaped mason's trowel having a blade of five inches and a hickory handle. It can be used to dig out roots or rocks, and thus smooth out the tent site. In addition, the cook will be using it much of the time as a pancake turner and in frying.

Tent ropes need not be heavier than No. 5 or No. 6 sash cord. Ropes should be sufficiently long so that you can go back twenty or thirty feet to a tree or a bush if you have to, rather than drive another stake or erect a pole.

Knots are a subject that should be studied at home, not at the moment they are required for use. Perhaps the most important to the camper is the *Taut-Line Hitch*. The use of this knot for all suspension ropes makes it possible to adjust the ropes after the tent has been erected, and permits you to take out any wrinkles. It is a knot which will not slip of its own accord, but which can be slipped manually along the taut part of the rope to any point, where it will remain. This provides a ready means of lengthening or shortening the tent suspension ropes. The knot used around tent poles should be the *Clove Hitch,* because here the knot can be slipped up and down the pole for adjustment without untying it. (See illustrations.)

Do not tie knots which require needless time to undo. Most knots can be completed with the end doubled back into the knot to form a loop so that a simple pull will untie the whole knot. The failure to add the last loop has been a fault in books on knot tying. Even

Taut-Line Hitch

Taut-Line Hitch (Improved)

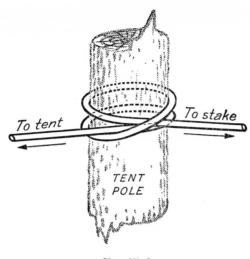

Clove Hitch

the *Bowline,* which is the great non-slip knot, should be finished with the end doubled back into a loop so that it can be untied with a jerk. Much time is saved in breaking camp where knots do not have to be laboriously untied. This is especially true if ropes become rain-soaked.

If stakes cannot be driven, tie the tent down to poles and lay rocks on the ends of the poles where they extend beyond the tent. If no rocks are available, use small logs. In the desert fill sacks with sand and tie the tent ropes to them.

New types of mosquito netting, developed during World War II for tropical use, are now on the market. Numerous kinds of marquisette, a net-like curtain material, if bought in a fine mesh make excellent insect netting. But all netting material must be thoroughly washed to remove the starch or filler, and then rinsed in one of the various newly developed commercial fabric softeners which may be bought in any grocery store. Then the netting will drape and close well at the openings. Since insect netting is exceptionally light, a generous amount of it should be carried. The edges of the netting should be reinforced with soft tape or hemmed for strength, and small loops should be sewn on at intervals so that the netting may be fastened to the tent. The netting should be liberally draped over any open canopy area. And do not overlook the advantage of erecting only the mosquito netting without the tent for a noon-day stop during the height of the insect season. Black netting, while funereal in appearance, permits a clearer view of the landscape because it does not reflect light.

## MODERN INSECTICIDES

DDT and other new insecticides developed during wartime are under the strictest examination in the various fields of insect control. Against the chigger DDT has no effect whatever; against the bedbug it is most effective. Against the two common pests of the wilderness—the fly and the mosquito—it has been fairly successful.

DDT comes in various sprays and powders, and in combination with other insect killers that work faster than DDT. It should be remembered that DDT in strong solutions with oil is poisonous to the skin. The safest and most convenient form for use in camping is the spray in which DDT is suspended in Freon gas. (Freon gas in solution is used in the coils of your refrigerator.) The spray will quickly cover the whole interior of a tent and will remain suspended long enough for every insect within the tent to get a fatal dose. Since Freon gas is retained under pressure, DDT when mixed with it is sold in a metal container with a spray valve. These containers are commonly called "bug bombs."

One drawback to DDT, besides the possibility of poison, is the length of time required before it becomes effective. For quicker results use a combination of DDT and malathion or lindane, a spray that kills immediately. The DDT with its delayed action will then take care of any later insect intruders. Sprays in this form can be obtained under various trade names.

For out-of-doors a number of insect repellents have been developed which can be rubbed on the face, neck, and hands. The cream types in tube form are the handiest and safest to carry where breakage is a concern. Spray types for skin and clothing are also available.

Dusts can be prepared for such insects as get into one's clothes and attack the body. These dusts are not easily prepared by the layman. DDT ground in talc or some other powder can be bought. They are prepared in strengths varying from $\frac{1}{10}$ to 10 per cent DDT.

The ink is scarcely dry on the latest insecticide bulletins of the

United States Agricultural Department before other, more effective, insecticides are being reported. For special insecticides in varying forms, it is well to consult the latest government reports. Bulletins are issued at frequent intervals, and effective new combinations are quickly made available commercially.

A head net and a pair of light leather gloves, while a nuisance, are the best guards against insect pests. Because black flies can and do crawl under nets, spray the net and gloves with a repellent.

The most overlooked insect deterrent is the age-old smudge pot. Use a No. 10 can. Fill the can with duff (pine needles and humus from the forest floor). Light the top and let it break into a good flame, then smother the flame and let the duff smolder like a pipe. The smudge pot is most effective on the black fly, but only moderately so on the mosquito. If no can or other disposable container is available, a smudge made on the ground will serve. The advantage of the pot is that it can be moved. The smudge should not be too close to the camp, but far enough upwind, about fifty feet, to allow a light smoke to drift through the camp. The effect will not be immediate; but when the smudge is some distance away the area of control is wider, and after a while the smoke becomes more effective.

## THE BED

Almost any sort of day on the trail can be endured if at its close you can sleep eight full hours in comfort. The body and spirit endure more abuse in the wrong type of camp bed than on the roughest trail. Yet a comfortable camp bed can be purchased at any good wilderness outfitting firm or sporting-goods store. You can also make your own sleeping unit.

Blankets are not suitable for wilderness beds. Their weight in relation to their warmth is excessive. The best blanket I know of, the Hudson's Bay 4-point blanket, weighs six pounds. Several of

Down Sleeping Bag (Commercial Type)

these will not have the warmth of a six-pound down robe, nor will they be as soft and snug. A down robe can be compressed into a much smaller space in the pack than any other form of bedding comparable to it in warmth.

A sleeping unit should be adaptable to great extremes of temperature. If you do not wish to buy one of the expensive down sleeping bags, here is how you can make an uncomplicated but satisfactory unit. The specifications are simple.

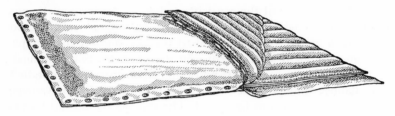

**Down Sleeping Bag (Homemade Type)**

Make two down quilts 90″ x 90″, with three pounds of down in each. From a good grade of gabardine make a flat tarp or cover 93″ x 93″, with the edges well hemmed or reinforced with tape. Spread this out to its full area. Lay the two down quilts on top of this tarp, and spread them out to their full area of 90″ x 90″. Fold the combination of quilts and tarp down the center. You should then have four folds or thicknesses of quilt approximately 45″ x 90″, with a tarp covering, one-half of the tarp on the bottom, the other half on top.

You could crawl in for a night's sleep without any further work on this unit if you could be sure to keep under and over you the two thicknesses of down quilt and one thickness of tarp. But the chances are that you would kick your way out of them before morning. To avoid this, have a tent and awning company fasten heavy glove snaps at the foot and open side of your tarp for closing the tarp cover. You will then come through snug and warm till morning. I do not like to use snaps more than two-thirds of the way up the side, because the upper portion is tucked around my head, and should be free from metal parts.

Because the snaps do not quite do the job of sealing the open side of the tarp, sew strips of material ten inches wide along the inside edge of the snaps on the tarp to act as sealer cloths. Just before snapping the sleeping unit shut, fold these strips around the open edges of the quilts to create a tight seal. Do this along the foot and the side to be snapped.

If it is not too cold, you can sleep beneath one layer of quilt. If the weather is warm, cover yourself with the tarp only. In extremely cold weather get in between the two upper and under layers, with the tarp covering all.

The quilts are best made of goose or domestic duck down, since eider down is not available. If you have a difficult time buying down, get enough high-grade down-filled pillows and remove the down. The cost will not be much higher. The quilt material should be a good grade of lightweight, feather-proof Bohemian ticking.

The chances are that you will not be able to buy quilts 90″ x 90″; and if you can they will be much too fancy for the wilderness and perhaps a little steep for your pocketbook. My suggestion is to make your own. Sew the material for the top and bottom of the quilt together on three sides, leaving one end open, thus creating a large square flat bag approximately 90″ x 90″. Now, sew parallel seams straight up and down from the bottom to the open end of your bag at six-inch intervals. You will then find that you have fifteen tubes into which to stuff the goose or duck down. Do this a fistful at a time, so that the feathers will be uniformly distributed, and do it out in the country somewhere. If you choose the spring of the year when the birds are nesting, they will use every stray feather for their nests. If you try doing this indoors, you will have feather-down in everything, including the pancake sirup.

After all of the down has been inserted, close the open end of the quilt and sew it by hand. Later, sew it by machine. What you now have is a quilt with tubular filled areas of down. Do not sew across this unit through the down. If you do, the down will start to work through the sewing. From time to time fluff the down back and forth through the tubes by pounding on them. This will keep the quilt soft and uniform.

Dry-cleaning firms now clean these down units so that you do not have to concern yourself about sheets unless you are very fastidious. A wool-flannel sheet on the inside—or even a wool blanket if weight is not too great a consideration—gives a warm feeling in winter camping.

In making up your bed, be sure that the ground is cleared of brush and reasonably leveled; a few boughs laid on the ground will help create a level surface. A ground cloth should then be laid. This cloth is subject to much abuse, and I find the best material to use for it is a good grade of unbleached muslin filled solid with a solution of three parts paraffin and one part beeswax melted together and ironed into the cloth. Every few seasons you will have to throw away your ground cloth and make a new one. It becomes moldy and torn, and looks "beat" after a season or two. This is bound to happen, since it takes all the abuse from the ground; and if your trips are over the great Canadian Shield it will get even harder wear from the abrasive rocks.

Place your air mattress on top of the ground cloth. The air mattress should not be inflated beyond a point where, if you sit on it, you can feel the contour of the ground under you. This allows the air mattress to conform to the shape of your body. When you lie down on it, enough air will be displaced so that your body will be held off the ground.

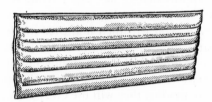

Rubber Air Mattress

The pillow should not be placed under your head but under the head of the sleeping unit. You can then draw the sleeping unit up around your neck, and the pillow will not interfere. Folded clothes can be used instead of a pillow, and if they are inserted under the sleeping bag they will be soft enough.

Some wilderness travelers still insist on bough beds. Even when made in the best "shingled" fashion, bough beds are good for no more than half the night. Toward morning they can be distinctly uncomfortable. I know such strictures will be blasphemy to some, and because I like the fragrance of balsam I compromise by placing a few boughs at the head and the foot of my bed. After all, it seems utterly foolish to omit an air mattress. The short air mattress weighs three pounds and saves endless hours of work on a trip; besides it is more comfortable. The full-length mattress in the light-weight types weighs little more.

In winter, when snow is cleared away for a tent, a certain amount of snow—about six inches—should be left for ground insulation. Boughs are placed over this snow; but instead of leaning them slightly and shingling one bough over the other as in the bough bed, the boughs are laid flat, and only enough are used to cover the snow area. The floor cloth is then laid over the boughs, and a wool blanket is placed on the floor cloth. On the blanket goes the air mattress, topped by the sleeping unit. Pressure of body weight reduces the insulating value of the sleeping bag on the underside. The blanket compensates for this. Any packsacks which are empty during the night can be slipped over the foot of the sleeping unit like a sock, thus adding much warmth.

### Packsacks, Duffel Bags, Tumplines, Containers, Food Bags

One of the chief shortcomings of many wilderness outfits is the method, or lack of method, used in packing and carrying the equipment. It is not so easy a problem as at first appears. The most common failure probably is stuffing too many small items in one large packsack, resulting in a confusion of broken containers and damaged equipment, to say nothing of frayed nerves.

In the matter of shipping equipment, it should be borne in mind that too many persons employed in handling freight are notoriously careless. When you ship your outfit, remember that it may be in such hands for most of the journey; pack it accordingly. It will be dragged over dirty, oily floors and dropped from trains onto station platforms. It will be loaded in a ship's hold, perhaps under machine parts weighing tons.

### Shipping Containers

The need to make quick transfers from home to station, station to ship, and so on, calls for shipping containers that are not too large to set on the back seat, the floor, or the trunk compartment of a car, or in a plane, and even, on occasion, to pack with a tumpline on your back. Trunks are out. Foot lockers or light waterproof plywood cases, with a crossbar at each end for handles, are good. If made of wood, they should be well nailed and glued. In shipping they should be well lashed with rope. Pack the more fragile contents in buffers, using such items as clothes, socks, and other soft articles.

### The Packsack

Essentially, a packsack is a large canvas sack equipped with carrying straps for the shoulders and a head strap to help support the load just above the forehead. This head strap is commonly called a "tumpline," which is incorrect. (See "Tumpline" illustration and description in this chapter.) The common name for this packsack is Duluth packsack or Poirer packsack.

**Duluth or Poirer Packsack**

Knapsacks are smaller sacks with shoulder straps, used largely to carry personal items. There will be disagreement here because hundreds of patterns of packsacks, rucksacks, haversacks, and so on, have been developed with an overlap of nomenclature. The knapsack is often liberally supplied with pockets sewed to the sack proper for small items. Though these knapsacks find their way into wilderness trips, they are a nuisance. The single compartment of a packsack is admirably adapted to canoe and back-pack travel, as well as to travel by toboggan and dog team. Packsacks are unsuitable, however, for horse packing. (See "Panniers.") Packsacks are made in the following sizes:

No. 1—24″ x 26″
No. 2—26″ x 28″
No. 3—28″ x 30″

Nearly all packsacks are made with the closing flap too short. When the sack is loaded, either the straps do not reach the buckles or the flap does not fully close the packsack opening. For this reason I have mine made to order by having the flap extended six inches, or I add a short section to the flap on a standard packsack.

About the only other unit which lends itself to wilderness packing is the pack basket. Its advantage over the packsack is that when it is loaded with hard objects, such as canned goods, they will not press into your back or work through the packsack material. Pack baskets come with shoulder straps and a protective canvas cover. However, both the shoulder straps and the cover are badly adapted. The position of the shoulder straps makes the loaded basket unwieldy; and the cover, because it has to be slit to make room for the shoulder straps, does not offer the needed protection. My suggestion is to order the largest size basket alone, without the shoulder straps or cover. Then place the basket in a No. 2 packsack which has been first lined with a waterproof bag. This makes an excellent packing unit, comfortable to carry, and one that offers great protection to its contents. I once saw this combination tumble through a section of rapids, the whole pack coming through without damage.

Pack frames were made for the old prospectors who carried picks, shovels, and other unwieldy items on mountain trails. For the wilderness, pack frames and packsacks with frames are a nuisance. One

**Pack Basket**

theory is that they keep the load out and away from your back, and for that reason they are supposed to be cool to carry during hot weather. In practice the load extends too far out from your back and becomes unwieldy. As to coolness, this is a negligible factor. If you want to avoid a nuisance, do not take pack frames into the wilderness, but adopt the Duluth or Poirer packsack, which will enable you to carry a big load or a small one with equal comfort by adjusting the carrying straps.

At one time duffel bags were a part of my equipment because I liked to pack with a tumpline. I still use the tumpline, but I have discarded duffel bags because of their awkwardness. Such large items as sleeping bags and tents are exceedingly difficult to pack and unpack in a duffel bag.

Do not pick up a packsack by the straps, or the straps will soon tear loose from the canvas. This is a difficult tear to mend. Grasp the packsack by the "ears"—the canvas corners—and lift the pack to your bended knee. Slide an arm into a carrying strap and place your hand on the bottom of the pack; then, with a quick boost, toss it into place on your back. Now, while stooping, slip the other arm into the second carrying strap, draw the head strap up high on the forehead, and be off.

### The Tumpline

The tumpline was first referred to in the chapter on the canoe. It is very valuable in the North, where it is used by the Indians for most portages. The tumpline is a 2½-inch head strap to which two narrower 8-foot leather straps or lines are attached. Sometimes these narrower lines are attached to the head strap with buckles so that they can be adjusted after the pack is loaded on the back. Inexpensive tumplines can be made with a leather head strap and ropes, but they are not quite as adaptable as those with leather lines.

When carrying a load with the tumpline, place the head strap high on your forehead. The advantages of the head carry instead of the shoulder carry are the better position of the pack and less strain on the body. Your neck muscles are stronger than you realize, and with continued tumpline packing they will develop greater strength. Indians, who pack all their lives, amaze the white man with their tumpline packing ability. Special feats of 400- and 500-pound carries are known, but these are exceptional. The daily packing of 200 pounds over portage trails by Indians is not uncommon.

Another advantage of the tumpline is its adaptability. The commercial freight sent into the interior by canoe brigade comes in all sorts of packages, and the portaging of these variously shaped items is made practical with the tumpline. Several boxes, for example, can be stacked one on top of the other; the tumpline is then tied around them; the head strap is placed high on the forehead; and they are ready for portage.

The tumpline is also adaptable for canoe trips, when such items as duffel bags and bed rolls are easily portaged. Some packers combine several standard packsacks into one load, carrying it with the tumpline, rather than use the packsack straps for carrying.

Tumpline Packing Method

### Food Containers—Panniers

Friction-top cans are necessary containers for items like jam, butter, and so on, but they become a hazard if they are placed loose in the pack. There is always the danger that they may be crushed open and spread their contents over everything, or become dented. In the chapter "Pack-Horse Methods" I described kyacks, or panniers. In my own outfit these were made 20″ x 20″ of ⅛″ waterproof plywood. As will be recalled, they also had leather loops for hanging them on the packsaddle, ready for the hitch. These panniers, slipped into packsacks, can be used on canoe journeys. One of them will take all the friction-top cans; the other, partitioned, may be packed with small items likely to suffer damage through the canvas walls of a packsack. The leather loops are excellent for lifting the

Pannier for Friction-Top Cans

panniers out of the pack. My last set of panniers was made to open on the flat side, thus making it much easier to get at any one item. They were designed to take half-gallon friction-top cans. Strip sponge rubber, if glued to the top edge of the pannier, will provide a waterproof seal between the cover and the pannier proper, and will make the pannier waterproof. It is a luxury to open a pack and have only a few such large units to lift out, with everything easily accessible.

All dry food items should go into sailcloth bags waterproofed with paraffin. Such bags can be bought from sporting-goods firms and wilderness outfitters; or, if you prefer, anyone who can operate a sewing machine can readily make them up for you. These food bags should be round on the bottom, and wide rather than long, so that they can be placed upright without tipping over. A tie string should be sewed to the side of the bag, near the top, for closing. Use a wax crayon for labeling; thus, when the bags are washed, the labels will wash out too, and the bags can be used for other food items, if preferred. Use a hot iron for melting the paraffin into the material; then, while the bags are hot, place one on top of another to allow the paraffin to soak uniformly through all of them. Or the bags can be dipped in melted wax. Line each paraffined bag with a light plastic bag.

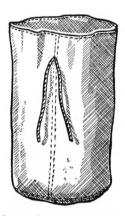

**Round-Bottom Paraffined Cloth Food Bag**

One of the most valuable containers for carrying fragile food items in a packsack is a No. 10 can fitted into a bag with a drawstring. I have carried eggs in such a container over rough trails without breakage. Other sizes of cans can also be used. This combination works well for breakable camp items such as first-aid equipment, films, and so on.

Liquids are few in the wilderness outfit; but such items as liquid cement, gun oil, vanilla, antiseptics, and the like, need safe containers. Liquid cement is best carried in a small friction-top can. Soft metal tubes may be crushed or break open, and are not safe containers without additional protection. Leading sporting-goods stores supply a gun-oil can which is leakproof. Bottles containing vanilla and antiseptics, I have found, come through safely if they are well wrapped with adhesive tape.

The most logical container for carrying liquids seemed to be plastic bottles. I was quite optimistic when they came on the market, but I was disappointed. They proved to be undependable. In addition, the soft plastic absorbed their contents, and those which contained food caused putrefaction. The harder plastics, though capable of much abuse, often crack, apparently through chemical change. In the city this would be a negligible matter; in the wilderness it poses a serious problem.

Plastic sacks or bags have their practical use only as liners for cloth bags. They are not dependable by themselves. Note: Observe carefully the method used in packing food items described in the chapter "The Wilderness Food Budget," page 184.

My method of packing the canoe trip essentials en route is as follows: First, the waterproof ground cloth is laid on the ground. On this go the air mattress, the tent (if dry), and the sleeping bags. All are rolled into the waterproof ground cloth. The whole is then strapped with the tumpline. (See illustration "Tumpline Packing," on page 131.

All that now remains is the food, the incidental small equipment, and clothes. Clothes are put into light bags with drawstrings to avoid leaving a clutter of small clothes lying around. All the small equipment, it will be recalled, was left in the compartment pannier; so, here too is a larger unit. The canned items, such as jam, butter, and the like, were also put in a pannier. Now, with the beds and the tent disposed of in the first unit, there are only two panniers to place in a packsack; the clothes bags should go in next to the back to soften your load. Food bags, returned to the packsack after each use, are already packed; cooking utensils in a compact nesting unit are placed in the top of the packsack or in the pack basket.

If you will analyze this, you will see that not a great deal was un-packed. All small items were left in the compartment pannier, and after use were put back. All canned items also remained in the pan-nier and were put back after use—much as you would set things back on a shelf. The point is that a few large units were quickly loaded into packsacks, the beds and the tent were rolled, and the trip was under way. No more than fifteen minutes should be needed to get ready.

Before packing your packsack, put a waterproof bag liner in it. Tightly close the inner bag with a tie string and strap down the flaps of the packsack. If the canoe upsets, everything will float, noth-ing will be lost, and security for your equipment is assured.

## THE AX

The blunt, woodshed variety of ax has no place in the wilderness. Your ax should be of high-quality, tough steel; it should have a straight-grained hickory handle, and the blade should line up with the center of the handle. The blade must be thin enough for easy chopping. It should be kept very sharp, and properly sheathed when not in use.

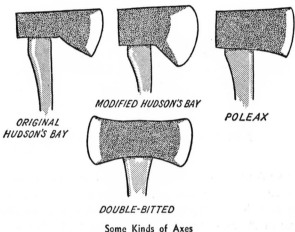

ORIGINAL HUDSON'S BAY

MODIFIED HUDSON'S BAY

POLEAX

DOUBLE-BITTED

Some Kinds of Axes

The ax commonly used on canoe trips is the three-quarter size, often referred to as a "boy's ax" or poleax. It is the cause of many accidents in the woods, even among experienced woodsmen. Owing to the shorter length of the handle, the ax may not swing clear of the body after a miss, and serious injury to an ankle or foot may result. A missed stroke with a full-handled ax will either swing clear of the body or end in the chopping block.

Organized camps should not permit the use of the three-quarter ax. The hazard is too great. However, it is a very handy instrument in the hands of an experienced axman. But it is not a tool for the beginner. A full-sized ax that weighs three or three and one-half pounds is best.

One of the best ax sheaths is made with two pieces of thin brass plate between two pieces of leather, riveted together with copper rivets. When this sheath is slipped over the blade, the blade is wedged between the brass plates, and does not touch the metal. A thong is fastened to each side of the sheath for holding it on the ax. If the proper lashing is made, the pull of the thongs will be up the center of the blade, and the bowknot can be made over the handle at the butt of the blade. (See illustration.)

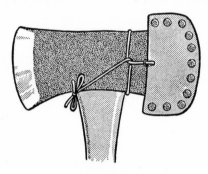

**Double-Bitted Ax Showing One Blade Sheathed**
**(Sheath Metal-Lined)**

Do not work nervously when swinging an ax. Most people are out of breath after a few strokes, and begin to miss. The secret of good chopping is to hit the right spot each time with little more than the weight of the ax in the blow. In cutting off a log, cut out large chips. This is possible only by starting the cut wide, so that the ax goes in at a slant, creating a wide wedge shape when the center of the log is reached. Cut halfway through on one side, then halfway on the other. On a log ten inches in diameter several ax-blade cuts will be required across the log. When making the cuts, do not make the first cut in the center but to one side. Make the next cut on the other side, then make the center cuts. Repeat these cuts at the opposite side of the chip. When the last cut is made, the whole chip will drop out. You will have a chip that will almost cover an average water bucket. As you go toward the center of the wedge cut, the chips, of course, will get smaller.

In cutting tent poles, make a single slanting cut on one side of a small tree, then on the other. The tree will fall over. Hold the tree at the butt end and cut off the branches, swinging the ax toward the top—not toward the butt end of the tree. In cutting tent stakes

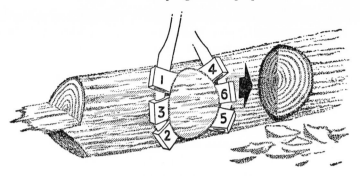

Relative Position of Ax-Blade Cuts

from such a pole, a chopping log should be used. Sharpen the stake ends as you hold them against a nearby tree or stump. An ax will not sink into the wood if it is driven across the grain. Chop at a slant.

In felling a fair-sized tree, make a wedge-shaped cut on the side of the tree facing where you want it to fall. Then go to the other side of the tree and make a similar cut a few inches higher on the trunk. The break will be from one cut to the other, and the tree will fall in the right direction unless it leans very badly the other way. Note the center of gravity.

Spectators are sometimes surprised by the accuracy of a capable axman. They are probably not as surprised to see a good golfer drive. Yet the necessity for proper stance, follow through, and concentration is the same for both. One of the best methods of gaining

Proper Cuts for Felling a Tree

accuracy with an ax is to place a match, sulphur side up, in the crack of a log or chopping block; then practice swinging the ax until you can split the head of the match, and incidentally light it.

The question of what type of ax is best, whether single or double-bitted, with straight or curved handle, is always controversial. Let me say that either a single or double-bitted ax can be balanced so as to perform with great accuracy. The single-bitted ax is convenient for travel in all seasons except winter. When the ground is open, and stakes must be driven, the flat side of a double-bitted ax is a poor tool for this purpose. In winter a double-bitted ax is best because extremely cold weather makes steel brittle, and the blade may break. The double-bitted ax gives you an alternate blade. Then, again, much more wood is cut in winter; and the thin blade can be used for chopping, the thicker one for splitting. The single-bitted ax is best with a curved handle, the double-bitted with a straight handle.

Here are some simple pointers on how to swing and hold an ax. Wear clothes that allow free arm swing. You must have a good stance, and this will not be possible if your feet are too close together. The distance they should be apart will depend on your height, but a spread of fourteen inches to two feet is best.

If you are right-handed, grasp the ax with your left hand near the end of the handle until your hand fits comfortably against the knob. Then place your right hand a comfortable distance down the handle toward the blade. This distance will vary with the ax and with your size, but it should be from about two-thirds to three-fourths of the distance from the left hand to the ax head. This position of the hands will enable you to lift the blade for the stroke.

If you are left-handed, reverse the position of your hands. However, if you are to become a skilled axman, you must learn to swing an ax both right- and left-handed. Start practicing both ways from the beginning of your training, because if your reflexes are built up for one side only, it will become increasingly difficult to learn to chop both right- and left-handed.

Now let us suppose that you are going to cut down a tree. The direction in which to fell it has been decided. Mentally mark the spot where the cut is going to be made. Then chop out a notch halfway into the tree as described earlier in the chapter. Because the notch is going to be wide at the start, it will give you a natural angle to the center of the tree. Follow the sides of this angle from the center, right out to the starting point of your stroke. This will be the angle of your swing. (See illustration on page 137.)

Watch this angle carefully. If you have any doubt as to why I say this, observe the average axman. Though he may be fairly accurate, he is apt to start the swing of his ax at different angles without being aware of doing so, and as a result he will be only moderately successful in making his cuts. Too many axmen hurry their back stroke by bringing the ax head back too soon, and thus do not get the full benefit of the energy they have expended.

Keep a "rear-view eye" on the ax as you swing it behind your shoulder. You need accuracy through the entire swing of the stroke, a much overlooked secret of chopping. Incidentally, this "rear-view eye" will prevent you from striking or hooking an overhead branch, a cause of serious accidents.

One last and most important point: In chopping, as in splitting, you may waste energy in freeing the ax from the cut. Actually, an ax does not stick as much in chopping as it does in splitting a knotty block of wood, but it does hold. What you should do is to twist the ax slightly at the end of each stroke. This will release it and at the same time split out the chip. This can be done after the blow is struck, and this is how such a twist appears to an observer. But a good axman applies the twist a split fraction of a second before all the energy is out of his blow.

Your knees should be slightly flexed when making the stroke. Bring the ax all the way up behind your shoulder, holding the handle as I have described. Do not give up this hold until you bring the ax forward, and then not until the ax is on the way down. In the hitting stroke, remember that the ax travels in an arc, first up and then down. When chopping right-handed, your right hand starts sliding down the handle toward your left hand as the ax begins its downward direction, and continues to slide until it touches the left hand, meeting that hand just a moment before the blade cuts into its mark. At that moment both hands are close to the end of the handle. When you chop left-handed the procedure is reversed.

If you tried to split a chunk of wood with one stroke of the ax and failed, your ax would stick fast in the wood. Or, if you stood the chunk of wood on a chopping block, and the piece split easily, the ax might go all the way through and stick in the chopping block. Here is how to avoid such ax "traps."

Set the block to be chopped on end. Grasp your ax as you did before, and bring it straight down. Just as the blade hits the wood, turn the blade. This, as you can see, is another case of close timing. By swinging the ax, and turning it at the last moment, a prying operation takes place, creating a forceful leverage and the blade will not stick. Thus, you split the chunk and at the same time almost tear it apart by your side-leverage twist of the blade. The energy in the side twist comes as part of the impact of the stroke. The ax will always stop near the top of the chunk, even though it splits the chunk in two.

If you are a beginner, don't try to split up the large piece of chunk into small pieces by holding it in one hand and cutting with the other. A trained axman can do it, but it is too dangerous for the beginner. If you watch a good axman closely, you will see that as the ax approaches his holding hand he momentarily takes his hand away from the wood and then recovers the larger section before it falls. But this requires experience and skill.

### THE KNIFE

On a wilderness trip you need three knives: (1) a belt knife; (2) what is called a "crooked" knife, which can be purchased from the Hudson's Bay House (their wilderness supply depot), Winnipeg, Canada; and (3) a penknife.

The thick chisel-edged belt knives, which are generally sold, are of little value in the wilderness. Get your belt knife too thin rather than too thick. Line the sheath with sheet aluminum so that the knife will not cut through it. Fold a sheet of aluminum over the back of the knife; cut it to fit the shape of the blade, but slightly wider, and then drill a row of holes along the edge. Then cut off several short stubs of copper wire, insert them in the holes, and peen down the ends to form rivet heads.

**Belt Knife**
**(Thin Blade)**

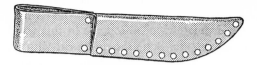

**Belt-Knife Sheath**
**(Metal Lined)**

The crooked knife is just what the name implies, a knife with a crooked blade. This knife is excellent for making a new paddle, replacing the broken parts of a canvas canoe, making snowshoe frames, and other woodcraft. When buying it, state whether you want it left- or right-handed, because it is designed for either hand. This knife is in common use in the North by the Indians. Where such knives are not available, the Indians make them out of flat files by annealing (removing the temper by heat and slow cooling), shaping, and then retempering them. I came upon an Indian carving out a paddle with such a knife, and realized more than ever its wide adaptability when I saw him creating masterful curves and formations in the white spruce.

**Crooked Knife**

A penknife should go into the first-aid kit. It will serve as a scalpel, and on occasion is handy for other very small work. Keep all your knives exceptionally sharp. Keep the penknife sterilized by boiling it or by plunging it into an antiseptic solution after every use so that it will be ready for any surgical emergency.

Reference has been made to thick and to thin knife blades. This matter of knife thickness, as well as the proper bevel for sharpening, has caused much confusion between knife makers and knife users. If a few points are understood, this confusion should not exist.

A knife that will hack the bones of a heavy carcass or, even worse, cut nails without destroying the edge, as claimed by some knife makers, must be made with a thick blade, have a blunt chisel-like bevel, and be exceptionally hard-tempered. The finest steel in the world would not withstand cutting bone or metal if it were not so constructed. Unfortunately, a knife made in this way is not suited for general wilderness use. Bone should be cut with a small saw or an ax, never with a knife. Ax-blade bevels are abrupt enough to withstand a limited amount of bone cutting.

In buying high-quality knives with blades thin enough for general wilderness use, knife users are often misled by the claims made for hard-tempered, chisel-edged knives, and then blame the manufacturer when the blade is dulled or broken by immoderate use. Another problem arises in sharpening when the knife blade is held flat against the whetstone. A thin, razor-like edge will of course result, but it will not stand up under normal all-around use. The angle between the stone and the blade when a knife is being sharpened should be about twenty degrees. Certain heavy, soft-tempered, chisel-edged knives are manufactured for throwing purposes. No high-quality knife can be thrown without, sooner or later, breaking off the point or otherwise damaging the blade or handle. A good knife is a fine instrument; it should be properly used and then carefully sheathed.

### WHETSTONE AND FILE

The secret of sharp knives is to have stones of such material as will create the finest possible edges. Emery and Carborundum— black stones which wear away rapidly and make a muddy smudge when oil is applied—are not a good choice. There is a stone on the market known as India stone, which is made by subjecting aluminum oxide to furnace heat until it is almost as hard as a diamond.

**Double-Faced Whetstone**

India stones come in various textures. There are also finishing stones, which are mined, called soft and hard Arkansas. Soft Arkansas is far from being soft, but the hard Arkansas is so hard and fine that the stone virtually polishes as it hones. The fine India and the soft Arkansas are the best combination of stones for the wilderness. Extraordinarily fine edges can be made with these stones. The India hones rapidly in the fine texture, and the soft Arkansas gives a razor-sharp finish. If still finer edges are desired, then a hard Arkansas "slip" stone, which is wedge-shaped and weighs less than an ounce, should be used as a finish stone. Use a hard Arkansas for sharpening your fishhooks. A fine knife should not be subjected to the coarse stones that are often sold as whetstones. Fine penknives and delicate tools should be honed only with hard Arkansas stones, or at least with the fine-textured India and soft Arkansas.

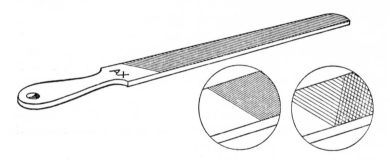

**Double-Faced Ax File**

Axes are made of tough, but not exceptionally hard, steel. A file will sharpen them. For this purpose use the file made especially for ax sharpening. It is coarse on one side and fine on the other. While the fine side of this file will do for the finishing job, you should finish all ax-filing jobs with whetstones. For this purpose, use a double-faced, four-inch whetstone—one side fine India, the other soft Arkansas. Regular ax stones are made round, but use the four-inch rectangular stone for all purposes on a wilderness trip. Hone tools daily, not at long intervals.

## REPAIR KIT

Repairs are an important consideration in extended wilderness travel. Such tasks as patching underwear, trousers, shirts, moccasins and rubbers, mending socks, repairing packsacks, and so on, require a fair degree of manual skill. Rough, temporary repairs are not always sufficient. However, several cements are now on the market for mending clothes, tents, and so on, simply by applying cement to the cloth patch and sticking it to the inner side of the garment or tent.

The harness stitch used on leather repairs is quite simple. Take a length of linen harness thread, draw it through a piece of beeswax, or the wax used by shoemakers to strengthen thread. Then run it over a candle or paraffin so that it will slide easily. Thread one needle on each end of the waxed thread. With an awl make a hole in the piece of leather or canvas you are mending. Run one needle through the hole and pull the thread through exactly halfway. Make a second hole for the stitch. Now run one needle through this second hole on one side, and the other needle through on the opposite side. Draw up the stitch, and repeat.

In mending buckskin or moosehide moccasins, use a three-cornered needle and a piece of waxed thread. Such needles can be purchased at a shoemaker's findings establishment. First wash the moccasin in lukewarm water and soap; then rinse and dry it. The best way is to let the moccasin dry in the smoke of a campfire, but not too near the heat. Place the piece of buckskin over the hole in the moccasin and sew round the edge of the patch. Pound the finished seam with a piece of smooth wood.

For repairing moccasin-rubbers (see "Footwear," Chapter 9), take along a few ounces of rubber cement in a friction-top can, some tire dough (or what is sold under the trade name Solo), and some tire tube patching rubber. The dough is used to build up the heel and the sole, the patching rubber to repair a rip in the upper rubber. For sole or heel patching apply the rubber cement and allow it to dry on the sole or heel long enough to become tacky. Apply a second coat and dry it in the same way. Then take a piece of tire dough, shape it roughly by hand, and press it on the sole or heel. Cover the top of the dough with rubber cement, and use your knife to trowel it down to the desired flatness. Do this at night and let it dry until morning, or longer, for best results. The same method applies to the tube-patching rubber. Cut a piece in the size needed, remove the protective fabric, and press the rubber patch over the tacky cemented surface.

To repair an air mattress, inflate the mattress if it is a small leak, but don't overinflate it. Place it in water; wherever it bubbles there is the leak. In a fabric-coated mattress, the repair is best made with tire dough rather than with rubber patching material. Dry the mattress thoroughly. Apply a half-inch or more of rubber cement to the area around the hole. Let it dry until tacky. Place a piece of tire dough over the hole, then press it firmly into the canvas. Because there is little pressure in an air mattress, you can use the mattress at once, but some drying is preferable.

Canoe repairs have been covered in the chapter "Canoe Travel and Procedure." For detailed items of the repair kit see Chapter 10, "The Itemized List of Camping Equipment."

## MATCH SAFETY UNITS

On the slender match rests much of the comfort and safety of a wilderness trip. There are several good ways to carry matches. My bulk matches are placed in a friction-top can with a wad of cotton over them to prevent jarring. I then seal the edge of the cover with a dripping candle, although this last precaution is perhaps unnecessary.

Another good method is to open the box of matches as it comes from the store, and pour melted paraffin over the matches until all the gaps between them are filled solid with paraffin. Let this harden and then slip on the cover. Sections of these waxed matches can be broken out and carried loose in the pocket without danger of their becoming wet from moisture or perspiration. Matches can also be dipped individually in clear lacquer and dried. Waterproof matches

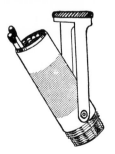

Match Safe

are now being marketed; but because they deteriorate, test them before you include them in your kit.

Several types of waterproof match safes are sold. Do not get one with a separate cover. That may get lost. Buy one with a hinged cover. (See illustration.) Always buy the best grade of wooden matches that will light anywhere. Books of matches and safety matches are an abomination in the woods. Do not take them unless you smoke, and then take paper matches for smoking only.

## THE COMPASS

In the chapter "Where Am I?" the compass was discussed at length. Somewhere on your compass, you should identify the ends of the needle. This may sound foolish, but many able men consider this a useful precaution. Any well calibrated compass of good quality will serve on average camping trips. For technical work precision instruments will be required, and bearings will be taken from celestial bodies, not from a magnetic compass.

## WATCHES AND OTHER INSTRUMENTS

Since you will have no opportunity to reset your watch unless you carry a portable radio, a wrist watch is not as a rule a good choice for wilderness travel. A pocket watch of such quality as to pass railroad inspection will maintain accurate time throughout the trip without the necessity of resetting it. Alarm watches are convenient for special rising, but are usually poor timekeepers.

An accurate watch is valuable as a compass. In the Northern Hemisphere point the hour hand on the sun. Halfway between the hour hand and twelve is approximately south. Reverse this procedure in the Southern Hemisphere.

Instruments used in making observations for latitude and longitude are expensive. Army surplus bubble sextants can be bought at a low price, but do not expect fixes closer than from three to five miles if the bubble artificial horizon is used and if the instrument is held in the hand. However, the instrument made by the Bausch & Lomb Optical Company for the government (now on surplus), which can be adapted to a natural horizon as well as to the bubble artificial horizon, is also adaptable for use with a mercury artificial horizon when used on land. The sextant must be mounted on some kind of permanent base for best results. It will then give readings to a fractional part of a minute of arc.

The instrument needed for the greatest possible accuracy in ground work is a theodolite. With this instrument positions can be determined within fifty feet or less.

Time is the important factor in taking celestial readings or in the use of astrocompasses. In using such instruments, you will, therefore, be required to carry a watch giving Greenwich mean time, a stop watch, and a small portable short-wave radio for time signals. (See the chapter "Where Am I?")

If the scope of your trip includes weather observations, you will need a set of two field barometers, a set of relative-humidity thermometers, and an anemometer (wind-velocity gauge). Obviously, these instruments will only be required in remote travel and on scientific expeditions, unless for instruction or for experimental work.

Pedometers (instruments measuring the distance you walk) are useful to check distances covered on foot. You will be amazed at the total distance covered by foot on a canoe trip.

The general instruments mentioned may be cut down to the compass alone, where weight is of first importance.

## VISION GLASSES

If you wear glasses, take a second pair for emergency. Safety lenses with hardened surfaces, capable of withstanding considerable abuse and offering great safety in travel through brushy country, have been developed. One pair of these will do. Glasses can be made for pistol and rifle shooting which offer a satisfactory compromise between target and sights. Consult your optometrist about them.

## FIELD GLASSES

Field glasses are important for the study of wildlife. Ordinary binoculars are usually too heavy and unwieldy for easy transportation. In recent years a variety of small pocket-size binoculars in 6- and 7-power has appeared on the market. These are very adaptable. In the mountains, on the arctic prairie and ice fields, or in other areas where great distances must be spanned to identify objects, it is well to carry a pair of these pocket binoculars, along with a pair of field binoculars of about 10-power. Objects are first spotted with the pocket binoculars, and more closely identified by using the field binoculars on some form of rest or tripod.

## SNOW GLASSES

For winter travel smoked glasses are essential, especially toward spring when the sun is high; otherwise snow blindness will occur. Polaroid glasses do very well if you can get a pair with double, adjustable lenses for variable light control. Intensity and angle of reflection can then be adjusted. A pair of welder's goggles fitting snugly round the eyes keeps out stinging, flying snow and are dark enough for heavy sun glare on snow. Do not use metal frames. They freeze to your face and cause injury. Where the goggles touch the skin, line them with wool felt or chamois.

If you lose your smoked glasses, carve a piece of wood to fit across your eyes and cut two slits in it for sight, with a hole for a cord at each end. If available, a piece of dark Polaroid or plastic held in place by a cord will do in a pinch. Some protection against snow glare can be had by blackening the area round your eyes with charcoal. If you wear ordinary glasses, hold them over the smoke of a campfire or smudge them with wet soot.

Some time ago it occurred to me that a dark mosquito netting might serve as protection from snow glare and blindness. I have not fully explored the idea, but so far my progress has been good. The netting relieves the need of glasses or goggles for snow blindness; in addition it keeps out blowing snow, and helps to prevent facial frostbite. I have not fully worked out the point of condensation, but I suggest that exploration parties in the arctic and antarctic take up the idea and exhaust its possibilities.

## CAMERA EQUIPMENT

Unless you wish to pursue some special phase of photography, there is only one place for the camera—on your belt, or preferably in your hand. The shutter should be set at the fastest speed and lens opening to suit the light. This will enable you to shoot a picture of wildlife in motion without fussing with the shutter. If you can take your picture at leisure, adjust the shutter for slower exposure; but always set it back after taking a picture.

The best way to carry a camera is in your hand, with a tripod attached and with the legs of the tripod collapsed to the second joint. Carry it as you would a gun. Pictures taken on a tripod, with slow speed and small lens openings, will bear great enlargement and have an improved depth of focus. There is no "fuzz" in tripod-taken pictures if the camera has been properly focused. Filters should be carried in a small pouch attached to the camera case or to the camera for easy access. If they are buried in your pack, the chances are that you will never find the time or opportunity to use them.

In deep woods, where light is very deceptive, use a photoelectric exposure meter. But here, as always with this instrument, you will need to adjust the meter reading to your own judgment. Hold the meter close to various patches of light and then do the same in deep shade; then hold it close to where your camera is set, and average the exposure. If you are in any doubt, expose for the shadows and let the high lights take care of themselves when you are using black-and-white film. If you are taking color stills or movies, underexpose slightly, rather than overexpose, in order to improve the color values. Use a filter to cut down the strength of the blues.

In using black-and-white film, work facing the light rather than with the light behind you, and increase the exposure to obtain fine half-tone values and beautiful high lights. If you are using color film, shoot with the light behind you, because color provides its own perspective. For interesting and unusual effects, you can on occasion shift the light to one side or even in front, but watch the exposure on such shots. It can be tricky. Sunlight is needed for color; but some fine color values are possible with diffused sunlight or overcasts, if good contrasts are visible..

Use repeating flash bulbs for night pictures and for deep shade in the woods. Your films should be kept in waterproof containers. If the camera does not have a built-in automatic release, then you should buy an auxiliary type of release, which can be adapted to your shutter. Telephoto lenses are needed for wildlife pictures; and you may want a wide-angle lens for certain crowded camera positions, but with a wide-angle lens considerable effect will be lost because of bad point of view and perspective. For obtaining good perspective, use one of two methods. Use a lens of long focal length, or assume a more distant point of view, and then enlarge the desired smaller portion of the negative.

## FISHING TACKLE

A steel casting rod with short joints, a couple of plugs, a half-dozen treble-hooked spoons, an extra line of good quality, two or three cable leaders, some light and some heavy sinkers, and a small assortment of hooks are all the equipment you will need for the North Country, unless you are going to fish in trout waters. Then a fly rod, flies, leaders, an assortment of hooks, and a few split-shot sinkers should be included. On some trips I have carried a linen line and a few spoons, catching all the fish I needed for food by trolling.

A Fiberglas rod can be substituted for the steel casting rod; if the rod is tied along the inside of the gunwale in the canoe it will be readily accessible at the foot of falls or other likely fishing places. A good reel should be used for free casting. (See the chapter "Fishing for Food.")

## FIREARMS

Years ago, when trips were so long that it was impossible to carry the amount of supplies needed, it was possible to use firearms to supplement the food budget. In Canada guns are now prohibited to aliens except during hunting seasons. This has greatly handicapped research groups and others who would shoot only for food and for scientific purposes. A notable example occurred when a group of university men asked permission to shoot a specimen of large game but were denied this scientific opportunity. Later, licensed hunters were permitted to ravage the area. It would be far better if special permits were allowed to research groups and to others traveling far into the Interior, to take only what game was necessary for food and specimens in the success of their work. There have been some exceptions in certain provinces and territories, in Manitoba, for example. But because Canada has suffered from trigger-happy individuals, both aliens and citizens, the result has been utter confusion in legislative control. Canada is now setting up rigid timber-cutting and planting controls, and will probably amend game and fish restrictions so that equitable, logical controls will be in effect.

In transporting firearms across international boundaries, for instance from the United States into Canada, permission must be obtained in advance from the national police, which in Canada are the Royal Canadian Mounted Police. After permission is received, the firearms must be declared to customs officials at the boundary, and a report should also be made to the Game and Fish Department. (See the chapter "Hunting for Food.")

## THE FLASHLIGHT AND OTHER LIGHTING UNITS

For many years I carried a Stonebridge folding aluminum candle lantern. This has been replaced by a more compact lantern that collapses into a small 2" x 4" unit. (See illustration.) But for most general-purpose use around the wilderness camp I use a flashlight, and make sure of its operation by placing several extra bulbs in the

Stonebridge Candle Lantern

base. For absolute assurance, I carry an identical pair of flashlights for interchangeable part replacements. Some late models have the advantage of being waterproof. Recent models with seal-beam heads now being developed will be a vast improvement in illumination and certainty of operation. The candle-lantern is the most dependable light; but if the flashlight is kept dry to avoid corrosion it is more convenient. The two-cell type with the light-head on the side, rather than at the end, has been the most successful because it can also be hung up as a lantern. Candles and batteries of equal weight burn for about the same length of time. Extra batteries should be

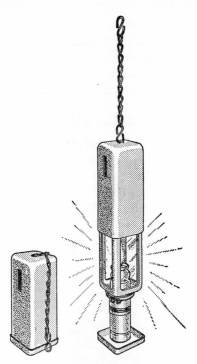

Small 2" x 4" Collapsible Candle Lantern

Flashlight (Two-Cell Type with Light-Head on Side)

Acetylene (Carbide) Light

Gasoline Lantern (Single-Mantle Type)

carried if the trip is to take more than two weeks. Acetylene (carbide) lights are satisfactory if jet wires are carried to keep the jets open, because they become plugged easily. This unit is excellent for reading purposes. On auto trips a gasoline lantern is valuable, and an extension light from the car battery will also give good light.

## DIARY AND PENCIL

A detailed record should be kept of every wilderness trip, showing routes, weather, type of country, and any experiences or events of note. In time such a diary will become priceless. A No. 1 pencil and a 5½″ x 8″ notebook, opening on the long side, is the handiest.

## FIRST-AID EQUIPMENT

Your first-aid equipment on a wilderness trip will depend on your own knowledge of the subject. On a long journey the full risk of accident or illness is thrown directly on the members of the party, and in any crisis they will usually have to be their own source of aid. For this reason every member should make a strenuous effort to acquaint himself with the major aspects of first aid and expect to act on occasion as a substitute physician. Injuries from an ax, a gun, or a fall are all possibilities, and should be avoided by every means.

For myself, I have found the training I received as a medical corpsman in the Navy valuable ever since. You can pick up a good deal of information by talking with your physician and surgeon, supplemented by a class in first-aid instruction. You should know how to use a local anesthetic administered hypodermically, and how to tie off an artery, because a tourniquet can be applied for a limited time only, or gangrene will set in. You should know how to reduce a fracture and how to apply splints.

Find out from your physician something about the use of the new antibiotics in an emergency. You may feel that this comes within the compass of professional use only, but when you are several hundred miles from civilization there is no choice. Without antibiotics the consequences may be serious. To do nothing would be gross negligence. For general use, bandages, cotton, adhesive tape, antiseptic, cathartic, an ointment, and a few aspirin tablets will be enough.

Many years ago I came across a device called an "inspirator," which was a piece of rubber tubing with a short piece of brass tubing inserted in one end; it was used as a bellows for fires that would not burn. Because any item of equipment taken into the woods should serve as many uses as possible, I decided to use a length of tourniquet rubber for the tube, and to make it serve as a tourniquet also. I have since found that it works well as an air-mattress inflator. Once I used it with a birchbark funnel in giving an enema. On another occasion I cut off a short length of rubber and made a slingshot out of it to obtain food during an emergency.

A more elaborate first-aid kit should contain a small lancet or penknife, a hypodermic syringe with local anesthetic and morphine, a pair of scissors, a pair of tweezers, a snakebite kit, a hemostatic forceps which can also be used as a needle holder, needles and sutures in a tube, dental forceps, gauze, cotton, bandages, plastic adhesive bandage strips (Band-Aids), a clinical thermometer, antibiotics for serious infections, Chlorazene tablets for general antiseptic use and for purifying water, boric acid, aspirin, a general ointment, and an alkalizing agent for the stomach, such as bicarbonate of soda. Much can be done with these few items if their use is understood.

One of the best methods I have found for sewing up an ax wound is to tape the area around the wound, leaving the wound exposed, and to make the stitches in the edge of the tape rather than in the skin. In this way the wound can be drawn together very well with little discomfort to the patient. An even simpler method is carefully to draw the skin together into its natural position and tape the wound at several spaced points with narrow strips of tape. This spacing of tapes permits the wound to drain. If the injury is to a hand or foot, the extremity should be immobilized with bandage, tape, and splint to avoid accidental reopening of the wound. You will, of course, want to consult a comprehensive manual such as the *Red Cross First-Aid Manual,* where bandaging is extensively illustrated. The liberal use of adhesive tape in making fracture splints, immobilizing sprained joints, or taping a broken rib deserves careful attention.

Learn and practice the manual method of artificial respiration and the best treatment for near drowning before starting out on a trip where drowning is a risk. The newest method for artificial respiration is treated at length in the Red Cross manual. In addition, learn the proper treatment for sunstroke, heat exhaustion, frostbite, and any other possible hazards to be encountered in the region in which you will travel.

There is a marked difference in symptoms and treatment between heat exhaustion and sunstroke. In heat exhaustion the body becomes cold and the temperature must be raised with heated rocks or heated sandbags, well wrapped to prevent burning of the skin. Sunstroke patients, on the other hand, need to have their temperature quickly reduced. They should be moved into the shade. If this is not possible, create shade with a tent, tarpaulin, or even a poncho. For heat exhaustion hot drinks should be administered, for sunstroke cold drinks, when the patient can take them.

The treatment of poisonous snakebites is described in detail on the snakebite kit, a common commercial item in country infested by poisonous snakes. Cut from the puncture of one fang to the other, and then make two cuts at right angles to this cut to form the letter H. When this cut is made in a fleshy part of the body, the risk of injury is small, and a liberal flow of blood will help to get rid of the poison. If the bite occurs in an area where you may not be able to do any cutting at all or where you face the danger of cutting tendons or arteries, then force the points of a scissors into the wound and open the scissors sufficiently for a flow of blood to release the poison. This will open the area parallel to the tendons with less risk of vital injury. The patient must not absorb more of the poison into his general circulation than is safe. If professional

Snakebite Kit

medical help is not available, you must do the best you can. A tourniquet on a bitten limb will prevent the poison from entering too freely into the bloodstream, but a tourniquet should not be left on too long if gangrene is to be avoided. Every twenty minutes some circulation must be allowed to return at the risk of absorbing some poison. The body can safely absorb some of the poison if it is released into the system very gradually. Follow the directions on the snakebite kit for treatment after the lancing. These kits generally are provided with a suction cup and with proper medication.

Ax wounds are relatively common. A severed tendon can be very serious, because surgery must be undertaken within about four hours. The sight of blood is often frightening, but as a rule it is not as serious as it seems to be. Bleeding can often be stopped by direct pressure with a compress on the wound rather than with a tourniquet. Infection is a constant danger. Cleanliness and sterilization, practiced in the best way possible under the circumstance, will go a long way toward avoiding infection. Do not be too free with antiseptics, for reactions from their use can be dangerous.

Gunshot wounds can, of course, be tragic, but a bullet in the body is not necessarily fatal. Bullets can remain in the body for long periods without causing great harm, and surgery performed at a later date can often take care of the situation without serious consequence. Needless to say, much depends on the individual wound. I simply point out that panic is out of order at such a time, and that many people now enjoy good health who at one time or another were shot. Internal and external bleeding from gunshot wounds can often be reduced by keeping the patient quiet and by allowing the blood to clot. If the wound is deep, and is not in a superficial part of the body, the patient must be moved with as little physical disturbance as possible.

Any kind of fall is dangerous in rough country, and is often accompanied by bruises and temporary shock. Far too often, bones are broken. Sections of birchbark lined with any soft material at hand, such as absorbent cotton, clothing, moss, or grass, make good splints for broken arms and legs, but should be reinforced on the outside with sticks liberally wrapped with adhesive tape, rope, cord, spruce roots soaked in hot water, or any other fiber available. A layman should be extremely cautious in trying to set a bone. If the fracture is not compound (that is, if the bones do not come through the flesh or seriously injure the tissue), or if an offset in the bone ends is not liable to cause a compound injury by additional disturbance, there is no harm in contriving a slight adjustment of the bone for splinting, but this is all that should be attempted. A broken hip or spine injury is, of course, a real problem. Here the patient's whole body must be supported if any movement is to be undertaken. If transportation is available within a reasonable time, the patient should be made comfortable on the spot, even though a tent has to be pitched over him. Many patients with minor injuries become serious cases because of needless immediate removal from the scene of the accident.

To transport a patient by horse, use two long poles and two horses. A stretcher can be made with blankets or canvas tarpaulin between the poles; the horses should be harnessed as in the shafts of a wagon. In moving a patient by canoe the middle thwart should be removed. If enough help can be had, four people should portage the canoe with the patient in it. They walk alongside, grasping the front and rear thwarts for handholds.

When a patient is moved by plane, either a commercial stretcher or a very short one contrived from poles and blankets should be used in getting a patient in and out of the plane. Where quarters are very cramped, you will have to create a splint for the whole body. An air mattress gives additional comfort in all types of transportation.

In moving a patient by toboggan or sled, either hand or dog team, take great care to keep the patient warm. If possible, two air mattresses should be used, one on top of the other, to ease the bumps. They will have to be supported with a frame of rope and short poles to prevent their rolling. At night the tent should be pitched over the toboggan or sled with the patient on it to avoid needless movement of the patient from toboggan to camp bed. The pitching of the tent should be done at intervals during the day to allow the patient a warm-up either with a Primus stove or with a wood camp stove. Hand warmers of the commercial type, heated rocks in a pail, or other artificial heat will help the patient's comfort. Food and drink, if the patient can take it, also help to maintain body warmth.

Fortunately, contagious disease is rare in the wilderness. But you can carry it in with you. For this reason, my advice to you is to go to a physician, especially if he is a man with some understanding of the wilderness, and obtain from him a definite program of specific and prophylactic treatment. Find out from him the various antibiotics you will need, the doses, and under what conditions it will be absolutely necessary to administer them. He will probably tell you to check the patient's temperature and other symptoms before you use them. Don't take liberties with these drugs unless the need for them is urgent. Most minor ailments will take care of themselves, and you cannot afford to indulge in antibiotic treatment unless the situation demands it.

Find out from your doctor how to tie off an artery. You will not be able to rely entirely on a tourniquet. A badly bleeding patient can be carried for many miles if the artery is tied off, whereas with only a tourniquet he may lose a limb or die from gangrene.

In addition, you should ask your doctor to show you how to use minor local anesthetics. It seems needless for a layman to work on a patient in the wilderness without some anesthetic aid. Certainly there is risk, and many surgeons have told me about them. But when I was in the medical corps during the war, I was sent out with only six months' training. When men were injured in the field, I administered potent drugs hypodermically and forgot about my lack of professional training.

Of course, laymen will make mistakes in advanced first-aid treatment. One day I arrived at a camp in the wilderness as preparations were being made to "cut out" a fishhook deeply lodged in the thick part of a man's hand. A fishhook does not like the idea of backing up. But if the pressure is made away from the barb, and if enough force is applied, fishhooks do back out. If they can be forced forward and the barb cut off, then backed up, the extraction is relatively easy.

Situations will of course occur where the layman must leave the operation to a physician. For example, you should not try to remove a fishhook when the risk of injuring a nerve or eyesight is high. It is better to tape the hook into the most comfortable position and wait for surgery.

On most trips medical help can be obtained within a week. On expeditions farther afield the situation is different. Then it is best to take along a doctor as a member of the party, preferably one who is involved in the scientific work of the expedition as well as in medical care of the personnel.

## MAPS

To get the best and also the cheapest maps, write to the central government of the country in which you will be traveling. These maps will show compass declination (the difference between True North and Magnetic North), canoe routes, winter trails, trading posts, portages, rapids, elevations, timber and swamp areas, and other information. For more isolated sections, of course, the information will be more limited. If you propose to travel in such isolated sections, plan to take notes to add to the existing knowledge. The government will be grateful, and you will be helping the next fellow. Many maps now available in Canada are on a scale of from two to four miles to the inch. Other sections vary. Frequently, geological maps are available, and are very informative as you go from one part of the country to another, noting changes. You may want to do a little prospecting.

Any map in regular use should be glued to a piece of thin plywood and covered with transparent varnish. Tie, screw, tape, or otherwise fasten your compass to the plywood for convenient orientation with the map. Both map and compass are then constantly available. Maps not in daily use should be kept in a rubberized, waterproof envelope or rolled and inserted in an aluminum tube, corked at both ends.

The relationship between compass and map is important. Unless the map can be read, the compass is only of moderate value. To read a map properly you must first identify your position in the area with the same area as it is shown on the map. A good map has all the features of the country designated by one means or another. If the map has been made by aerial survey, the land and water areas will be clearly defined. The aerial survey is really a photograph of the country from a high altitude. Other features are then added. Topography is indicated by showing the height above sea level at various points—sometimes by graphic designs.

Topography is important because it shows in which direction the water flows. If water flows in two directions from a given area, in the same manner as rain falling on a roof runs down both slopes, it is spoken of as a watershed. Frequently, there are no well-defined rivers to indicate which way the water flows. Nevertheless, even in an area of hundreds of connected lakes the water may still be flowing in one general direction. Often one lake will spill into another lake by means of an enormous waterfall—a vivid reminder that there is movement and direction.

A good map will show marsh, muskeg, or swamp; state, provincial, and territorial boundaries; portage, pack, or winter trails; canoe routes, declination, base lines, meridians, latitude and longitude, and other pertinent details.

Therefore, to read a map accurately and easily and to identify your position, you must learn how such details are shown. In wild regions there may have been no survey. In that case you must depend on an occasional native for information and on any early records of explorations. A large part of the wilderness has by now been surveyed by air, but much remains to be done.

In some of these wilderness regions there are surveys of a very general nature. These surveys are no more than a single east and west line, running across a large area of country, called *base lines*. Where the lines have been run north and south, they are called *meridians*. If the surveys are more detailed, they will even show ranges, townships, and possibly sections. However, in prolonged travel in wild areas, your position can be properly identified on the map only by degrees of latitude and longitude. Detailed identification can be made by subdivisions of latitude and longitude called *minutes* and *seconds*. An astronomical observation of your position would read so many degrees, minutes, and seconds of north or south latitude and east or west longitude. (See the Chapter "Where Am I?")

# 9

*
* *
* * *
* * * *

## Clothing and Personal Equipment

THE SUBJECT OF FOOTWEAR, NEVER SUFFICIENTLY UNDERSTOOD, IS still the most difficult of clothing problems.

On canoe journeys, especially in the spring and in the fall of the year, leather boots are hopelessly inefficient. You start out with a well-greased pair. In a day or two, they are soaked from the wet, spongy portage trails. It is useless to oil them while they are wet, and there is not time overnight to dry them out, for they must dry slowly or the leather will be ruined. The result is wet feet for most of the trip. The rubber-bottom, leather-top type of boot is better, but causes perspiration from condensation, especially when the tops are high. The boot with the six-inch upper is a fairly good compromise.

**Rubber Bottom, Leather Top Packs**

162

Some firms are now impregnating leather with new waterproof compounds, and this may prove a partial solution, if the porous nature of the leather is not sacrificed, but this seems impossible.

The Canadians sell a moccasin-rubber formed in the mold to fit a moccasined foot. Moccasins are worn over wool socks, then fitted

**Moccasin-Rubber and Moccasin**

closely with the moccasin-rubber. My early experience with this footwear was a revelation. For the first time I went throughout a trip with dry, comfortable feet. Smoke-tanned deerhide moccasins are lighter than a pair of socks, and two or three pairs can be taken on the trip. If you should step into water by accident, take off your wet socks and moccasins, and put on the dry set. The rubber is wiped dry, and comfort again restored. In a canoe, or around a dry camp, the rubbers can be quickly kicked off, to give you the lightness of foot that is such a joy. Even with the moccasin-rubber, the combination is light and springy.

For winter wear, when extreme cold keeps the snow dry, moose-hide moccasins with tops reaching just above the calf of the leg, and wool socks along with duffel socks, assure comfort.

Mukluks are the most satisfactory cold-weather footwear available. The real difference between a high moccasin and a mukluk is that the moccasin is worn against the sock, with the pants over it, while the mukluk comes up, like a boot, over the pants leg. To make a pair of mukluks, simply take a pair of moccasins, remove the narrow tops, and have a pair of wide canvas tops sewed on.

Moosehide Moccasin

Moosehide and Canvas Mukluk

A drawstring at the top, tied just below the knee, keeps the mukluks up and the snow out. Most mukluks worn in the arctic are made from hair seal, with the hair scraped off the hide of many of them. In some the hair is left on the leg part of the mukluk, while the foot is made hairless. The better sealskin mukluks have soles made from the square-flipper seal and tops made from hair seal. For dry, cold weather, the bottoms are made from smoke-tanned moose or caribou and the tops from hair seal. The Hudson's Bay Company at Winnipeg, Manitoba, or any outpost merchant should be able to dig up a pair of mukluks for you. They are not difficult to obtain.

The so-called "insulated boots" now appearing on the market

Sealskin Mukluk

which feature porous rubber, and which have dead air spaces, are good from the point of view of insulation; but, as with other rubber goods, condensation soon ruins their insulation value. In addition, they are prohibitively heavy, especially for long trips afoot or on snowshoes.

## SOCKS

Four kinds of socks are common in the North—the ordinary knitted wool socks, Finn socks, duffel socks, and fur socks. The Finn sock is pounded wool similar to a loosely packed felt. It is excellent material if it is uniformly packed, but most of these socks are poorly made, lumpy, and uneven. The sock which has won more converts in the North than any other is the duffel sock. This generally is ankle high, and made of a fine-grade, heavy blanket-like material cut to fit from a pattern. Fur socks are usually made from young caribou that have been killed in late summer (generally August), but other furs can be used.

Socks are now being made from extruded synthetic fibers, such as nylon, Dacron, Orlon, and so on. A combination of socks made from wool and synthetic fibers offers strength and warmth—something wool was not able to offer alone. In some cases the nylon sock is worn over the wool sock; in others the wool sock is worn outside the nylon. And where a wool sock has been sandwiched between two of the nylon socks, the wear of the wool sock is increased. All seem to offer some advantage. Nylon woven into wool adds strength, especially in reinforcing the toe and heel of the sock.

## UNDERWEAR

It is difficult to insist on or even to recommend light wool underwear for summer use. Yet it is a sensible choice. Nothing is quite so clammy on a cold, rainy day as cotton underwear; and it does not absorb perspiration very well. My suggestion is to take along cotton shorts, if you must, and put on wool underwear when the need arises. From my own experience, the wool underwear will be worn on the first night out, and the cotton shorts abandoned on the nearest limb. From then until the end of the trip, you will wear the wool underwear. Do not buy the one-piece union suit; it is a nuisance. Get two-piece underwear. If you wish to strip to the waist, you can take the shirt off like a sweater. You will find many other good points in the two-piece type. If you get it with a crew neck and dye it red or blue, it makes a very comfortable and attractive garment for utility wear as the only upper garment worn. For winter underwear, see Chapter 5.

## OUTER SHIRT AND WINDBREAKER PARKA

For additional warmth, wear a soft, loose-fitting all-wool shirt over your crew-neck undershirt. Do not get the stiff weaves. They impair freedom of arm movement and are not as warm as the softer materials. You will need a windbreaker over the wool shirt. Mine is of very light, closely woven poplin with a parka hood, and almost reaches to my knees. It is water-repellent rather than waterproof, so that condensation will not take place. It wards off a sudden light shower. When black flies and mosquitoes are bad on the portage trail, I put up the parka hood. Around a campfire on a cool night, the hood cuts off the drafts at the back of my neck. Although extremely light, it wards off the wind, and, with the wool undergarments, makes an excellent cold-weather combination. Get it large and free with plenty of room in the hood. Use buttons, not zippers, for the opening at the front, and put in a pucker cord for the hood. It can be made with no opening at the neck as a slipover garment, but it is then more difficult to get on and off. See Chapter 5, under "Winter Camping." Buttons on the parka hood and loops on the fur hood trim, make it easy to convert the parka to winter or summer use. (See illustration.)

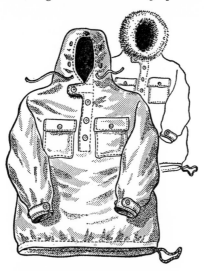

Windbreaker Parka for All-Season Use

## THE RAIN SHIRT AND THE PONCHO

For many years I used a poncho as a protection against rain. It covered the pack on the trail, and avoided the condensation which forms inside the sleeves of the ordinary raincoat. It served as a fly to supplement the main shelter, and it also served as a sail. In short, it had various uses. But it had one very bad feature: it did not permit proper freedom in paddling, in using an ax, or in other activities. Eventually, a garment appeared on the market which solved the problem—a combination of poncho and sleeve-type rain cloak, known as a "rain shirt." This garment is 105 inches around the bottom, so that when you are sitting in a canoe the full skirt can be draped around your feet. Deep kimono-type sleeves of the raglan cut, and the fact that there is no close body fit to this garment, prevent excessive perspiration and offer freedom of action. Several years of testing this rain shirt have established the following conclusions:

By using the featherweight, 16-inch, ankle-fitting rubber boot, the rain shirt described above, and a sou'wester type of rain hat instead of the hood which is optional with the rain shirt, and which is very impractical, you can remain out in the rain all day without serious concern for the weather. You can work, fish, or otherwise occupy the time during prolonged rains. In addition, if you pack all your equipment in waterproof containers, traveling and camping in the rain become feasible. This is perhaps the greatest achievement in camping that a traveler in the North can aspire to, since rain lasting for days or even weeks becomes very discouraging, and may create an insurmountable problem to many campers.

Rain Shirt, Sou'Wester, and Ankle-Fitting Boots. Inset Is Hood Type.

## TROUSERS

Trousers should be of pure soft wool, fitted with elastic knitted wool cuffs. When the cuffs are tucked into moccasins or boots, the pants form an overlap on the footwear to seal out snow. For extremely cold weather a pair of light, tightly woven cotton windbreaker trousers or short alpaca pants should be worn over the wool trousers. Avoid breeches. (See Chapter 5, under "Winter Camping.")

Blue jeans and dark gabardine trousers are good for warmer weather. "Shorts" in most wilderness areas do not offer enough protection against insects, abrasions, sunburn, and the elements to be of any practical use.

## FELT HAT

A good quality felt hat is a valuable head covering in the wilderness. If it is dipped in a solution of one ounce of lanolin to a half-gallon of gasoline, it will ward off quite a shower. In the hot sun the hat will be cooler if it is not creased. Get it a size smaller than you usually wear and take out the leather band. It will absorb moisture better and will not blow off easily. A leather hatband should be fitted around the outside of the hat to keep it to size.

## BUCKSKIN GLOVES OR MITTENS

Buckskin gloves are a comfort on cold fall mornings, but when your trips continue into late fall it is well to adopt the buckskin mitten instead of the glove. For pack-horse trips and general use in roping, a gauntlet glove is preferred by some; but buckskin gloves without gauntlets are still my choice for work of this kind. For winter mittens see Chapter 5, under "Winter Camping."

## BANDANNA

The bandanna handkerchief is handy throughout the day in countless ways from its use as a neckpiece to that of an emergency towel or a potholder. It can be easily washed and dried on the pack.

## MONEY WALLET

Your wallet should be carried in your back pocket and secured by a safety pin instead of by a button. Money belts are a nuisance. For extremely warm weather it is a good idea to wrap dollar bills and other valuable papers in wax paper before putting them in your wallet, or the wallet itself can be wrapped in wax paper, or stuffed into a rubber tobacco pouch.

## TOILET ARTICLES

In the wilderness you should shave. You will feel better if you do. Take along a shaving kit. Toilet soap can be carried in a soap container or in a rubber tobacco pouch. One towel will be sufficient for your needs. You can wash it as often as you wish. A toothbrush, toothpaste, a mirror, and a comb will complete your toilet articles. One roll of toilet paper per week for two people is ample.

## WINTER CLOTHING

For winter clothing, see Chapter 5, under "Winter Camping." For wilderness travel women have adopted the sensible solution of wearing men's clothes. In Chapter 5 the subject has been gone into in some detail. I might add one more suggestion. When your wife picks out her wilderness outfit, let her try the men's or boys' departments first. She will have a better chance of finding what she needs there than in the ladies' outdoor department. The reason for this is that manufacturers have been bending over backward to give a feminine touch to wilderness clothing equipment, and too often their alterations in design have destroyed the usefulness of the original garment.

# 10

# The Itemized List of Camping Equipment

THE FOLLOWING LIST IS DESIGNED FOR A WILDERNESS JOURNEY OF one month. If your trip is to be longer, certain items such as socks, flashlight batteries, and so on, will have to be reconsidered. Winter items are covered in Chapter 5, under "Winter Camping."

### *Personal Equipment for One*

| | |
|---|---|
| Wool underwear, medium weight, 2-piece | 2 pairs of drawers |
| | 1 shirt |
| Wool socks, medium weight | 4 pairs |
| Wool outershirt, lightweight | 1 |
| Wool pants | 1 pair |
| Belt and/or suspenders (braces) | 1 |
| Wool jacket or stagged wool shirt | 1 |
| Windbreaker parka of poplin | 1 |
| Moccasins, light moosehide or smoke-tanned | 2 pairs or more |
| Rubbers, moccasin type or 6-inch rubber packs | 1 pair |
| Hat of treated felt | 1 |
| Bandanna handkerchief | 1 |
| Gloves or mittens of buckskin | 1 pair |
| Rain gear | |
|    Rain shirt | 1 |
|    Rubber boots, featherweight, 16-inch ankle-fitting | 1 pair |
|    Rain hat, sou'wester type | 1 |

| | |
|---|---|
| Rubber gloves or mittens | 1 pair |
| Wallet | 1 |
| Pocket watch, railroad type | 1 |
| Compass, cruiser's | 1 |
| Match safe, waterproof type | 1 |
| Matches (see "Provision Check List," Chapter 11) | |
| Belt knife | 1 |
| "Crooked" knife | 1 (optional) |
| Glasses, vision (if needed) | 2 pairs or 1 safety type |
| Glasses, sun | 1 pair |
| Razor | 1 |
| Mirror, metal | 1 |
| Toothbrush and container | 1 |
| Dentifrice | 1 tube |
| Comb | 1 |
| Soap container (rubber tobacco pouch) | 1 |
| Soap, toilet (see "Provision Check List," Chapter 11) | |
| Hand towel | 1 |
| Head net, insect | 1 |
| Diary, 5½″ x 8″ with side opening | 1 |
| Pencils, No. 1 | 2 |
| Map | 1 |

### Camp Equipment for Two

| | |
|---|---|
| Tent, all-weather or convertible *A* type | 1 |
| Ropes, tent and tracking | 1 set |
| Mosquito net of fine mesh marquisette | 1 |
| Combination DDT and lindane spray for insects | 1 16-ounce can |
| Canoe, prospector type, aluminum | 1 |
| Paddles | 3 |
| Down sleeping bags | 2 |
| Air mattresses, 30″ x 72″ or ¾ length | 2 |
| Packsacks, No. 2 | 3 |
| Panniers to go into packsacks | 2 |
| Tumpline | 1 |
| Ax, 3½ pound, or ¾ size, 2½ pound | 1 |
| Ax sheath | 1 |

| | | |
|---|---|---|
| Whetstone, double-faced India and Arkansas | 1 | |
| File, 6-inch ax type | 1 | |
| Flashlight or candle lantern | 1 | |
| Extra bulbs (carried in flashlight base) | 3 | |
| Extra batteries | 1 | set |
| Candles for lantern (if carried) | 6 | |
| Fishing rod and reel: casting, fly rod | 1 | or both |
| Fish lines: casting or trolling | 2 | |
| Lures: spoons and plugs | 6 | |
| Lures: flies, spinners, trout plugs | 12 | |
| Sinkers: heavy, deep trolling | 3 | |
| Sinkers, split-shot | 12 | |
| Fishhooks of miscellaneous sizes | 12 | |
| Hone for fishhooks, ½-ounce size | 1 | |
| Carbine or rifle, with sling | 1 | |
| Small-game arms, pistol or shoulder | 1 | |
| Shotgun in goose and duck area | 1 | |
| Ammunition, high power | 20 | rounds |
| Ammunition, small game (.22 caliber) | 50 | rounds |
| Ammunition, shotgun shells | 20 | rounds |
| Cleaning equipment and gun oil | 1 | set |
| Camera, vest-pocket and/or cinema | 1 | |
| Extra lenses, telephoto | 1 | or more |
| Film | 50 | exposures or more |
| Filters | 1 | or more |
| Tripod with universal head | 1 | |
| Exposure meter | 1 | |
| Flash bulbs (repeating type) | 1 | assembly |
| Automatic shutter release if none is provided in camera shutter | 1 | |
| Alarm clock or alarm watch | 1 | (optional) |
| Sextant with artificial horizon, or theodolite | | |
| G.M.T. watch | | For expeditions |
| Stop watch | | where positions |
| Short-wave radio | | must be found |
| Plotting equipment | | |
| Nautical Almanac | | |
| H.O. 214 Tables | | |

Cooking utensils

| | |
|---|---|
| Aluminum cooking pail, 6-quart size | 1 |
| Aluminum cooking pail, 4-quart size | 1 |
| Aluminum cooking pail, 2-quart size | 1 |
| Cups, heavily tinned or porcelain with split handles | 2 |
| Frying pan, steel with straight sides | 1 |
| Aluminum plates | 2 |
| Aluminum bowls | 2 |
| Forks | 2 |
| Spoon, mixing | 1 |
| Spoons, eating | 2 |
| Chain shaker (milk shaker for mixing dry milk) | 1 |
| Reflector oven of aluminum alloy | 1 |
| Dutch oven, on pack-horse trip only | 1 (optional) |
| Brush, vegetable, for dishwashing | 1 |
| Detergent for dishwashing (see "Provision Check List" in Chapter 11) | |
| Towels, dish | 2 |
| Trowel, mason's 5-inch, for cooking and tent trenching | 1 |
| Can opener | 1 |

Toilet paper (see "Provision Check List" in Chapter 11)

Repair kit

| | |
|---|---|
| Awl | 1 |
| Harness needles | 4 |
| Moccasin needles, 3-cornered type | 4 |
| Darning needles | 4 |
| Sewing needles, assorted sizes | 1 paper |
| Buttons, assorted sizes | 1 dozen |
| Thread | 1 spool |
| Yarn for mending socks, small skein | 1 |
| Cloth patches, miscellaneous | 6 |
| Leather, about 6" x 6", for reinforcement | 1 piece |
| Buckskin, about 12" x 12", for moccasin patching | 1 piece |
| Tire dough, for mending rubbers | 1 small can |

| | |
|---|---|
| Rubber cement, for mending rubbers | 1 4-ounce can |
| Patching rubber, for mending rubbers | 1 can |
| Plastic canoe glue | 4 ounces |
| Pliers, small side-cutting type | 1 pair |
| Copper wire | 1 small coil |
| Canoe patching, cloth | ⅓ yard |
| Screwdriver (2 sizes), small, for camera, etc. | 2 optional |
| Canoe nails, assorted sizes, for canvas-wood models only | 1 small box |

First-aid and medicine kit

| | |
|---|---|
| Lancet, small, or penknife | 1 |
| Hypodermic syringe with large and small needle | 1 |
| Hemostatic forceps | 1 |
| Needles and suture in tube | 2 |
| Forceps, dental | 1 |
| Clinical thermometer | 1 |
| Tweezers | 1 |
| Scissors | 1 pair |
| Tourniquet, rubber, 30 inches | 1 length |
| Adhesive tape, 2 inch x 5 yards | 1 roll |
| Gauze | 1 small packet |
| Bandages, gauze, 2-inch width | 1 roll |
| Plastic adhesive bandage strips | 1 box |
| Cotton | 1 small packet |
| Antibiotics | on prescription by |
| Novocain, in vials | your physician for |
| Morphine, ¼ grain | emergency use only |
| Alkalizing agent for the stomach | 25 tablets |
| Paregoric for the stomach | 2 ounces |
| Aspirin | 25 tablets |
| Cascara (cathartic) | 12 tablets |
| Snakebite kit, for poisonous snake regions only | 1 pocket-size kit |
| Ointment, general | 1 flat |
| Campho-phenique | 2 ounces |
| Boric acid crystals | 1 ounce |

### Winter Items, Personal Equipment
### for One

| | | |
|---|---|---|
| Parka of quilted down, pile, or fur | 1 | |
| Wool stocking cap (under parka hood) | 1 | |
| Wool outershirt | 1 | |
| Windbreaker parka, lightweight | 1 | |
| Wool pants with knitted ankle cuffs | 1 | pair |
| Alpaca short pants | 1 | pair |
| Wool underwear, full-weight, 2-piece | 2 | pairs of drawers |
| | 2 | shirts |
| Mittens of fur or moosehide, with duffel wool liner | 1 | pair |
| Overshoes, wool tops | 1 | pair |
| Moccasins of moosehide, or mukluks | 1 | pair |
| Wool duffel socks | 3 | pairs |
| Wool socks, regular type | 4 | pairs |
| Snow glasses | 1 | pair |
| Snowshoes | 1 | pair |
| Sleeping bag, double combination unit of down or caribou fur | 1 | |

### Winter Items, Camp Equipment
### for Two

Tent: double *A* type with stove
    or
    arctic pyramid with Primus stove
    or
    all-weather reflector type
    with open fire     }    1

Stove: sheet metal with pipe for double tent
    or
    with oil-unit adapter or Primus type
    for treeless area     }    1

Swedish saw, 30″ folding type    1

Hand toboggan and traces with breast straps
    or
    hand toboggan, dogs and harness
    or
    dog sled and dogs with harness     }    1 outfit

| | |
|---|---|
| Dog food (see Chapter 5, under "Winter Camping") | |
| Tarpaulin for toboggan or sled | 1 |
| Lash rope for toboggan or sled | 1  50-foot |
| Carpenter's plane for icing sled runners | 1 |
| Winter foods (See "Simplified List of Winter Foods," pages 243 and 244) | |

## GO-LIGHT OUTFITS

If you plan to travel light, carrying all of your equipment on your back, the strictest selection must be made.

For such a trip tent materials should be of a light, closely woven percale, which is lighter than sailcloth. The tent should be reduced to the smallest possible dimensions. The convertible *A* tent is the best model for such a trip. (See Chapter 8, under "The Tent.")

Cooking utensils should be light in weight but able to withstand the abuse of a direct fire. A round (not oval) mess kit is available with a cover that serves as a plate. The mess kit should be of light steel. Do not use an aluminum mess kit. Food burns and sticks to it. Cooking pails should be as small as possible, but the largest pail should be at least a two-quart size. A two-quart pail into which a second pail and two nesting tin cups will fit is ample for a go-light trip. Baking bannock in the mess kit will replace baking in the reflector oven. Two spoons, two forks, and a dishtowel complete the outfit.

The sleeping unit should consist of a medium-weight wool or down quilt with tapes sewed along the edges for glove snaps, so that it can be folded and snapped together as a sleeping bag. No outside protective covering is necessary on the wool-filled or down sleeping unit, where weight is essential. An air mattress (feather-weight pattern), 26 inches by 48 inches, and a lightweight poncho complete the sleeping equipment.

Clothes for both men and women should be of the same general type as described for longer trips. Skirts are an abomination in the woods. Even for the ladies there is no substitute for the felt hat. (See "Felt Hat" in Chapter 9 and Chapter 5, under "Winter Camping," for added material on women's clothes.)

Food lists for go-light packs may be taken from the regular food list in this book. The camp items have been selected for extreme lightness, and will apply equally well to light packs. (See "Go-Light Check List," pages 178, 179 and 180, for all camp items needed.)

## ONE-DAY TRIPS

Day trips are important in the training of any outdoor enthusiast, since the problems of maintaining comfort in all types of weather, cooking foods under difficult weather conditions, and the task of traveling all day in a wild country are comparable to the conditions experienced from day to day on extended trips. In addition, an emergency may involve remaining out all night.

All one-day hikers should be equipped with packsacks which allow full arm freedom for climbing where hand support is needed and for other diversions. Packsacks should be large enough so that they can be used for overnight trips. A partly filled pack of larger size, buckled higher on the back, hangs better than a small pack loaded to bulging proportions. Use the No. 1 or the No. 2 Duluth pack for a general all-around pack. (See "Day-Trip Check List," pages 180 and 181.)

## GO-LIGHT CHECK LIST

The following list is the minimum that should be taken on a go-light trip. Circumstances and individual ability to pack will determine how much of the items listed on pages 171 through 175 can be added. For yourself alone, follow the list as given. For two, double the items marked with an asterisk.

| | |
|---|---|
| *Wool underwear, medium weight, 2-piece | 2 pairs of drawers |
| | 1 shirt |
| *Wool socks | 2 pairs |
| *Wool outershirt | 1 |
| *Wool pants | 1 pair |
| *Belt or suspenders (braces) | 1 |
| *Wool jacket, lightweight | 1 |
| *Windbreaker parka, lightweight | 1 |
| *Moccasins, buckskin or moosehide, lightweight | 2 pairs |
| *Rubbers, moccasin type or 6-inch rubber packs | 1 pair |
| *Hat, treated felt | 1 |
| * Bandanna handkerchief | 1 |
| *Poncho, lightweight, or rain shirt | 1 |

| | |
|---|---|
| *Wallet | 1 |
| *Compass | 1 |
| *Match safe, waterproof type | 1 |
| Matches | 1 box (16-cubic-inch size) |
| *Belt knife | 1 |
| *Vision glasses (if needed) | 1 pair |
| Cooking utensils | |
|     Aluminum cooking pails | 2 |
|     *Steel mess kit with cover | 1 |
|     *Fork | 1 |
|     *Tablespoon | 1 |
|     Dishtowel | 1 |
| Ax, 2½ pound, ¾ length | 1 |
| Ax sheath | 1 |
| File, 6-inch | 1 |
| Whetstone, small size double-faced (India and Arkansas) | 1 |
| Flashlight, vest-pocket size | 1 |
| Flashlight bulb | 1 extra |
| *Map of region | 1 |
| Combination DDT and lindane spray for insects | 1 small can |
| First-aid packet | 1 |
| Camera, vest-pocket | 1 |
| *Hand towel | 1 |
| Toilet soap | 1 bar |
| *Toothbrush and dentifrice | 1 |
| Razor | 1 |
| *Comb | 1 |
| *Toilet paper | 1 roll |
| Mending kit | 1 |
|     Needles | small assortment |
|     Thread | " " |
|     Buttons | " " |
|     Patches | " " |
| Fishline | 1 |
| Fishhooks | small assortment |
| *Diary and pencil | 1 each |

| | |
|---|---|
| Tent, convertible *A* type (see "The Tent," pages 114 and 116) | 1 |
| Ropes, No. 5 sash cord for tent | 1 set |
| Mosquito netting for tent | 1 |
| *Packsack, No. 1 Poirer or Duluth | 1 |
| *Down sleeping bag with snaps | 1 |

For a cold-weather go-light trip refer to Chapter 5, under "Winter Camping."

## DAY-TRIP CHECK LIST

The following items should be included on day trips. The list is planned for one. Where two or more are in the party, all items marked with an asterisk should be duplicated for each member. Most items will be worn, and not carried in the pack.

| | |
|---|---|
| *Wool underwear, medium or lightweight 2-piece | 1 pair of drawers |
| | 1 shirt |
| *Wool socks | 1 pair |
| *Wool outershirt | 1 |
| *Wool or gabardine pants | 1 pair |
| *Belt or suspenders (braces) | 1 |
| *Low leather boots or moccasins and rubbers or 6-inch rubber packs | 1 pair |
| *Windbreaker, cotton jacket or lightweight parka | 1 |
| *Hat of treated felt for sun and rain | 1 |
| *Bandanna handkerchief | 1 |
| *Wallet | 1 |
| *Compass | 1 |
| *Match safe with matches | 1 |
| *Belt knife or pocket knife | 1 |
| *Poncho, lightweight | 1 |
| (For hiking, the poncho serves better than a rain shirt because it covers the pack and is a shelter cloth for rain.) | |
| Cooking utensils | |
| Aluminum Cooking Pails | 2 |
| *Mess kit with cover | 1 |
| *Fork | 1 |

| | |
|---|---|
| *Tablespoon | 1 |
| *Nesting cup | 1 |
| Dishtowel | 1 |
| *Vision glasses (if needed) | 1 pair |
| Ax, ¾ length with sheath | 1 |
| Flashlight with extra bulb | 1 |
| Ropes for stretching poncho in rain | 4 pieces of No. 5 sash cord, 20 feet each |
| *Map of region | 1 |
| *Head net for insects | 1 |
| *Insect repellent | 1 small tube |
| First-aid packet | 1 |
| Camera, vest-pocket | 1 |
| *Hand towel | 1 |
| Toilet soap | 1 bar |
| *Comb | 1 |
| Toilet paper | ¼ roll |
| *Packsack, No. 1 Poirer or Duluth | 1 |

For cold-weather day trips refer to Chapter 5, under "Winter Camping."

# 11

## The Wilderness Food Budget

THE NOTION THAT OUTDOOR COOKING MUST BE SOMETHING ROUGH and ready is akin to the equally absurd idea that you can sleep on the hard ground in a single blanket for a good night's rest. Both are false. Both typify the novice. A frying pan full of bacon plus a pot of coffee seems to feature most camp cooking. With proper fire control and attention to simple details, anyone can prepare well-balanced meals outdoors. On an extended trip full meals are indispensable. In remote areas each member of the party should have a fair knowledge of cooking; otherwise his inability to sustain himself if separated from the group becomes a risk.

The following list of foods and the directions for their preparation are slanted entirely for wilderness travel. This implies light weight and limited bulk. The great strides made in dehydration and in prepared and precooked commercial items not only make this possible but also give the wilderness traveler almost anything he wants in his diet. Earlier methods of dehydration should not be confused with modern ones. Where potatoes and other dehydrated vegetables once had a peculiar medicinal taste, it is difficult today to detect them from fresh vegetables. Fresh foods should of course be used wherever possible.

As an example of saving in weight and bulk, consider a hundred-pound sack of potatoes. The peelings weigh twenty pounds. The water in the potatoes weighs sixty-three pounds. Thanks to modern dehydration, the equivalent of a sack of potatoes can be tucked into a corner of your packsack, weighing only seventeen pounds. If you were to load a No. 2 packsack (the popular pack used on canoe trips) with dehydrated vegetables and fruits, and carry it over a portage, the equivalent in fresh products would require the combined efforts of six men to portage. You will agree that it is useless to haul along sixty-three pounds of water when it can be dipped out of a lake. Approximately a thirty-minute soaking of the newer type of dehydrated vegetables is all that is required. Dehydrated vegetables should not be soaked overnight. This will result in poor flavor and even in spoilage. It is now possible to arrive in camp and have cooked vegetables without delay, while such items as "instant" potatoes are ready with the addition of heated milk.

The precooking of commercial foods, especially cereals, has given the wilderness traveler another important advantage. Cereals now cook in from ten seconds to five minutes, where formerly they required a half-hour.

Despite the wide range of foods now available through dehydration, your wilderness menus should be kept as simple as possible in keeping with a balanced diet. This can never be emphasized enough, but only experience on the trail will prove to you the value of the suggestion. The trouble with a complex food list is that many of the items will never be used. *The ability to extract variety from a few ingredients is the secret of good outdoor cooking.* There are no jaded appetites to pamper in the wilderness. Hard work and fresh air tend to make any well-cooked meal attractive.

At one time I used to pack several types of breakfast cereal, but I found that unconsciously we turned to the bag of oatmeal until it was used up, and somehow we never tired of it. Now I take only one breakfast cereal. For a time I included a variety of dried fruits. Now the list has been reduced to apples, prunes, and raisins, with an occasional addition of figs or apricots, the latter for their high vitamin-C content.

Because tastes differ widely, a comprehensive food list is given. Recipes will follow the list of food items. These recipes are designed for the limited cooking utensils carried in the wilderness, and are free from the procedures found in most cookbooks. The direct method of mixing ingredients used in these recipes may bother cooks who are accustomed to mixing the various food components separately to gain the best possible texture or flavor. If texture or flavor is sacrificed to simplicity (an essential in outdoor cooking), the sacrifice is only slight. The recipes have been tested and used for some years in the wilderness, and will be found wholly adequate to most tastes. The "direct from food bag to kettle method" used is cheerfully accepted by most wilderness cooks—and especially by the hungry traveler.

The best utensils for the wilderness are simple aluminum pails hung over an open fire. The frying pan, however, must be made of steel, because food sticks to aluminum frying pans. A difficulty experienced by most people in outdoor cooking over an open fire is control of the fire. Much has been said and written about cooking over a bed of coals and other formal procedure; but the wilderness traveler coming off the trail wants his supper as soon as it can be prepared, and he cannot be bothered with formal procedure that takes a great deal of time. Supper should go on the kindled fire at once, without ado or ceremony in woodcraft. Usually you do not want to take time to wait for the fire to burn down to a bed of glowing coals. Coals will be available in time for you to prepare fried foods, for this is one of the last functions in preparing a meal.

The following list of foods represents the outside limit of variety that I carry on my trips. Following this is a condensed list from which substitutions can be made to fit individual tastes. If you are doubtful where to obtain your supply of dehydrated foods, write to your Government Department of Agriculture or to the larger wholesale food-supply houses. Local merchants have some of these items on hand, especially the precooked varieties.

*All food items listed hereafter should be packed and carried in a paraffined cloth bag with a plastic bag liner unless otherwise indicated.*

### Potatoes

The potato is one of our best staple foods, and is now known to be a so-called "protective" food. Dehydrated potatoes come in various shapes—diced, julienne, and "instant." In this last form the potatoes have been cooked and dehydrated, so that only hot milk and butter need to be added to make excellent mashed potatoes. Powdered milk can be added to the dry "instant" potatoes, in which case hot water is used for the liquid ingredient. (Dehydrated sweet potatoes are another excellent product.) Potatoes are high in carbohydrates, contain vitamins C, $B_1$, and G, and are rich in potassium, with an alkaline ash.

### Carrots

Dehydrated carrots are a valuable item in the diet; they are a good source of vitamins A, $B_1$, and C, and are rich in iron, with an alkaline ash. Carrots are valuable in overcoming night blindness and other eye ailments.

### Vegetable Greens

Spinach, turnip greens, mustard greens, and so on are available in dehydrated form. They are a valuable source of many of the vitamins, such as A, $B_1$, C, and G, and are rich in minerals, with an alkaline ash. If you like greens, they are a good item to take.

### Onions

Dehydrated onions are an excellent item in preparing many foods, and are tasty alone when creamed, fried, or boiled. They are a good source of vitamin C, with some $B_1$ and G.

### Cabbage

Cabbage is available in dehydrated form. Fourteen pounds of field cabbage are required to make one pound of dehydrated cabbage. You can tuck the equivalent of a couple of bushels of field cabbage in a small corner of your packsack. Cabbage is a good source of vitamins A, $B_1$, C and G, with an alkaline ash.

### Celery

Celery does not lend itself too well to reconstitution (the replacing of water after dehydration), but it is excellent in flavoring soups and vegetable soup mixes. Home-dried celery tops reduced to powder form also make excellent flavoring for soups. Celery is a good source of vitamins A, $B_1$, and G.

### Vegetable Soup Mixes

Assorted vegetables dehydrated and mixed are available. They are easy to prepare, but soups made from them are not substantial enough for the trail, and I do not take more than a small amount.

If cooked and prepared as heavy soups or stews, they are better for the wilderness.

## Sweet Corn

Good meals can be prepared with dehydrated sweet corn as a base. It is an acid ash food and should be avoided by those with hyperacidity. Sweet corn is a good source of vitamin $B_1$, a fair source of vitamins C and G, and is rich in iron and copper.

## Beans

As a general rule, beans require far too much time to cook, and therefore are of little value in wilderness travel. Only enough should be taken to supply a stayover in some spot. They are excellent in a permanent camp. Where travel is continuous I do not carry the unprocessed kind. Unfortunately, commercially precooked beans and bean flour are only fair substitutes. Navy and lima beans are popular with most tastes. Beans are high in vitamin $B_1$ and G, and are rich in vegetable protein and minerals, with an alkaline ash.

## Peas and Pea Flour

Split peas are an excellent food item; but, like beans, they take much too long to cook. For many years pea flour has been the better choice. Some of the earliest fur-trade ration lists include pea flour. Peas are high in vitamin A and are a good source of $B_1$ and G. Pea flour compressed into stick form is sold under the trade name Erbswurst. A piece broken off and boiled makes a thick pea soup.

## Tomato Paste and Dehydrated Tomato Flakes

Tomato flakes are more convenient from the point of view of weight, but I find that a more palatable item is tomato paste. This is nothing more than tomatoes reduced through dehydration beyond the purée stage to a paste. In spaghetti dishes it is a valuable item. It makes a good cream of tomato soup and, diluted, a fair tomato juice. A dash in the stew helps. It comes in small sealed cans, containing a few ounces, and goes a long way. It is a good source of vitamins A and $B_1$ and is high in C. Carry it in the smallest sealed cans for individual meals.

## Oatmeal

Oatmeal is a standby as a breakfast cereal. It can also be used in baking breads. Get the quick-cooking kind. Oatmeal is a good source of vitamin $B_1$ and minerals, and is a high carbohydrate food.

## Prepared Breakfast Foods

Prepared, ready-to-eat breakfast foods such as Corn Flakes are too bulky for wilderness packs, but they can be compressed. This makes them less appetizing in appearance but not in actual taste. If you insist on carrying Corn Flakes in their original form, then put the packages in a corrugated carton and place them in a pack-sack. Corn Flakes make quick lunches with rich liquefied whole milk; they are also good for breading fish. Bulk is the only objection. Grape-Nuts can be carried with no concern for bulk. Simply remove them from their original container and repack them in a paraffined cloth bag with a plastic liner.

## Wheat Granules

Wheat granules are available in plain granules and are a valuable item. A better tasting one, however, is the malted wheat granule. It is a good source of vitamin $B_1$ and minerals, and is a high carbohydrate food. Wheat granules come in patented package form. Remove them from their original container and repack them as you would Grape-Nuts or any other dry cereal.

## Rice

Before a really good dehydrated potato was available, rice was the staple starch food in the wilderness, and the alternative to spaghetti. Though I now take less rice, I still find it a valuable item on the list. Eaten boiled and as rice pudding it is excellent. Rice contains vitamins A, $B_1$, G, and minerals, and is a high carbohydrate food. Despite the high vitamin claim for unpolished rice, I find such rice poor for puddings and flat for general use. I much prefer the polished. Wild rice is sometimes available in the wilderness; in cities the cost of it is prohibitive. Precooked rice in packaged form is available. It requires boiling water but no actual cooking; however, because the rice must be left to stand near the fire for ten to fifteen minutes, little time is saved. In addition, with precooked rice there is some loss in flavor and body when it is compared to freshly cooked raw rice.

## Spaghetti and Macaroni

These were the alternatives to rice before the better dehydrated potato became available. Spaghetti and macaroni are good items for Italian dishes and cheese dishes. They contain vitamins $B_1$ and G and minerals, and are a high carbohydrate food. Get the short kind.

## Noodles

The best noodles are made at home from egg yolks and flour. They can be made on the trail with dehydrated eggs, flour, and water, but the commercial noodle saves you this trouble. Where fresh eggs are used, add enough flour to egg yolks to make a stiff dough. Roll the dough out thin and cut it into strips. Noodles are a good substitute for spaghetti, macaroni, or rice in some dishes. Egg yolks are a very rich and sustaining diet, and are high in vitamins A, $B_1$, and G.

## Corn Meal

Corn meal is a good item but cooks too slowly. Omit it where time is important. It makes the proverbial mush, which can be eaten as cereal, or later fried in slices. Corn meal makes very tasty breads. Get the yellow kind. This is a rich source of vitamin $B_1$ and minerals, has a good protein content, and is a high carbohydrate food. It has an acid ash, however, and should be avoided by some people.

## Rice Flour

Rice flour is one of the ingredients in many commercial ready-mixed pancake flours. The addition of rice flour makes pancakes more tender.

## Soybean Flour

Soybean flour is a good item and should be part of the wilderness fare. A tablespoonful stirred into stews gives a rich and tasty thickening. It is a high protein food. The Chinese regard the soybean as a valuable substitute for meats. In biscuits and pancakes it adds a nut-like flavor.

### Flour

Enriched white flour is most practical for a wilderness diet, despite the nutritional argument in favor of the darker kinds, because it has the most general use. One-sixth of the white flour should be what is known as cake flour. This is a plain flour which does not possess the gluten content of regular flour. Pancakes and sweet rolls made of cake flour will be tender because of the absence of gluten. Keep the two flours in separate bags and mix them when needed. Enriched flour is high in vitamins $B_1$ and G, and is a high carbohydrate food. Prepared pancake and biscuit mixes should be well packed against moisture to prevent spoiling, if you take them.

### Yeast

When yeast is carried on long trips, it should be of the dry, fast-rising granular type. It is used for the traditional sourdough pail and, now and then, in freshly raised yeast bread where extensive layovers allow it. Yeast is high in vitamins $B_1$ and G. Drop it in the cereal bag in its wrapped package for protection.

### Soda

Soda is used for the sourdough pail, and acts as an acid neutralizer and rising agent. It also serves the same purpose in sourmilk pancakes.

### Baking Powder

Do not buy the alum baking powder, but get the cream-of-tartar kind. It will be much easier on your stomach. Baking powder is the popular leavening ingredient in the wilderness, although the sourdough method is superior from a health standpoint. Remove it from the store can and carry it in a friction-top can.

### Cornstarch

Cornstarch will form a base for puddings and other foods, and should be included, unless commercial puddings are taken. This is the basic item in the preparation of blanc mange, to which various flavors and fruits may be added to make desserts.

### Lard and Vegetable Fats

If you use bacon as liberally as most campers do, the fat from your fried bacon will supply all that is needed for frying your fish and meats. Vegetable fats are preferable to lard, since they fry at a higher temperature and thus do not soak into the food. For general use oleomargarine keeps well. Remember that fried fish and meat are not as good for you as boiled or baked. Bake your fish in a reflector oven or prop it up before a fire—not over it—impaled on two sticks. Carry fats in a friction-top can.

### Meats

Side bacon, Canadian bacon, and various canned meats are the best items that can be carried. Ham spoils in time but it is good at the start of a trip. Fish you can get from wilderness waters. Pork shoulders, canned under several trade names such as Spam, Spork, and so on, and corned beef are on my list, but you may not like them. Canned roast beef is another meat liked by most people that is good for the trail. My own choice is Canadian bacon with a limited amount of side bacon and a variety of canned meats. Meats contain vitamins A, $B_1$, C, G, protein and minerals. Bacon and ham if not canned should first be wrapped in parchment paper (rice paper), then placed in a cloth bag. When time permits on the trail, they should be removed, hung up in the shade, and allowed to air for several hours. Watch out for bears. Your smoked meats should be wrapped in cloths dipped in vinegar and dried to retard mold, then wrapped in parchment paper and placed in paraffined bags.

### Eggs

Dehydrated eggs are an important item in wilderness travel. The secret of their use scrambled is to flavor them with bacon, ham, or cheese. They have wide use in the general preparation of food. One pound of dehydrated eggs equals about five dozen eggs. They are high in vitamins A, $B_1$, G, and in minerals.

### Cheese

Cheese will become moldy on an extended trip, but it should be used as long as weather permits. Here taste must determine choice.

English Cheddar is very good for general-purpose cooking. Cheese is a good source of protein, minerals, and other food elements. It is especially high in vitamin A and in calcium. Sew small packages of cheese tightly in cheesecloth and dip them in melted paraffin. Then place these in cloth bags that have been dipped in vinegar and dried. The acid in the vinegar will retard mold.

Dry cheese is a valuable complement to spaghetti dishes and in omelets made of dehydrated eggs, and it keeps well.

### Butter

The best way to carry butter is in half-pound sealed cans. However, I have found that by packing butter in friction-top cans, thus removing all air pockets, it will keep well. There is also a much improved tropical butter on the market. I have let a can of this stand through the heat of a long summer, then opened it and found it fresh. It is harder to spread than ordinary butter but it is an excellent product. Ask your local dairy association where you may buy it. It is high in vitamin A. (Oleomargarine keeps better than butter, and in warm weather it should replace the latter for prolonged trips.)

### Dehydrated Whole Milk

Dehydrated whole milk is a highly important item. It is useful for cocoa, chocolate milk, and as a drink by itself; but it finds an even wider range of uses in the preparation of staple foods. It is perhaps the best-rounded food we have. Powdered whole milk contains butter fat; when it is mixed with water a pound of it will make a gallon of standard milk. As cream, it can be mixed as rich as desired, but one-half cup of powdered milk to two cups of water will serve most cream uses. Once liquefied milk is mixed, it will spoil just as quickly as fresh milk. Therefore in warm weather only enough should be mixed for immediate use. If cooler temperatures permit, mix the powdered milk twenty-four hours in advance to obtain the best flavor. Leave this liquefied milk in the chain shaker or mixer described in Chapter 12, "Wilderness Cooking." Fat-free milk is also available, but it is very flat tasting until you become accustomed to it. Its advantage is that it mixes instantly in water by simply stirring.

Powdered whole milk has an excellent balance of vitamins A,

$B_1$, C, G, minerals and protein. Powdered milk packed in cans sells at double or more the cost of bulk powdered milk. If there is a milk-drying plant near you, get the bulk powdered milk.

Canned condensed milk, while sometimes substituted, is heavier and bulkier to carry than whole or powdered milk, and is not as palatable to most tastes.

### Coffee, Tea, and Cocoa

The concentrated coffees are now so vastly improved that they should satisfy most coffee drinkers; they are also a great saving in weight, bulk, and time. Despite the fact that I am a coffee drinker, in the woods I prefer tea. This is common with many coffee drinkers. Tea is easier on the digestion, and is a quick bracer. Coffee, of course, has no equal for breakfast. Caffeine-free coffees have been much improved in flavor, and come in all forms. Both regular coffee and the "instant" kind should be carried in air-tight or friction-top cans.

Tea can be had in "instant" and tablet form, and in tea bags, but my choice is bulk tea.

As for cocoa, the ready-mix kind is the most convenient. Either hot or cold liquefied dry milk can be added for the drink desired.

### Dehydrated Fruit Juices

The methods used successfully in the drying of blood plasma have been applied to the dehydration of citrus fruits. Thus today the vitamin C deficiency, once such a problem in wilderness fare, has been solved, reducing scurvy to a minimum. Orange juice, lemon juice, grapefruit juice, and other juices are available for the wilderness breakfast. A tablespoonful of orange powder makes an eight-ounce glass of orange juice. The lemon powder is more highly concentrated. My choice is to combine the lemon and orange powders. This lends a little more tartness to the orange juice. It is an excellent drink to start the day. It is a simple beverage to prepare for the quick noonday stop. Citrus fruit juices are good flavoring, and a combination of soda and citrus juice makes an excellent pancake leavener. A little of the citrus fruit powder added to applesauce improves the flavor. Dusted lightly on a coffee cake, it adds zest. Concentrated juices in liquid form canned, that do not need refrigeration, are available and very good, especially the lemon.

Modern concentrated and dehydrated fruit juices are high in vitamin C. Carry them in friction-top cans or in their original sealed cans.

### Dried Apples

Dried apples are a valuable item to take in the woods. They can be stewed; they can be blended with cooked cereal; they make good cobblers; they top a coffee cake well, baked in the reflector oven; with sugar they can be reduced to jam; and they serve in other ways. Dried apples contain vitamins A, $B_1$, C, G, and minerals.

### Raisins

Raisins are a valuable adjunct when used in rice pudding and in biscuits, or when stewed with apples for sauce. They are rich in iron, are a good source of vitamins $B_1$ and G, and have an alkaline ash. Raisins are a high carbohydrate food, and therefore a good between-meals snack along the trail. Get the kind that is loose, not the pressed type.

### Dried Figs

These are unsweetened, light-colored cooking figs. Since figs have a slightly laxative effect, they are a good item to use during the first few days of a trip when you are adjusting yourself to different fare and water. They are a good source of vitamins $B_1$ and G, and have an alkaline ash. They are easy to stew.

### Prunes

Prunes are well known for their peristaltic action on the intestines to help regularity. Because they have an alkaline ash, and increase acid in certain organs, they should not be used by those avoiding an acid diet. Prunes are a valuable source of vitamins A, $B_1$, and G. Eaten raw, prunes have a high caloric value, and are therefore good to chew along the trail.

### Dried Peaches and Apricots

Both peaches and apricots respond well to drying and are flavorful. They are an excellent source of vitamins A, $B_1$, C, and G. (Apricots, especially, are very high in vitamin C and might serve as a substitute for citrus fruit juice when this is not available.)

### Preserves

Jam is an indispensable item on the wilderness food list. It satisfies more than anything else your craving for sweets and acids. Added to butter on a hot biscuit, jam makes an excellent simple dessert. My choice is a good quality of strawberry preserves where the fruit has not been overcooked. Jam can be made on the trail from dried fruits or from wild berries in season, adding sugar and plain gelatin. (See Chapter 13, "Wilderness Recipes and Menus.") Preserves are high in vitamin C. Carry them in a paraffin-lined can with a friction top.

### Peanut Butter

Peanut butter is a very nourishing and substantial item for the noonday stop. It makes a good combination with jam in sandwiches. Put it on your wilderness provision list. Peanut butter, a high energy food, contains vitamins A, $B_1$, and G. Carry it in a friction-top can.

### Sugar

Do not stint on sugar. Concentrated sugar substitutes can be obtained, and will cut down on weight. Dehydrated lemons call for so much sugar in lemonade that sugar substitutes must be carried where large quantities of lemonade are desired. Sugar is a high-carbohydrate food. (Some may prefer a portion of this ration in the form of brown sugar.) If you make your own jam on the trail from dried fruits or from wild berries in season, allow for additional sugar; or, if you use sugar substitutes, add gelatin to give the jam sufficient body.

### Cinnamon

Cinnamon is needed for rice pudding, cinnamon toast, and coffee cake baked in the reflector oven.

### Vanilla

Vanilla is used to flavor puddings, pancake sirup, breadstuffs, dried fruit sauces, and so on. Tape the bottle well with adhesive tape to prevent breakage and place it in the bag with the cereal for protection. (Unfortunately, plastic bottles have not proved safe containers for vanilla.)

## Salt

Take the iodized salt sold in cardboard containers. Either place the original container in a paraffined cloth bag or empty the salt into a friction-top can which has first been lined with paraffin.

## Pepper

I use pepper sparingly, but you may feel that you cannot enjoy your food without it. Carry pepper in a screw-top hard rubber or metal shaker.

## Vitamin Tablets

The minimum-daily-requirement type of vitamin tablets should be included as an extra precaution to afford sufficient vitamin intake, but they will not take the place of food or wholly make up for an unbalanced diet.

## Plain Gelatin

This is not the product sold as Jello-O but is the basic animal element from which most of these patent food items get their jelling agent. The use of gelatin has been much overlooked in camp cooking. Its great value lies in the fact that it supplies a base from which innumerable dishes can be made. Puddings, jellied meat or fish loaves, desserts with citrus fruit powders, pies, cooked dried fruits, and many other improvisations are possible with gelatin as a thickening agent or binder. It is an all-protein food. Use in proportion to liquid as stated on the gelatin package. One envelope of gelatin will congeal two cups of liquid. Always soften gelatin with cold, not hot, liquid before stirring in hot ingredients. The reader will, of course, recognize that many of the smaller items, such as gelatin, cinnamon, and so on, can be consolidated in a paraffined cloth bag lined with a plastic bag.

## Prepared Mixes and Precooked Foods

Up to this time we have considered many basic foods and the separate ingredients which make up numerous recipes. In conclusion, I do not wish to overlook the importance of great developments in specially prepared foods, many suitable for the trail. Piecrusts, bread and cake mixes, cheese spreads, dry sirups which need only water and heating, and a vast number of other foodstuffs on the store shelves will no doubt replace some of the basic items already listed, for the sake of expedience. Where a camper has a limited knowledge of cooking, many of the problems are solved by these prepared mixes, and I heartily recommend them. They should, however, be tested before stocking up on them, and special consideration ought to be given to their keeping qualities under varying temperatures. The ever-expanding variety of these foods has made wilderness food budgets simpler; and it should be borne in mind that because ready-mixed products are easier to carry than a number of separate ingredients, both packing and cooking are simplified.

Ready-mixed items should be removed from their original packages in order to save space and to avoid broken containers, and then packed as shown in the early part of this chapter. Mixes which do not lend themselves to dry packing should be put into friction-top cans. Cut out the recipes from the packages and put them inside the bags or cans used to repack the individual food items.

The following three items are included in the food budget because they are usually purchased with groceries:

### Soaps and Detergents

For washing clothes use Naptha soap. For dishes use one of the new detergents. Thanks to them, stubborn grease can now be removed from camp utensils even in cold water. Transfer the detergent from its original box into a paraffined cloth bag lined with a plastic bag.

For toilet soap, a bar of the new detergent type which lathers quickly in any kind of water is the handiest, I find. For the grimier cleaning jobs I include a bar of Lava soap. Carry these in a soap container or in a rubber tobacco pouch.

### Toilet Paper

Increase your amount of toilet paper if you also intend to use it as paper toweling, or substitute paper toweling of the softer, more absorbent types for all use.

### Bon Ami

A half-bar or less of Bon Ami must be carried to keep the reflector oven shiny, or it will not bake properly.

### Provision Check List
(A one-month supply for two men)

| | | |
|---|---|---|
| Flour, white | 24 | pounds |
| Flour, cake | 4 | " |
| Flour, soybean | 2 | " |
| Corn meal | 2 | " |
| Oatmeal | 8 | " |
| Malted meal | 2 | " |
| Rice | 5 | " |
| Grape-Nuts | 2 | " |
| Hardtack or Ry-Krisp | 2 | " |
| Potatoes, dehydrated and "instant" | 9 | " |
| Carrots, dehydrated | 2 | " |
| Onions, dehydrated | 8 | ounces |
| Vegetables, dehydrated (greens, leafy) | 8 | " |
| Sweet corn, dehydrated | 1 | pound |
| Tomato paste | 1 | " |
| Spaghetti and/or macaroni | 3 | pounds |
| Apples, dried | 3 | " |
| Peaches and/or apricots, dried | 2 | " |
| Raisins | 2 | " |
| Prunes and/or figs | 2 | " |
| Preserves | 5 | " |
| Orange and lemon powder | 3 | " |
| Milk, dehydrated (whole or fat free) | 8 | " |
| Eggs, dehydrated | 4 | " |
| Peanut butter | 2 | " |
| Butter and/or oleomargarine | 5 | " |
| Vegetable shortening | 2 | " |
| Canned meat | 10 | " |
| Canadian bacon | 5 | " |
| Side bacon | 5 | " |
| Cheese, fresh | 4 | " |
| Cheese, dehydrated (grated) | 8 | ounces |
| Coffee, regular | 3 | pounds |
| (if "instant," then 12 ounces) | | |
| Tea | 1½ | " |
| Cocoa | 1 | pound |
| Cornstarch | 8 | ounces |

| Soda | 2 ounces |
| Dried yeast, granular quick-rising type | 2 " |
| Baking powder | 12 " |
| Sugar | 10 pounds |
| Concentrated sugar substitute | 2 ounces |
| Salt | 2 pounds |
| Pepper | ½ ounce |
| Cinnamon | ½ " |
| Vanilla | 1 " |
| Vitamins, minimum-daily-requirement type, 60 tablets | 4 ounces |

Total food list 150 pounds, or 2½ pounds per man per day.

| Laundry soap, Naptha, bar or package type | 2 bars, or 1 package |
| Toilet soap, Lava and/or face soap | 2 bars |
| Detergent | 1 box |
| Bon Ami (for cleaning reflector oven) | ½ bar |
| Toilet paper | 4 rolls |
| Matches | 1 box (16 cubic inch size) |

The following list includes foods which can be used as alternates to those in the writer's list where tastes differ. It shows the foods now being dehydrated by modern means and available at dehydrating plants:

| | |
|---|---|
| Artichoke | Chard (Swiss) |
| Asparagus | Cherries |
| Bananas | Chili, pods and powder |
| Bean flour | Citrus fruit peel |
| Beans, green | Cranberries |
| Beets | Cucumber |
| Blueberries | Currants |
| Bouillon (meatless stock) | Dates |
| Broccoli | Dulse |
| Broths, powder form | Egg plant |
| Cabbage | Endive |
| Cauliflower | Garlic powder |

Grapefruit juice
Grapes
Horseradish
Kale
Leek
Lettuce
Mincemeat
Mint
Nectarine
Okra
Paprika pods
Parsley
Parsnips
Pears

Peppermint
Peppers, green, red, or sweet
Persimmon
Pimientoes
Pumpkin
Radish
Raspberries
Rhubarb
Rutabagas
Salt, vegetized (onion, celery, etc.)
Spinach
Squash
Tomatoes, green
Watercress

This does not exhaust the list. If further information or some special dietary food item is required, inquire of your Government Department of Agriculture.

# 12

# *Wilderness Cooking*

THE READER WILL HAVE OBSERVED THAT SUCH ITEMS AS FRESH EGGS, fresh vegetables, fresh milk, and other foods found in settled areas have not been included in the wilderness food budget. However, the dehydrated eggs, vegetables, milk, and other items listed will provide tasty dishes not easily distinguished in flavor from the fresh product. Care should be given to reconstituting these foods. Vegetables should be soaked for thirty minutes, then placed on the fire and allowed to simmer slowly for about forty-five minutes. They should be tested for tenderness with a fork to determine when they are fully cooked. Some "instant" kinds require no soaking.

## THE CHAIN SHAKER

Reconstituting eggs and milk, I found, was a problem in the woods until I developed the *chain shaker* or *mixer*. This is nothing more than a common shaker supplied with a length (about 16 inches) of well-plated wire chain. The chain used with an ordinary friction-top can will serve the same purpose. The proper amount of dry egg or milk powder and water, along with the chain, are put into the mixer. A few rapid shakes and the eggs or the milk are well mixed and ready. (See illustration.)

## COOKING KIT

The cooking kits usually supplied by sporting-goods stores need some culling out before they are ready for wilderness use. The frying pan is generally of aluminum, and food will stick to it and

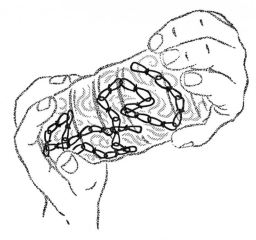

**Chain Shaker or Mixer**

burn if you are cooking over an open fire. Replace it by a steel pan with steep, though not flaring, sides to prevent a bannock from sliding out of the pan when propping the pan before a fire. The cups also are likely to be aluminum, and will burn your lips. Replace them with heavily tinned or porcelain cups with split handles for nesting. The table knives that come with the kit are scarcely ever used, since they are usually replaced by a belt knife.

**Split-Handle Porcelain Cup**

A set of cooking utensils for two should include the following:
  One 6-quart aluminum cooking pail with cover
  One 4-quart aluminum pail with cover
  One 2-quart aluminum pail with cover
  Two heavily tinned or porcelain cups with split handles for nesting
  One steel frying pan with steep sides (the pan about 8 to 10 inches in diameter)

Two aluminum plates

Two aluminum bowls

Two spoons

Two forks

One 5-inch mason's trowel (This item, besides its use for cooking, has other camp uses. See page 119).

A cooking kit made in England, and sold in Canada and in the United States, has covers made in the form of inverted pans or bowls—a valuable innovation for the camper because covers are not generally useful. With the three pails in this kit, the three covers provide extra utensils with no additional weight.

## THE REFLECTOR OVEN

Perhaps no one item of camp equipment has contributed more luxury to wilderness fare than the reflector oven. Hot breads, biscuits, cakes, pies, puddings, roasted meat and fish—all these and more are readily prepared outdoors in the reflector oven.

Because a lively flame is needed, small pieces of dry wood should be collected for such quick work as biscuits that require only twenty minutes to bake. Large fish and meat roasts can be cooked with

Firewood is placed upright to give height to flame.

The Reflector Oven

rougher and larger wood, since this job requires several hours, and you do not have to be fussy about the nature of the fire so long as it is moderate.

In the standard type of reflector oven which has a 60-degree reflecting angle, the bottom will bake faster than the top unless the fire is raised a few inches. This is best done by laying several pieces of green wood for the base of the fire to get it higher than the lower edge of the oven for uniform top and bottom baking. If time permits, you can increase the efficiency of the oven by providing a small backlog at the side of the fire farthest from the oven. The same thing will be accomplished if you build the fire against perpendicular rock formations, which are numerous in the North Country, or if you lean your fuel against a green wood support.

The oven should be placed about eight inches away from the flame. Experience will soon teach you how far away to set it, depending on the size and intensity of the flame. It is wise to keep a handful of small dry sticks on hand for the final "flashing"—the quick browning of the top of your baking just before you remove it from the fire. (See illustration of reflector oven and fire.)

The Dutch oven is treated at length in Chapter 4, "Pack Horse Methods." (See illustration.)

In arctic areas transporting fuel for cooking is a problem which forces the traveler to use every economy he can. One economical method is the use of a pressure cooker. With such a utensil the cooking time can be cut down considerably, with consequent saving in the fuel supply. The handles of such utensils should be supplemented with heavy wire bails if they are to be hung over an open fire of heather, willow, driftwood, or other fuels available in the arctic. Most cooking in the arctic, however, is done on a Primus stove. (See illustration.)

Another method of fuel saving, and a great saving in cooking operations, is to use wide-mouthed Thermos bottles or Thermos jugs. Oatmeal, for example, is brought to a boil and placed in the Thermos unit. Cooking continues by means of the trapped heat. Overnight, or between meals, the process goes on. The luxury of sitting down to a hot meal without setting about the task of cooking will be evident. Place Thermos units in whatever additional insulating material is at hand—bedding or clothes—to retain the heat longer.

In the arctic, Primus stoves, or other heating and cooking units, should be protected with a barrel-like shield of some kind so as to retain their heat.

## COOKING FIRES

Lighting a fire after days of rain will give you no difficulty if you have a sharp ax. Water does not penetrate far into a log. Choose a dead tree that is leaning or standing. Hit it with the butt end of the ax to hear if it will ring. Cut a short length of log with the ax and split it. The center will be as dry as bone. From this, split some kindling. Then take your hunting knife and cut some of the kindling into "feather sticks," pieces of kindling with the shavings attached. Lay a piece of the kindling on the ground; lean the "feather sticks" against it, with the shavings downhill, and touch a match to them. Lay small pieces of dry kindling crisscross on the fire. Gradually add larger stuff. When the fire is well under way, put on the wet outer part of your wood. It will dry off quickly and burn well. Birchbark will burn on wet days, but it burns reluctantly when it is very wet.

Even on dry days you may experience some difficulty in getting a fire started promptly. One of the chief difficulties is that in a forest area the moisture is still in the ground whether rain has fallen recently or not.

Your most common mistake will be to smother your fire with fuel. No matter what sort of design you build with your wood, remember that you must burn a vast amount of oxygen, and that if you pack the fuel too closely there will be no room for the oxygen to burn. The rule to follow is roughly this: Allow a space between every stick of wood about half as wide as the thickness of the sticks themselves for the flames to come through. Too wide spacing destroys the combustion chambers of your fire, and may also cause it to go out.

You may also fall into the common error of starting a fire, getting it going, and then adding fuel that is too heavy. What happens is that a pocket burns out in the center of your combustion area and the fire dies because you have gone too fast from small kindling to large pieces of wood. A fire should grow gradually from one size of wood to another until it is blazing.

When you build a wood fire in a stove you have easy combustion once the fire is well under way. In fact, if you put only one stick of wood in the stove it will burn. Outdoors, one stick will usually go out. The reason is that two sticks, side by side, form in principle a combustion chamber such as you have in a stove. Additional spaces between the sticks form additional combustion chambers. The better the combustion chambers, the better the fire.

You should adopt the same principle in the kindling of a fire. Two "feather sticks" propped up and sufficiently close together to form a combustion chamber, and with an area underneath for a draft, are the secret of getting a quick fire. This principle will apply to whatever fuel you use for kindling—birchbark, tinder, duff from the forest floor, spruce, or other twigs. A combustion chamber and a draft below, with proper spacing of tinder for general circulation of air and flames, bring results.

Under the lower green branches and on the lower part of the trunks of small spruce trees, you will find quantities of very fine dead twigs. These are about the best type of kindling for a quick fire during dry weather. They are also useful shortly after a rain because they are so well suspended for aeration that they dry quickly. In a spell of wet weather they are not good. You will probably have to cut fuel in any event for a continued fire; and since the center of such cut fuel is bone dry you can cut a few "feather sticks" while doing your chopping. Unless there are other slightly larger unchopped pieces of dry fuel lying around which you can add to the flash flame, spruce twigs flare up and go out. For this reason I maintain a general rule of splitting firewood and bone-dry kindling from it at the same time.

Almost certainly your first cooking fires will be ten times as big as they ought to be. These holocausts are the downfall of most camp cooking. If you had a fire in your own kitchen one-tenth as large as the fires on which most camp food is cooked, you would send out a fire alarm immediately. It is impossible to get near a fire like this to control the cooking, to say nothing of the scorched cooking utensils and the frustrated spirits that are the result.

Cut a sufficient quantity of small sticks about eight inches long; stack them up near the cooking fire and feed them on a few at a time as they are needed. Very little fuel will be needed for the entire cooking process. If more than one cooking pail is to be set on the fire, build a long, narrow fire or keep several separate small fires going under the cooking pails. I have often wondered why there is such a reluctance to have a small narrow fire or several small fires instead of one large inferno. Different kinds of cooking call for different degrees of heat. You may want one small fire that has burned down for frying away from the cooking fire, where it will be cool and convenient. Of course, the small fires should all be in the same general area, so that you can move a burning stick from one fire to another as cooking progresses. You wouldn't think of having a stove with one big burner for all your cooking. Four flames are better than one big one on the stove, and the small narrow fire or several separate fires are also better outdoors.

Campfires for cheer and warmth are of course larger. But here again you can practice moderation to advantage. If cooking must go on at the same time, rake or carry off a batch of hot coals on a sheet of birchbark to a cool place and do your cooking there, adding fresh hot coals as you need them.

Every year forest fires exact their toll. Some are set by lightning, some by bottles left carelessly exposed for the sun to make a burning glass of them, and many by cigarettes thrown out of car windows. The camper sets a shameful number. He does it in a typical way. A camper cooks his dinner and eats it while the fire burns down and apparently is out. Only a few gray ashes remain. He is fed and contented, and takes off in his canoe, on his saddle horse, or hikes away to fish, as the case may be. He is gone for several hours while the dead-looking fire slowly creeps through the humus, perhaps from under his rocky fireplace, underground, or over the duff, slowly smoldering. Then it finds some lively tinder on which to get going. Soon a billow of smoke and fire rises. If the Forest Service sees it, men are dispatched to the scene, men who otherwise would be working and developing areas for our pleasure. Their constructive work stops. They must fight to prevent the loss of forests and the loss of human and animal life. Bulldozers are brought in to tear down trees to create a firebreak. Men sweat and fight twenty-four hours a day, without sleep, for here is the arch enemy—fire, ready to plunder and destroy a wilderness paradise!

The camper, who is caught in the area, is drafted into service. His valuable camp equipment has gone up in flames hours ago; his lungs are full of smoke; and if he has been responsible he wishes that he were dead. The chances are that he will have to answer to the authorities for a serious crime, caused by leaving a small pile of gray ashes.

The next time he may pour a bucket of water on the fire and go about his business of breaking camp. In a week, three weeks, or three months, the fire which he thought he smothered with one pail of water has slowly grown into an inferno from one small spark that was not quite out, smoldering underground and remaining invisible to the Forest Service sentinels. Again the camper has devastated a wilderness paradise, and again he has perhaps caused the loss of human and of animal life.

What should you do? *Soak your campfire!* Then stir the ashes and their surroundings with a stick and soak them again. Continue to do so until not a semblance of smoke, steam, or heat remains. You cannot afford to do less.

This is not a pretty picture, but the United States Forest Service, the Canadian Forestry Association, and a number of State Forest men have asked me to say something in this book that would reach and impress the camper.

If you are using the convertible type of tent described in an earlier chapter, your rainy-day fire will not be exposed but will be under the protection of the tent fly. If you are not using this type of tent, you should carry a separate canopy and stretch it so that you can cook in a rain. If you are caught out with no shelter and have to build a fire, look for a rotten birch tree, shake the pulp out of a section of the bark, and build a fire inside it as it lies horizontal on the ground. Use a part of the bark for kindling. When the tube of birchbark is on fire, you will have a good start against anything but a downpour.

It is not necessary to fight smoke around a cooking fire. The idea that smoke will follow you to any side of the fire you go is fact, not fancy. Smoke will move into the partial vacuum any object near a fire creates. For this reason build your fire against a rocky ledge or some other vertical surface—never against a log or a tree. The log may be hollow and start a forest fire. If no ledge is handy, use a poncho, a floor cloth, or some other article that can be stretched a safe distance from the flame; or lean your canoe on its side a short distance away. This will help to carry off the smoke.

In the North Country where rock forms much of the earth's surface, cooking pails are best hung over a fire by resting a pole at an angle on a rock or log and weighting one end of it on the ground with another rock or log. The cooking pail is then hung on the opposite end of the pole in a small notch made with a knife. Several of these poles can be pointing into the fire. (See illustration.) Where

(A) Cooking Pail Supports. (B) Green Pole Grate over Long Narrow Fire. (C) Green Pole Grate over Small Single Fire.

the earth is soft, a crane can be made of two crotched sticks with a pole across them. Several cooking pails can be suspended from the pole by pothooks made from smaller crotched sticks, notched at one end for the bail, and hung on the main pole. Rocks, properly spaced, can be used on which to support cooking pails. Two green logs placed parallel or at an angle may also be used to support the cooking pails. The fire is built between the logs. However, this principle is not generally understood. The common notion is that two large logs are laid on the ground and that a fire is built between them. In actual practice, this is too laborious.

The proper method is to use two green poles a few inches in diameter; lay them parallel or slightly at an angle to each other, and support them off the ground at each end by crosspieces. The crosspieces should be notched to keep the poles from rolling. Such a wooden grate will conveniently support your cooking pails and frying pan at the proper height from the cooking fire. This arrangement is admirably suited to the long, narrow fire mentioned earlier. The green poles will allow you a surprising number of fires without burning the poles. (See illustrations.)

## FOIL COOKING

Cooking in foil has become popular in organized camp and picnic group activities. It has also crept into wilderness cooking, where it has a number of enthusiastic supporters. The theory is that in foil cookery the ordinary utensils can be dispensed with, thus offering a primitive approach to cooking without the difficulties of the genuinely primitive method. In any event, it has the fascination of novelty. But, as with all novelties, you should be careful not to go overboard about it until you are thoroughly aware of the principles involved.

The simplest and most common example is to wrap a piece of meat, a potato, or a whole meal in foil and thrust it into the fire, or into hot ashes, and after it is cooked eat it directly out of the foil wrapping. Serving dishes can be made out of foil by modeling them by hand, or over the top of a small stump. You can make a plate, a can, or whatever form you choose. The most popular way to cook solid foods is to make a bag out of a sheet of foil, insert the food, and close the bag at the top with long strands of flexible copper wire which can be easily retrieved. The foil for this type of cooking should be of the heavier gauge 18-inch width especially made by manufacturers for this purpose.

Some firms make a wire basket with a bail (wire handle) and with a foil container ready to be dropped into the basket. Another item is a long-handled wire frame made to hold a foil container, both shaped like a frying pan. The foil containers can also be used inside ordinary camp cooking pails or fry pans, although at some risk of warping your utensils. The general theory is obvious. You dispose of the foil containers after use and thus avoid dishwashing.

In practice the wire frames, plus the disposable foil containers and a roll of foil, do not save any weight on a camping trip; aluminum pails will weigh about the same, or even less. Wire frames have to be scoured after each exposure over an open fire to remove the soot. There is also some question as to the actual saving in dishwashing. If you decide to use foil without the frames, there is of course a saving, except for knives, forks, and spoons.

If you have made up your mind to fry your meat or vegetables in foil, get a green crotched stick and spread a sheet of foil across it. Or shape a frying pan out of the foil and attach it to the crotched stick by wrapping the edges of the foil around the fork of the crotch to hold it. If wood burned down to a bed of glowing embers

**Aluminum Foil Frying Pan**

is well flattened, the foil can be laid directly on the coals, but the meat should be placed on the foil immediately to avoid burning the foil. Or you can set the foil directly on the hot ground, where a fire has been burning for a half-hour or more.

Reflector ovens can be made from foil by building a frame of wood and by stretching sheets of foil over it. (See illustration. See also methods for baking with a reflector oven on pages 202 and 203.)

**Foil Reflector Oven**

Much of the trouble with cooking in foil lies in the fact that sound cooking principles are sacrificed. For example, no good cook who wanted to bake a potato would completely seal it in foil. All of the moisture would be retained in the potato. A baked potato, prepared properly, is mealy and light, and the secret of success is puncturing the peel to allow some of the moisture to escape. A potato baked in foil is like a potato boiled with the peel on. It retains the bitter taste of the peel. Peeled potatoes cooked in foil are a slight modification of the boiled potato. An apple, on the other hand, lends itself quite well to baking in foil, since here the retention of moisture is desirable.

A piece of raw meat sealed in foil and laid on the fire is very edible, but it is not roasted meat. Like the potato, the meat holds its moisture and tastes more as though it had been boiled. There is no objection to the food value of boiled meat, but it tastes flatter than roasted meat. Actually, for a straight diet of meat, the meat should be boiled and the liquid drunk to obtain the most food value. If meat is to be cooked in foil, it should be browned thoroughly before wrapping, which makes this kind of cooking a fairly elaborate affair. Meat cooked in this way compares in taste to meat done in a pressure cooker.

The most popular method of foil cooking is to wrap meat and several vegetables in the same bag of foil and cook them in an open fire. But, again, if you do not like water-cooked meat, the meat will be tasteless, and will resemble what is popularly called a boiled dinner. To seal a steak in a piece of foil and lay it in the fire is wrong in principle. Steaks need to be exposed, and should be fried or broiled in an open foil pan—very hot—for about $3\frac{1}{2}$ minutes on each side. Pork chops, while covered for a part of the time, need to be fried slowly and thoroughly; but to roll them in a piece of foil and stick them in an open fire is a good way to ensure culinary disaster.

Most foil cooking is done in a hot fire where foods are burned or otherwise ruined in the process. The proper method is to build a fire and let it burn down. Rake away the embers from the hot ground, place the foil-wrapped foods on the ground, rake the hot embers and ashes over them until they are completely covered, then lay on fresh wood and build up the fire and allow it to burn until it is once again a mass of glowing embers. This provides steady heat and does not scorch the food and the foil. When time is nearly up, place your tea or coffee on the fire so that everything will be ready at the same time. Stewed fruit for dessert will have to be taken off the fire earlier in its foil wrapping to allow it to cool.

As I have said, foil cooking is a novelty and it can be fun. But it does not lend itself to a serious wilderness trip, and it should be confined to social groups, organized camps, or day trips. Furthermore, if you already know how to cook with standard equipment, your foil cooking will be greatly improved. The principles of cooking, once you have learned them, can be applied successfully to any new method.

Foil cookery, "bean holes," barbecues, tin-can cookery, dough-on-a-stick, cabobs, weiner roasts, and so on, are pleasant social pursuits. Most of us would be better adjusted if we followed out such programs. But in this book we must be careful to make a distinction between social pastimes and the needs of wilderness travel. To confuse the two is to detract from both. Even in organized camps for boys and girls it is good to teach the fundamentals of cooking three meals a day quickly and with the proper utensils before indulging in novelties.

Let me add in conclusion that foil has a wide range of usefulness for the serious traveler. It can be used as an emergency match safe, as film wrapping, as a photographic reflector, and in many other ways almost too numerous to mention.

# 13

## Wilderness Recipes and Menus

### JUICES

*Apple Juice.* To 1 quart of water, add 1 cup of dried apples. Stew for 40 minutes. Remove from the fire. Drain off the juice for drink. Add sugar and a small amount of lemon powder to taste. Cool. (The apples remaining may be eaten with rich milk.)

*Orange Juice.* To 1 cup of water, add 1 level teaspoon of orange powder and a small amount of lemon powder to taste. Some sugar may be added, if desired. If concentrated liquid juice is carried, dilute according to directions on the can.

*Tomato Juice.* To 1 quart of water, add 1 small can of tomato paste. Mix thoroughly. Add 1 level teaspoon of salt, 1 level teaspoon of sugar.

### BEVERAGES

*Coffee.* To each cup of rapidly boiling water placed in a cooking pail, add 1 rounded tablespoon of coffee. Stir and set aside for 7 minutes to settle the grounds. Do not put coffee in before water boils. It is sure to boil over, unless constantly watched.

A wine-clear coffee can be made by adding a pinch of dehydrated egg powder to the finished coffee, but clearing coffee in this way destroys some of the body. Coffees are blended in order to obtain this body.

For "instant" coffee of the soluble kind, use a level teaspoonful to each cup of boiling water.

*Tea.* Into a pail of boiling water, add tea according to strength desired: 1 level teaspoon of tea to 1 quart of boiling water makes mild tea. Do not boil tea. Remove it from the fire at once. Let it steep 5 minutes.

Drop a tea bag into a cup. Pour on boiling water and take out the tea bag when the color tells you the tea is the desired strength. If lemon is desired in tea, add a pinch of lemon powder.

*Milk.* To each cup of powdered milk, add 4 cups of water. Shake this in the chain shaker or mixer described and illustrated in "Wilderness Cooking," Chapter 12. For best results, let the mixture stand at least 10 hours—preferably 24. This greatly improves the taste. Such procedure will be governed by temperatures, because powdered milk once mixed in liquid form must be treated like fresh milk. However, either as a beverage or for cooking purposes, this milk can be used at once.

For cream, mix powdered milk double-rich. In place of butter for bread, mix it into a paste, and salt to taste.

*Cocoa.* In a cooking pail mix 2 heaping tablespoons of cocoa, 4 heaping tablespoons of sugar, 2 heaping tablespoons of powdered whole milk, $\frac{1}{8}$ teaspoon of salt. Add just enough cold water to make a smooth paste. Now stir in 1 quart of water. Stir this mixture vigorously until well blended. Place it on the fire. Bring it to the boiling point.

Cocoa can also be made from skim milk, if you want it fat-free.

*Chocolate Milk.* Make cocoa as above, and chill. More water may be added, if desired. A flatter-tasting kind can be mixed cold by the above recipe. It should, however, stand from 1 to 12 hours.

*Lemonade.* To each cup of water, add $\frac{1}{2}$ teaspoon of lemon powder and sugar to taste. (In place of sugar, 1 to 2 tablets of concentrated sugar substitute for each spoonful of sugar can be used.)

If concentrated juice is used, dilute it according to the directions on the can.

The numerous synthetic fruit powders to be dissolved in water for cold drinks are not sufficiently fortified with vitamin C and other qualities of dehydrated lemons and oranges; nevertheless, they provide a simple method to make a cold drink. Recently a product has been introduced on the market in the form of a large flavored tablet which, when dissolved in water, carbonates and creates a drink much like "soda-pop." When this item is developed into a well-balanced and vitamin-fortified product, it should be a valuable item for camp use, since carbonated water properly flavored and sweetened is an appetizing drink with a cold lunch.

## SOUPS

*Potato Soup.* Into a cooking pail place ½ cup of "instant" potato and 1 level teaspoon of salt. Add slowly 1 quart of hot liquefied dry milk, stirring constantly to avoid lumping. To this, add 1 level table-spoon of butter, and stir until melted. A half-teaspoon of dried, powdered celery tops adds greatly to the flavor. The celery should be added to the milk when heating it.

*Cream of Potato and Onion Soup.* Prepare this in the same way as the above, but add ¼ cup of boiled, dehydrated onions to the recipe, or an envelope of dry onion-soup mix.

*Cream of Tomato Soup.* Into a cooking pail put 4 level table-spoons of flour, 4 level tablespoons of butter or fat. Place this over a slow fire and cream the flour and butter together. Remove it from the fire. Add 1 quart of liquefied milk slowly, a little at a time, mixing it until smooth.

In a separate cooking pail mix 1 small can of tomato paste, 1 quart of water, ¼ teaspoon of soda, and 1 level teaspoon of salt. Hang both cooking pails over a slow fire. Stir the creamed mixture constantly until it is thick. Remove it from the fire. Now stir the tomato mixture slowly into the creamed mixture. Return this to the fire and cook it for 5 minutes.

*Navy Bean Soup.* Into a cooking pail put 6 cups of cold water, 3 slices of diced bacon, 1 level tablespoon of butter or fat, 1 level table-spoon of salt, ¼ teaspoon of pepper, 1 heaping tablespoon of dehy-drated onions, and 1 cup of precooked navy beans. Cook this at least ½ hour—the longer, the better. About five minutes before removing the soup from the fire, add 1 plump tablespoon of soybean flour, and stir.

Diced canned meat or corned beef may be added to this recipe, if desired. (Also, in place of precooked navy beans, ½ cup of bean flour may be substituted.)

*Pea Soup.* Into a cooking pail put 6 cups of cold water, ¼ cup of dehydrated carrots, 1 level tablespoon of dehydrated onions, ½ cup of dehydrated potatoes, ¼ can of tomato paste, 1 level teaspoon of salt, ¼ teaspoon of pepper, 1 cup of pea flour, 5 slices of diced bacon. Cook this for ½ hour.

*Vegetable Soup.* Into a cooking pail put 2 quarts of water, 2 level teaspoons of salt, 3 slices of diced bacon, ½ can of canned or other meat, ¼ cup of dehydrated carrots, ½ cup of dehydrated potatoes, 1 heaping tablespoon of dehydrated onions, 1 heaping tablespoon of rice, ¼ can of tomato paste. Soak this for ½ hour. Then cook it over a slow fire for ½ hour or longer—preferably longer.

*Vegetable Soup with Fresh Meat Stock.* Vegetable soup made with fresh meat stock is not practical for normal wilderness travel because of the 3- to 4-hour cooking time required. But if rainy weather or other reasons permit, and if fresh meat is on hand, use a joint or other bony cut of meat. Place it in a cooking pail. Cover it well with cold salted water. Simmer this over a slow fire for 3 to 4 hours. Water will have to be added from time to time, as it boils away.

About ½ hour before the meat stock is ready, add soaked dehydrated vegetables and rice as given in the above recipe for Vegetable Soup.

*Vegetable Soup Mix.* Dehydrated vegetable soup mixes, containing numerous mixed vegetables, can now be had; they can be substituted for the vegetables given in the above recipes. Take 1 cup of dehydrated vegetable soup mix to 2 quarts of water. Soak and cook this mixture as in the Vegetable Soup recipe.

*Dumplings.* These are sometimes desired in soups. Mix 1 cup of flour, 1 level tablespoon of egg powder, 2 level tablespoons of milk powder, 1 level teaspoon of baking powder, ½ teaspoon of salt. Add enough water to make a soft dough. Drop the dough by the spoonful on the finished soup. Cover and simmer this slowly for 15 minutes.

*Soups in general* are not a very sustaining diet on a wilderness trip. Heavy soups or stews, however, are sustaining. When soups are desired, it is best to keep the water content as low as possible.

*Creamed Mulligan.* Into a cooking pail put 2 quarts of water, 3 level tablespoons of rice, 1 cup of dehydrated carrots, 1 cup of dehydrated white potatoes, ¼ cup of dehydrated onions, 4 slices of diced bacon, ½ can of pork shoulder or other canned meat, 2 level teaspoons of salt, ¼ teaspoon of pepper. Soak these ingredients for ½ hour. Cook them for at least ½ hour over a slow fire.

Into the chain shaker or mixer, put 2 level tablespoons of white flour, 1 level tablespoon of soybean flour, 4 level tablespoons of milk powder, 2 cups of water. Shake this well. Stir this mixture slowly into the mulligan. Cook it for 10 minutes longer. If the water has boiled away, add hot water.

*Stew with Fresh Meat.* Cut 2 pounds of meat into 1-inch pieces, salt and dredge them with flour. Brown the meat thoroughly in a frying pan with fat. Soak ¼ cup of dehydrated onions for ½ hour. Place the meat and the onions in a cooking pail and cover them with water mixed with the stock left in the frying pan. Cook this for 1 hour. In the meantime soak a cup of mixed dehydrated vegetables for ½ hour. After the meat has cooked the full hour, add the vegetables and cook the stew for ½ hour longer.

*Winter Trail Stew.* Actually, this is simply stewed meat which can be eaten with "instant" potatoes or rice, or added to cooked vegetables; but for winter use it is better to eat the stewed meat alone.

Cut 10 pounds of fresh meat into 1-inch pieces, and dredge them with flour. Brown the meat thoroughly in a frying pan with fat. This browning for 10 pounds of meat will have to be done in portions. After browning each batch of meat, add ½ cup of water to the deposit left in the bottom of the frying pan; mix and save this stock.

Put the browned meat in a flat baking pan, pour the stock over it, and bake it in an oven for 2 hours. Add water, if needed. The finished meat should be quite moist but not soupy. Set the pan where it will freeze solid. From time to time run a knife through the stew as if to cut it into bricks. This will fissure it enough to break it into bricks after it is completely frozen. When it is frozen, set it on the stove just long enough to free the frozen stew from the pan. Then remove it outdoors and break it into bricks. Put the bricks into individual plastic bags and pack them in a food box or paraffined cloth bag. Add the salt when reheating the stew for a meal, not when first preparing the stew.

*Fish Chowder.* Take cold, boiled, baked, or fried fish. Bone it carefully, separating it into small pieces. Into a cooking pail put from 2 to 4 cups of this fish, 2 quarts of water, ⅓ teaspoon of pepper, 2 level teaspoons of salt, ½ can of tomato paste, ¼ cup of dehydrated onions, 2 slices of diced bacon, 1 cup of dehydrated potatoes. Let this soak for ½ hour. Cook it over a slow fire for ½ hour or longer. Stir in 1 heaping tablespoon of soybean flour about 10 minutes before removing it from the fire. This makes a heavy chowder. Add water if desired.

## SPAGHETTI OR MACARONI

*Spaghetti Boiled.* Into a cooking pail put 3 quarts of water, 2 level teaspoons of salt. Place this on the fire. When the water starts boiling, pour in 1 cup of spaghetti. Cook this rapidly for 20 minutes. The water must be kept boiling or the spaghetti will stick. Stir it now and then. Remove the spaghetti from the fire and drain it. If desired, the cooked spaghetti may be washed with hot water in a cooking pail to make it more attractive.

*Spaghetti with Cheese.* Prepare the spaghetti as in boiled spaghetti. Add dry or grated cheese to taste. If grated cheese is used, then heat the spaghetti and cheese over a slow fire, or place them in the reflector oven to melt the cheese. With dry cheese no additional heating is necessary, unless desired. Butter may be added to improve the flavor.

*Spaghetti Italiane.* Prepare the spaghetti as in boiled spaghetti. While the spaghetti is cooking, take 3 slices of diced bacon, ¼ can of canned meat, 1 level tablespoon of presoaked dehydrated onions, ¼ teaspoon of pepper, ½ teaspoon of salt. Place this mixture in a frying pan and fry it slowly until brown. Then add ½ cup of tomato paste, 1 cup of water, and reheat.

Pour this mixture into the prepared spaghetti. Cook it for 15 minutes over a slow fire to blend the flavors. Watch your liquid. The spaghetti must not be soupy, but should be moist. Be careful not to burn it in the final cooking.

*Spaghetti with Fish or Meat Creamed.* Prepare the spaghetti as in boiled spaghetti. Add 1 or 2 cups of boiled, baked, or fried, boned fish. In a separate cooking pail or a frying pan, put 3 level tablespoons of butter or fat, 3 level tablespoons of flour. Heat these slowly and cream them together. Remove this mixture from the fire and add 2 cups of liquefied milk—a little at a time—stirring until it is smooth. Put this back on the fire and stir it constantly until it thickens. Mix the spaghetti, fish, and cream sauce. Reheat this combination over a slow fire. Add salt and pepper if needed.

Prepare this dish with meat in the same way, using canned meat or whatever cooked meat is on hand.

*Spaghetti with Eggs Creamed.* Prepare the spaghetti as in boiled spaghetti. Into the chain shaker or mixer put ½ cup of egg powder, ½ cup of water. Shake this well. Pour the egg liquid into a greased frying pan. Heat it over a slow fire until it is stiff. Cut this egg preparation into small squares and combine it with the spaghetti.

Into a frying pan put 3 level tablespoons of butter, 3 level tablespoons of flour. Heat these slowly and cream them together. Remove this mixture from the fire and add 2 cups of liquefied milk—a little at a time—stirring until it is smooth. Put this back on the fire and stir it constantly until it thickens. Pour this mixture on the spaghetti and eggs. Mix it carefully so as not to mash the egg squares. Reheat this combination over a slow fire.

## RICE

*Rice Boiled.* Two methods can be employed for cooking rice. For the first method put 10 cups of water and 2 level tablespoons of salt into a cooking pail. When the water boils rapidly, add slowly 1 level cup of rice. Cook the rice for 20 minutes, or until the kernels can be mashed between the fingers. The water must be kept boiling or the rice will stick. Stir the rice now and then. When the rice is done, remove it from the fire and drain off the excess water. This is the best way to cook rice over a campfire. However, if water is short, here is the second method:

Pour 2 cups of cold water, 1 cup of rice, and 1 level teaspoon of salt into a cooking pail. Bring this to a boil. Then either raise the cooking pail above the flames or reduce the fire until the water and rice boil moderately. Cover the rice and let it boil for 14 minutes. Remove the cover and set the rice aside for 5 minutes to allow it to steam dry. All of the water will be absorbed by the rice, and the vitamin quality will be higher.

Precooked commercial rice needs only to be added to boiling water with salt. Pour 1 cup of precooked rice and ½ teaspoon of salt into a cooking pail containing 1¼ cups of boiling water. Cover the rice and remove it from the fire. To allow the rice to swell, let it stand for 15 to 20 minutes in a warm spot.

*Rice "Portage."* Prepare and drain the rice as for boiled rice. Into the chain shaker, put 1 heaping tablespoon of egg powder, 2 heaping tablespoons of milk powder, and 1½ cups of water. Shake this well. Pour this mixture into the rice. Bake it in the reflector oven for 15 minutes, or longer.

If a faster method is desired, cook the milk and egg mixture until it is thick. Then add it to the rice, folding it over and over with a large spoon.

*"Portage William Tell."* Prepare Rice "Portage" as above. Add 1 cup of cooked dried apples, 2 heaping tablespoons of sugar, ¼ teaspoon of cinnamon or ½ teaspoon of vanilla extract. Eat it hot or cold. It is best cold.

*"Portage Black-Eyed Susan."* Prepare the Rice "Portage" recipe. Add 1 cup of raisins 5 minutes before the Rice "Portage" is fully baked. For flavoring, add 2 level tablespoons of sugar, ¼ teaspoon of cinnamon or ½ teaspoon of vanilla. Eat it hot or cold. It is best cold with rich liquefied milk.

*Rice Patties.* Prepare 1 cup of rice as in the basic boiled rice recipes. To the rice, add 1 level tablespoon of egg powder, 2 level tablespoons of powdered milk, 1 level tablespoon of white flour, 1 level tablespoon of soybean flour. Mix this well. Then add just enough water, if needed, to form the mixture into patties. Fry them brown. Eat the patties with butter or sirup.

## POTATOES

*Potatoes Boiled.* Into a cooking pail put 1 cup of dehydrated white potatoes and 6 cups of cold water. Soak these for ½ hour.

Add 1½ level teaspoons of salt. Simmer the potatoes over a slow fire for ½ hour, or until they are tender. Then drain them.

*Potatoes Mashed and Potato Patties Fried.* Into 4 cups of liquefied hot milk, stir 1 cup of "instant" potatoes, using a whipping motion. Add 1 level teaspoon of salt, 1 level tablespoon of butter, and serve. "Instant" mashed potatoes are excellent when made into patties and fried.

*Potatoes Fried.* Prepare dehydrated potatoes as in the recipe for "Potatoes Boiled." Drain them well. Fry them in fat or butter. Season them with salt and pepper to taste. Dehydrated potatoes do not lend themselves very well to frying.

*Potatoes Creamed.* Prepare dehydrated potatoes as in the recipe for "Potatoes Boiled." Drain them. Into a separate cooking pail or frying pan, put 2 level tablespoons of butter or fat and 2 level tablespoons of flour. Heat them on a slow fire and cream them together. Remove this mixture from the fire. Slowly add 1 cup of liquefied milk. Mix this until it is smooth. Return the mixture to the fire and cook it until it is thick. Pour this cream sauce over the potatoes and mix them gently. Season it with salt.

*Potatoes au Gratin.* Prepare 2 cups of dehydrated potatoes as in the recipe for "Potatoes Boiled." Into a buttered reflector oven pan, place a layer of potatoes to cover the bottom of the pan. Sprinkle the potatoes with dry grated cheese and salt, and dust them with flour. Add bits of butter. Now add another layer of potatoes, and repeat the process until all of the potatoes are used up. Cover them with liquefied milk nearly to the top of the pan. Place the pan in the reflector oven and bake the potatoes until the top layer is nicely browned.

*Potatoes Scalloped.* Prepare 2 cups of dehydrated potatoes as in the recipe for "Potatoes au Gratin." Omit the cheese.

*Potatoes Scalloped, with Meat or Fish.* Prepare 2 cups of dehydrated potatoes as in the recipe for "Potatoes au Gratin," omitting the cheese. To alternate layers of potatoes add such items as cold diced canned meat, dried beef, venison, or other cold meats or fish on hand.

## BEANS BAKED

Beans are best prepared ahead of time, because they require a long period of cooking. Soak beans overnight, then boil them until the skins start to curl. Place the beans in a deep baking pan together with enough of the water they were boiled in to keep them moist, and add the following ingredients in the proportions of: 2 cups of beans; 1 small chopped onion or 1 tablespoon of dehydrated onions; ¼ pound of bacon or side pork, diced; ½ teaspoon of salt; ½ teaspoon of dry mustard; and 2 tablespoons of brown sugar or molasses. Bake the beans from 5 to 8 hours, keeping the pan covered. Uncover them for the last half-hour to allow any excess moisture to evaporate and to allow the beans to brown.

## CREAMED MEATS AND FISH

*Creamed Chipped Beef.* Separate ½ pound of dried beef into small pieces. Place the beef in hot water for 10 minutes, then drain off the water.

Into a cooking pail or a frying pan put 2 level tablespoons of butter or fat and 2 level tablespoons of flour. Cream them together into a smooth paste over a slow fire. Then slowly add 1 cup of liquefied milk to this mixture and stir it until it is well blended and smooth. Return the mixture to the fire and cook it slowly, stirring constantly, until the cream sauce thickens.

Add the dried beef to this cream sauce and reheat it. Serve the creamed chipped beef on hot biscuits or with macaroni, rice, or potatoes.

*Creamed Canned Meat.* Take 1 to 2 cups of canned meat and cut into small pieces. Add these to a cream sauce prepared as in the recipe for "Creamed Chipped Beef." Season it with salt. Serve it hot as in the preceding recipe.

*Creamed Fish.* Take 1 to 2 cups of cold, boiled, or fried fish. Bone the fish carefully, separating it into small pieces. Add the fish to a cream sauce prepared as in the recipe for "Creamed Chipped Beef." Season it with salt. Serve this hot on hot biscuits, macaroni, rice, or potatoes.

## EGG POWDER

*Creamed Eggs.* Into the chain shaker put ½ cup of egg powder, 1 level teaspoon of salt, 1 cup of water. Mix these ingredients with a few rapid shakes of the shaker. Pour this mixture into a greased frying pan. Cook this egg mixture slowly until it stiffens. Cut this into inch squares.

Add the egg squares to a cream sauce prepared as in the recipe for "Creamed Chipped Beef." Fold the egg squares gently into the cream sauce. Serve this hot on hot biscuits, macaroni, rice, or potatoes.

*Cheese and Eggs Baked.* Into the chain shaker put 1 cup of egg powder, 2 heaping tablespoons of milk powder, and 2 cups of water. Give the shaker a few rapid shakes. Then pour this mixture into a greased reflector oven pan. Cover the surface with grated cheese. Place it in the reflector oven. Bake the egg mixture until it stiffens— about 15 minutes. Season it with salt.

*Omelet.* Into the chain shaker put 1 cup of egg powder, ¾ cup of milk powder, 2 cups of water, and mix these ingredients with a few rapid shakes of the shaker. Season this with salt.

Soak 1 level tablespoon of dehydrated onions ½ to 1 hour. Drain them. Into a frying pan put several slices of bacon, chopped up. Fry them until done. Remove the bacon and put the drained onions in the bacon fat. Fry them until brown. Drain off some of the fat. Add the milk and egg mixture and then the bacon. Turn the mixture as in scrambled eggs.

Scrambled eggs made with egg powder alone, are not as palatable as fresh eggs. Therefore such mixtures as the omelet or the cheese and egg combination are best.

## FRUITS

*Blueberries Raw.* Melt white sugar with a very small amount of water. Pour this through the blueberries. Cream (made with powdered milk) may be added.

*Apricots.* Stew 2 cups of dried apricots in 4 cups of water for 40 minutes. Add sugar to taste.

*Peaches.* Stew 2 cups of dried peaches in 4 cups of water for 50 minutes. Add sugar to taste.

*Pears.* Stew 2 cups of dried pears in 4 cups of water for 40 minutes. Add sugar to taste.

*Prunes.* Stew 2 cups of prunes in 4 cups of water for 50 minutes. No sugar is required. Or, pour boiling water over the prunes, and let them stand overnight.

*Raisins.* Stew 2 cups of raisins in 4 cups of water for 10 minutes. No sugar is required.

*Apples.* Stew 2 cups of dried apples in 4 cups of water for 40 minutes. Add sugar to taste. Lemon powder, cinnamon, or vanilla may be added for zest.

*Figs.* Stew 2 cups of cooking figs in 4 cups of water for 15 minutes. Add sugar to taste.

## ON ADDING SUGAR

There is a difference of opinion as to whether sugar should be added while dried fruit is cooking or after it has cooled. When sugar is cooked, it loses much of its sweetening power through evaporation. When sugar is added after the fruit has cooled, it does not combine with the fruit so well. My practice is to add the sugar immediately after the fruit is cooked and let it stand for several hours, if possible. This combines the stewed fruit and sugar adequately.

## JAM

*Jam from Dried Fruits or Fresh Berries.* Cook dried fruit in as little water as possible until it is half done. Drain off any juice. To the fruit add an equal amount of sugar. Cook this for 30 minutes or until the jam thickens. Better yet, keep the juice as low in content as possible, and add plain gelatin at the rate of 1 envelope (4 come in a package) to 1½ cups of liquid.

Gelatin must be softened in cold water before adding it to a hot liquid.

For jam from fresh berries, add the sugar to the raw berries—the same amount of sugar, in weight, as berries. Use as little water as possible, just enough to prevent burning at the start. Then cook the jam until it is done. Or, add plain gelatin as in the preceding recipe.

## CEREALS

*Oatmeal.* Into a cooking pail put 4 cups of water and 1 level teaspoon of salt. Bring this to a vigorous boil. Stir in 2 cups of rolled oats. Cook the "quick" kind for 1 to 3 minutes, depending on the type.

*Farina or Malted Meal.* Into a cooking pail put 6 cups of water and 1½ level teaspoons of salt. Bring this to a vigorous boil. Stir in 1 cup of farina or malted meal. Cook for 3 minutes.

*Commercial Patent Cereals.* A number of patent cereals are on the market which are fortified with wheat germ. Use these as directed on the package.

*Corn Meal.* Into a cooking pail put 5 cups of water and 2 level teaspoons of salt. Bring this to a vigorous boil. Stir in 1 cup of corn meal. Cook the corn meal for 5 minutes until it thickens. Then, either hang the cooking pail high above the fire and allow the corn meal to steam for 30 minutes, or place the pail of corn meal inside a larger pail, which has several pebbles at the bottom, along with water, to support the smaller pail and serve as a double-boiler. Cook the corn meal in this double-boiler for 30 minutes longer.

*Rice.* Into a cooking pail put 10 cups of water and 2 level teaspoons of salt. Bring this to a vigorous boil. Stir in 1 cup of rice. Boil this vigorously for 20 minutes more. Then drain off the liquid. Eat the rice with sugar and milk as a cereal. (Also see the recipe "Rice Boiled" given earlier in this chapter.)

*Tacrumbs.* Crumble hardtack (Ry-Krisp). Eat this with sugar, raisins, and milk. If desired, the raisins may be dropped into boiling water for 5 minutes to soften them, then drained. Also, the crumbled hardtack or Ry-Krisp may be toasted in the reflector oven to give it added flavor as a dry cereal. Bread crumbs, so toasted, will also take the place of dry cereal; in fact, they are very good with milk and sugar.

*Grape-Nuts.* This patent dry breakfast food is eaten cold with heavy milk or cream (made with powdered milk).

## ON ADDING FRUIT TO CEREALS

Fresh berries, when available, are always a valuable complement to cereals, both cooked and dry. Some dried fruits, particularly apples, figs, and raisins, lend themselves to cooked cereals. Always cut up dried fruits into small pieces, however, before adding them, especially if uncooked.

*Dried Apples* do best if partially precooked for about 20 minutes, which can be done in the salted cereal water, before adding the cereal. Then cook both together until the cereal is done, adding more water for any moisture that may have boiled away.

*Figs* should be chopped up and cooked for 10 minutes before being added to the cereal.

*Raisins* may be added with the 3-minute cereals and cooked for the full time. With rice and corn meal, or where longer cooking is required, add the raisins 5 minutes before cooking is complete. This allows ample swelling but does not break down the fruit, which if cooked too long dominates the taste of the cereal.

## BREADS

*Toast.* Place slices of bread or biscuits in the reflector oven. Toast them with a fast fire. Or, prop up the reflector oven pan, or the fry pan, with the toast close to the fire.

*Cinnamon Toast.* Toast bread or biscuits in the reflector oven. Butter the toast, then sprinkle it with a mixture of cinnamon and sugar. Return the toast to the reflector oven until the sugar melts.

*French Toast.* Into the chain shaker put ½ cup of egg powder, 6 level tablespoons of milk powder, 1½ cups of water, ½ teaspoon of salt. Mix these ingredients with a few rapid shakes of the shaker. Pour it into a pan and dip slices of bread or biscuits in this mixture. Fry them slowly in butter or fat until they are brown.

*"Lightning" Coffee Rolls.* Cut biscuits in two, flatwise. Into the chain shaker put 2 level tablespoons of egg powder, 1 level tea-

spoon of orange powder, ½ cup of water. Mix these ingredients with a few rapid shakes of the shaker. Make a small swab of cloth and paint the biscuits on all sides. Place them, cut side up, in the reflector oven pan. Sprinkle them with sugar. Bake them in the reflector oven just long enough to melt the sugar and brown them slightly.

*Hot Biscuits.* Into the mixing pail put 2 cups of flour, 1 heaping tablespoon of powdered milk, 3 rounded teaspoons of baking powder, 1 level teaspoon of salt. Mix these ingredients. Then with the fingers work in shortening the size of an egg, or 5 tablespoons of melted shortening. Grease the reflector oven pan and have a hot fire going. Add ⅔ cup of cold water to the biscuit mixture. Mix the dough as little as possible. Drop it with a spoon into the greased reflector oven pan. Bake the biscuits for 20 minutes, or until they turn a golden brown.

This dough may also be rolled out, cut into round biscuits, and then baked; but this is a nuisance when the above method is so much more expedient and produces the same results.

Paint the top of the biscuits with a mixture of egg and water (1 part of egg powder to 3 parts of water) to get a rich golden brown color. Or, paint the biscuits with liquefied milk, 8 parts to 1 part of sugar.

Commercial biscuit mixes are more convenient but cost more.

*Corn Bread with Bacon.* Into a mixing pail put 2 cups of hot water, 1½ cups of corn meal, 1 level teaspoon of salt, 2 level teaspoons of shortening. Allow the mixture to cool.

In a separate dish mix 2½ level teaspoons of baking powder, 2 level tablespoons of egg powder, 6 level tablespoons of milk powder. Add this to the corn mixture. Pour the whole mixture into a greased reflector oven pan, and sprinkle the top with diced bacon. Bake this for 30 minutes.

*Corn Bread North Country Style.* Into a mixing pan put 2 cups of corn meal, 1 cup of flour, 1½ level teaspoons of salt, 2 heaping tablespoons of egg powder, 1 heaping tablespoon of sugar, 3 level teaspoons of baking powder, 2 tablespoons of melted shortening.

Add cold water to make the batter just heavy enough to pour into a greased reflector oven pan. Bake this for 30 minutes, or until the corn bread turns light brown on top.

*Bannock.* This has been the bread of the wilderness traveler for centuries, and still is very popular among woodsmen of the old school, some preferring it to bread baked in a reflector oven. Bannock is simply bread baked in a frying pan before an open fire. It can be made as rich or as plain as desired. Prepared according to any one of a hundred different recipes, it is still bannock. Men traveling hard invariably make their bannock quite simple and make a number of them at one time for use on the trail. Bannock is best, however, when fresh and when eaten hot. Sourdough bannock is the one most palatable for continued use; but with the cream-of-tartar type of baking powder I find that no bad effects are suffered from baking-powder bannock. Commercial biscuit mixes are also satisfactory.

*Sourdough Bannock.* A small pail with a friction-top cover is carried for the primary sourdough. Into this pail put 2 cups of flour, 1 level tablespoon of sugar, and ½ cake of yeast. Let this mixture set for at least 3 days. It will get strong and alcoholic in odor. Stir the mixture before using it. Remove 1 cup of this liquid batter into a mixing pan. Add ¼ teaspoon of soda—no more. Mix this. A chemical change will take place, because the alkali soda will combine with the acid of the sourdough to form a valuable rising compound.

Now, to replace what you took from the sourdough pail, add the equivalent in flour and water. Set this liquid batter aside for later use. As the mixture gets stronger, increase the soda slightly. In the mixing pan where you have the sourdough and soda, add 1 rounded tablespoon of milk powder, 1 level teaspoon of salt, 1 level tablespoon of sugar, and 1 tablespoon of melted shortening. Add enough flour to make a dough stiff enough to spread out easily in a frying pan, using a mixing spoon. If too stiff, it will not be as good as a medium mixture. Grease the frying pan well. Drop the dough into it. Spread it out evenly. Set it near the fire and let the dough rise for 20 minutes.

Now hold the pan high above the open fire. Fry the mixture very slowly. You will almost certainly burn the first batch. As the bread begins to rise well—in about 10 minutes—place the frying pan on the ground. Prop it up with a stick so that the fire reflects on the surface of the loaf. When it is a rich golden brown color, it is ready. Test it by sticking a wood sliver into it. If the sliver comes out clean, it is done. It can be turned over, once the loaf is well along.

The loaf can also be baked by starting it low on the ground and gradually propping it up as the crust forms. When it is half done, turn it over and bake the bottom side the same way. You will probably like the first method best even though it is a bit more work.

A sure method of baking bannock is to build a fire on the ground until the bare ground is hot enough to sizzle from a drop of water. Place the pan with the bannock on the hot bare ground, then over the top place a piece of tin or a tin plate. Heap hot coals on the tin and allow the bannock to bake for 15 minutes. The loaf bakes uniformly and the method is almost failure-proof. In principle it resembles the Dutch oven. (See "Dutch Oven" in the chapter on "Pack-Horse Methods.")

*Bannock with Baking Powder.* This is the usual and easier way of making bannock.

Into the mixing pan put 1½ cups of flour, 1 heaping teaspoon of baking powder, 1 level tablespoon of sugar, 1 level teaspoon of salt, 1 heaping tablespoon of milk powder, and 1 tablespoon of melted shortening. Mix these thoroughly. Add water to make a medium dough. Drop the dough into a greased frying pan. Bake the bannock as described in "Sourdough Bannock."

Using commercial biscuit mixes is even easier. Also, see "Pancakes No. 2" recipe for leavening.

*Pancakes No. 1.* Into a mixing pan put 1 cup of cake flour and 1 cup of regular flour, 1 level teaspoon of salt, 3 level teaspoons of baking powder, 1 level tablespoon of corn meal, 1 level tablespoon of sugar, 3 level tablespoons of egg powder, 4 level tablespoons of milk powder, 1 level tablespoon of shortening, and 1 level tablespoon of soybean flour. Add water to make a batter. Beat this until it is smooth. Drop the batter on a lightly greased *hot* pan. When bubbles form in the batter, turn it over.

*Pancakes with Blueberries.* Blueberries in season added to the above recipe make a traditional North Country pancake.

*Pancakes No. 2.* For many years I carried a sourdough pail for pancakes and biscuits, but I found that a similar combination could be made more easily and quickly by the use of an acid and a soda. The citrus powders, lemon, orange, or grapefruit, combined with soda, make an excellent pancake leavener.

Use the same mixture as the "Pancake No. 1" recipe, but omit the baking powder and add ½ teaspoon of soda and 1 level teaspoon of powdered lemon juice. This can also be used to make biscuits and bannock.

*Sirup for Pancakes.* Into a cooking pail put 2 parts of sugar to 1 part of water. Melt this on a slow fire. Add vanilla, maple flavor, or orange powder when it has cooled. Brown sugar and water may be substituted for the above. Commercial dry sirup mixes are available to which water may be added. These come in envelopes for the trail. Many other commercial food items are similarly packed for the trail.

## DESSERTS

*Piecrust, Pies, and Cobblers.* Mix cold, 2 cups of flour, ⅔ cup of shortening. Then add 4 to 6 tablespoons of water, 1 level teaspoon of salt. Add the water slowly. Mix this just enough to hold the mixture together. Or, use commercial piecrust mix. For a rolling pin use a peeled round stick.

For pies, divide the batch. On a floured surface—a canoe paddle will do—roll out ½ of the batch for the bottom of the pie; ½ for the top. For wilderness use, the simple and easy way to make pies and cobblers is in individual bowls or small pans. For 2 pies divide the piecrust dough into 4 parts. Flatten out ¼ of this pie dough between your hands and line the bowl. (No rolling is necessary, a great convenience in the woods.) Fill the lined bowl with blueberries, cooked dried apples, or other filler. Add a liberal amount of sugar and some small pieces of butter. Flatten out a second piece of piecrust and place it on top. Pinch down the edges. From the remaining dough make your second pie in the same way. Place the pies in the reflector oven for about ½ hour. A little egg powder, mixed with water, painted over the crust, will give the pie a nice golden brown color. Sprinkle a little sugar on the egg mixture.

*Custard.* A soft cream pie filling, which can also be eaten as a cup custard, is easy to make. Into the chain shaker put 2 heaping tablespoons of powdered milk, ½ cup of sugar, 1 level teaspoon of salt, 1 heaping tablespoon of cornstarch, 1 heaping tablespoon of dehydrated eggs, 1½ cups of water. Mix these ingredients thoroughly by rapidly shaking them in the shaker. Pour this mixture into a cooking pail and cook it for 10 minutes, stirring constantly, until it thickens.

A better way to avoid stirring is to use a double-boiler method. For a simple double-boiler for small amounts, use a mixing bowl for the custard and allow it to float in a cooking pail of boiling water. If the bowl is flat enough, it will not upset. Cook the custard in this double-boiler for 20 minutes. Cornstarch is improved with cooking. Although the cornstarch foods will cook in less time, there is apt to be a slightly raw taste to undercooked cornstarch.

Various custards, puddings, and trade-name desserts in a variety of flavors are on the market. Those requiring cooking are superior to the "instant" kind requiring no cooking.

*Bread Pudding.* Into a heavily buttered reflector oven pan crumble 4 cups of leftover biscuits, corn bread, or any other dry bread on hand. Over this pour a mixture of 1 heaping tablespoon of egg powder, 3 heaping tablespoons of milk powder, ½ cup of sugar, 1 level teaspoon of salt, 1 teaspoon of vanilla, and 3 cups of water. The mixture should be somewhat soupy. Place it in the reflector oven and bake it for 20 minutes, or until the pudding has set firmly. Serve it with rich milk and more sugar if desired. Raisins may also be added for variety.

*Cornstarch Blanc Mange.* It is important to know this basic recipe. A number of desserts can be made from it simply by adding whatever fruits or fruit juices you prefer. The basic recipe follows:

Into a bowl or cup, put 3 level tablespoons of cornstarch, ¼ teaspoon of salt, ½ cup of liquefied milk, 4 level tablespoons of sugar. Mix these ingredients.

Into a cooking pail, put 1½ cups of liquefied milk. Bring this to a boil. Now add the cornstarch mixture, stirring it constantly over a slow fire until the mixture thickens. Cover the pail. Cook the mixture slowly for about 20 minutes. Stir it now and then.

When the above mixture begins to set, stir in what fruit you have —blueberries or cooked dried fruits from which the juice has been drained, or you may add orange or lemon powder (2 level teaspoons of orange powder or 1 level teaspoon of lemon powder).

Eat the blanc mange with rich milk when it has cooled.

By browning 2 level tablespoons of sugar, 1 tablespoon of water, and adding this to the blanc mange, a caramel pudding is easily made.

*Chocolate Pudding.* Add 2 level tablespoons of cocoa to the blanc mange.

The use of plain gelatin should not be overlooked in supplying body to wilderness items such as puddings where this is usually accomplished with eggs or cornstarch. Use it in the proportion of 1½ cups of liquid to each envelope of gelatin.

## CAKE

To bake a cake outdoors is no more difficult than to do it at home. Here is a basic cake recipe that can be varied in several ways:

Into a mixing pail put 2 cups of cake flour, 1 cup of sugar, ⅓ cup of egg powder, ½ teaspoon of salt, 1 heaping tablespoon of baking powder, ⅓ cup of milk powder. Mix these dry ingredients well. Then work in ½ cup of melted butter. Add water to make a stiff batter. Next, add 1 teaspoon of vanilla. Beat the batter until it is smooth. Pour this into a greased reflector oven pan, and bake it for 25 to 30 minutes. Test the cake with a wood sliver; if the sliver comes out clean the cake is done.

Here are a few variations:

*For Raisin Cake,* add ½ cup, or more, of raisins to the batter.

*For Chocolate Cake,* add ½ cup of dry cocoa.

*For Apple Cake,* soak 1 cupful of dried apples for ½ hour. Mop them dry. Then place apple slices on top of the batter just before putting it into the oven.

*For Fig Cake,* chop up figs into small pieces. Mix them with the batter.

The list of cake recipes is limited only by your own taste and ingenuity.

*Boiled Cake.* The secret of boiled cake lies in the fact that fruit flavors can be brought out and combined with the batter by boiling. Proceed as follows:

Into a cooking pail put 1 cup of apricots, apples, or any other dried fruit you have on hand, ½ cup of butter, ½ teaspoon of salt, and ⅓ cup of milk powder. Add water to about an inch above the ingredients. Cook this until the fruit has broken down and can easily be mashed. Be careful not to allow the fruit to cook dry while at the same time maintaining a thick porridge-like mixture. Cool this mixture. Now add ⅓ cup of egg powder, 1 cup of sugar, 1 teaspoon of vanilla. Combine 1 cup of cake flour with 1 heaping teaspoon of baking powder; add this to the mixture. Then add enough flour to make a thick batter. Pour this into a greased reflector oven pan and bake it for about ½ hour; or test the cake with a wood sliver. If it comes out clean, the cake will be done.

*Variations of Boiled Cake:* Raisins, figs, pitted prunes, fresh berries and other such items may be used in boiled cake. The vanilla may be replaced with a level teaspoon of orange or lemon powder for variety. Half the fruit may be cooked to porridge and blended with the batter while the other half is chopped up and added to the batter just before the cake is placed in the oven.

*Advantage of Cake Flour:* Of the flour I take into the woods, ⅙ is cake flour. This is not a patented product but simply plain white flour that has a low gluten content. Because gluten has binding ingredients, it tends to toughen cakes. In baking cakes, cake flour should be used. However, good cakes can be made from regular flour. Use slightly less of the regular flour. You will find that pancakes are much improved in texture with cake flour. A variety of commercial cake ready-mixes are available, and they are excellent for camp use. Buy those already containing eggs, and use liquefied powdered milk.

## MEAT

*Fresh Meat.* In warm weather, when newly killed meat is to be kept fresh for a short period, it can be cut into ½-pound pieces and dropped into furiously boiling salted water. Cook for 10 minutes or more; then dry them just long enough to rid the meat of surplus moisture. If the pieces are then placed in a flour sack and hung in the shade where a current of air will aid further drying, the meat will keep well for a week or more.

*Jerking (Drying) Fresh Meat.* This is the best way of preserving fresh meat for an extended period. Find an open place in the sun and build a rack of poles on which strips of meat an inch in diameter and about a foot long can be hung. Use no salt. A smudge of fire should be kept going under the rack to ward off flies and to give the meat a slightly smoked flavor. Drying will take several days. If it rains, the meat must be covered with ponchos weighted with poles. The sticks of meat when dry will be hard and can be eaten raw. If you want to cook the meat, first soak it in water, and then fry it or roast it. For quick stews, pound the meat into small pieces rather than cut it. The butt of the ax is excellent for this procedure.

*Pemmican.* This is the cold-weather meat ration of the North, and one of the most highly sustaining foods known. For 10 pounds of pemmican, use 5 pounds of jerked meat ground or well pounded, ½ pound of brown sugar, ½ pound of seeded raisins, and 4 pounds of suet. Use no salt. Melt the suet and mix it with the ingredients mentioned. Shape the pemmican into bricks; pack the bricks individually in plastic bags, and then in a paraffined cloth bag.

Pemmican can be eaten uncooked, but it lends itself well to the preparation of rice, spaghetti, dehydrated vegetables, and to frying. When frying pemmican, cut off slices and dip them in flour after first salting them; then fry them slowly. When boiling pemmican, place the desired amount in a cloth sack and drop the sack in salted boiling water. Pemmican also makes a good heavy soup with dehydrated vegetables. It should be made just thick enough to stir; cook the pemmican and the vegetables together. You may not like pemmican at first, but you will develop a taste for it.

*Meat Balls.* Meat balls should be of the Swedish type. Use 1 pound of beef, ½ pound of veal, ½ pound of lean pork—ground together twice. Combine the meat with 1 slice of bread or biscuit soaked in milk, 1 heaping tablespoon of egg powder, 2 level tablespoons of tomato paste, 2 level teaspoons of salt. (Omit salt if the meat balls are to be frozen for the trail. See "Winter Food Items," page 243.) Shape the meat into balls, brown them in a frying pan, and then place them in a reflector oven pan. Add enough water to the meat balls to reach nearly to the top of the reflector oven pan. Bake them for 1 hour or more. A cooking pail can be used instead of the reflector oven, with enough water barely to cover the meat balls. Cover and simmer them over a slow fire for the same length of time.

Where time is important, the pure ground meat alone in the form of meat balls can be fried. Because of the pork ingredient, however, ordinary meat balls must be fried thoroughly and slowly. Meat balls made of beef alone, of course, can be fried quickly.

The water which was added to the meat balls will simmer down and leave a rich deposit in the pan. This can be made into a very tasty sauce or gravy to pour over the meat balls.

*Roasting Fresh Meat.* Roasting is by far the tastiest way to prepare fresh meat. Slow roasting in a reflector oven, if time and travel permit, is the perfect method. The direct rays of the fire, the heat of the oven, and the frequent basting give meat so cooked a very fine flavor.

The meat should first be browned in a frying pan to seal in the juices and to add to the taste, then placed in the reflector oven pan with a small amount of water and allowed to roast slowly. Because moisture evaporates quite rapidly in a reflector oven, the juice in the pan should be basted over the meat as often as possible. Turning the roast in the pan will also help to keep it moist. Add more water as it evaporates. When the meat is about half done, salt it, to give penetration to the salt. If it is salted when first placed in the oven, the meat will lose too much juice.

*Frying Meat.* This is the common method of cooking meat in camp, but many cuts of meat do not lend themselves well to frying. Steaks are best fried, and should be done at high heat—in about 7 minutes to be at their best. Chops and tenderloins fry well if done slowly. They are best roasted, although there is some difference of opinion as to the tenderloin. Meats not shaped or intended for frying can be cut into small chunks, then flattened with a blow from the flat side of an ax blade. This tenderizes them. Commercial tenderizer may also be used.

*Frying Bacon.* Bacon is more difficult to fry than most people realize. It usually is fried too fast. Bacon should be fried slowly and turned often to be at its best. The excess fat in the pan should be drained off several times during the frying, and saved.

For variety, bacon may be dipped in sugar and fried. This gives it a golden brown color and a very rich flavor. It may also be fried until it is nearly done; the fat is then drained off, and the bacon placed in a pool of milk in the reflector oven pan, sprinkled with brown sugar, and baked until the milk is almost evaporated.

*Fowl.* Fowl should be cooked in the same way as any other meat. If fowl is fried, the pan should be covered and the fowl cooked slowly. The meat can also be cut away from the bone in small pieces, then fried or stewed, and creamed. Fowl thus stewed or creamed makes a tasty meal when poured over hot biscuits.

Wild duck requires rather deliberate and lengthy roasting. Stuffing can be made with a mixture of 1 cup of dry crumbled biscuit or bread seasoned with a heaping tablespoon of dehydrated onions, a level teaspoon of salt, 4 slices of bacon cut small and fried, and a pinch of sage, if you have it.

Duck makes a good soup or mulligan. Chop the duck into small pieces, brown them well in a fry pan, then add plenty of water and cook them for at least an hour. A half-cup of rice can then be put in and cooked until all is done, seasoned with a level teaspoon of salt. Or, a cup of dehydrated, mixed vegetables can be added after they have soaked for an hour, and the whole cooked until the vegetables are tender. Season this with a level teaspoon of salt.

For speed in preparing partridge, only the breast should be used. The breast contains nearly all the meat. Break the skin and tissue at the apex of the breast. Bend the apex back toward the neck until the breast is torn loose from the body except at the neck. Insert one index finger through one side of the wishbone and the other index finger through the other side, and pull. The wings will come off with the breast, leaving the entrails, feathers and other parts of the bird to be thrown away. (There is a small amount of meat on the legs and back, but this method of cleaning the bird is excellent where time is the important consideration.) Now, twist off the wings. Take your sheath knife and cut down close to the breastbone, then away from the breastbone. Make these cuts on both sides. You now have two boneless, solid pieces of partridge breast. Hit them with the flat side of your ax in much the same way as your butcher flattens a tenderloin steak. From the time you started until the meat is ready to eat, you should not have used more than eight minutes.

I used this high-speed method for years when I traveled through the country living largely on the natural food supply. Mealtime was often dictated by the sight of a partridge along the trail, and hunger prompted the method of preparation.

*Gravy.* When you are frying or roasting meat or fowl, a rich brown fatty deposit is usually left in the bottom of the pan. Do not use too much of the fat. Into the pan put 1 level tablespoon or more of flour. Stir this over a slow fire until it is brown. Then add hot water and cook the mixture until it thickens. Milk can be used instead of water for a cream gravy.

Presoaked, dehydrated onions may be added and cooked with the gravy. Add salt if needed, but be careful not to oversalt.

## FISH

Fish lends itself well to both roasting and frying. A large fish can be steaked and fried, but it makes a tasty meal when baked slowly in a reflector oven. Treat fish in the same way as roasted meat, but salt it early. Commercial bread crumbs or potato meal is best for dusting fish before frying. Use plenty of fat in frying fish.

## EMERGENCY RATION

Armies all over the world have searched for years to find a lightweight and sustaining food that will provide nourishment during critical periods. One which I have developed and find satisfactory is made of corn meal, dried meats, and other ingredients ground into granule form. It is taken a tablespoonful at a time, stirred into cold water; or it can be eaten dry and swallowed with a drink from a stream, spring, or lake. It swells in the stomach and gives a comfortably full sensation. It is prepared as follows before each wilderness journey, and should be thrown away at the end of the trip if not used:

Parch ½ pound of corn meal in an oven until it is brown. Dry ¼ pound of thinly sliced dried beef or jerked meat in the oven until it will crumble into granules. It can be ground fine in a coffee mill or meat grinder if thoroughly dry. Add ¼ pound of brown sugar, 1 ounce of dehydrated lemon powder, 1 ounce of plain gelatin. Mix these ingredients thoroughly and place them in unused tobacco pouches, issued to each member of the party and carried individually.

Do not use additional salt unless jerked meat is used, because dried beef is very salty. If jerked meat is used, add 1 level teaspoon of salt to the mixture.

One of the best emergency rations which can be carried in the pocket, and which lends excitement to the taste, is a heavy, high-grade fruit cake. On one expedition into the arctic where I set up the food budget, I included 40 pounds of fruit cake, heavily loaded with nuts, fruit, dates, and similar rich foods. It proved a most valuable and tasty item.

## TEN-DAY SUGGESTED MENU

What to cook is sometimes a problem in the midst of plenty. Planned menus relieve the cook of some of the burden of his task, and on occasion suggest other items to cook. Weather, travel circumstances, and other factors will alter the menu; but here is a ten-day schedule to follow, and if necessary repeat. One or two loaves of baker's bread can usually be bought on the first day on the trail. By the second day the reflector oven will be in use. In the following menus the orange juice is made from the citrus powder. The eggs are dehydrated. Fruits are dried stewed fruits. Milk is whole dehydrated milk or fat-free milk.

### First Day

| *Breakfast* | *Lunch* | *Supper* |
|---|---|---|
| Orange juice | Orangeade | Tea |
| Coffee or cocoa | Cold canned meat | Heavy vegetable |
| French toast | Fresh baker's bread | soup with meat |
| Stewed figs or | Butter and jam | Buttered toast |
| prunes | | Stewed apples |

The First-Day Menu is very light. Stewed figs or prunes are given to ensure regularity. Do not overeat for the first day or two. Let your system get accustomed to the change in water and to the overstimulation of the fresh air and exercise. There is a tendency to overindulge in pans of fat bacon and other constipating foods on the first few days out.

## Second Day

| *Breakfast* | *Lunch* | *Supper* |
|---|---|---|
| Orange juice | Lemonade or milk | Tea |
| Coffee or cocoa | Cheese | Fish or ham, fried |
| Canadian bacon | Fresh baker's bread | "Instant" mashed |
| Malted meal | Peanut butter and | potatoes |
| Stewed figs or | jam | Stewed apricots |
| prunes | | Hot corn bread |

## Third Day

| *Breakfast* | *Lunch* | *Supper* |
|---|---|---|
| Orange juice | Orangeade or milk | Tea |
| Coffee or cocoa | Leftover fish or ham | Spaghetti dish with |
| Oatmeal cooked | Leftover corn bread | meat or cheese |
| with apples | Butter and jam | Fruit cake |
| Bacon | | Chocolate pudding |

## Fourth Day

| *Breakfast* | *Lunch* | *Supper* |
|---|---|---|
| Orange juice | Lemonade or milk | Tea |
| Coffee or cocoa | Grape-Nuts with | "Instant" mashed |
| Hot biscuits | milk | potatoes |
| Butter and jam | Leftover biscuits | Boiled carrots |
| Canadian bacon | Peanut butter and | Fried corned beef |
| | jam | Peach cobbler |

## Fifth Day

| *Breakfast* | *Lunch* | *Supper* |
|---|---|---|
| Orange juice | Orangeade or milk | Tea |
| Coffee or cocoa | Cheese | "Instant" mashed |
| Malted meal with | Ry-Krisp, butter | potato patties, |
| apples | and jam, or fruit | fried |
| Canadian bacon | cake | Creamed chipped |
| | | beef |
| | | Hot biscuits |
| | | Stewed raisins |

## Sixth Day

| *Breakfast* | *Lunch* | *Supper* |
|---|---|---|
| Orange juice | Milk | Tea |
| Coffee or cocoa | Corned beef | Corn bread with |
| Oatmeal with raisins | Leftover biscuits | bacon (recipe on |
| Canadian bacon | Peanut butter and | page 227 |
| | jam | Stewed peaches |
| | | Fruit cake |

## Seventh Day

| *Breakfast* | *Lunch* | *Supper* |
|---|---|---|
| Orange juice | Orangeade or milk | Tea |
| Coffee or cocoa | Leftover corn bread | Rice patties |
| Plain oatmeal | Cheese | Canadian bacon |
| Side bacon | Dry raisins | Butterscotch pud- |
| Stewed figs | | ding |
| | | Fruit cake |

## Eighth Day

| *Breakfast* | *Lunch* | *Supper* |
|---|---|---|
| Orange juice | Orangeade or milk | Tea |
| Coffee or cocoa | Cold boiled rice | Creamed mulligan |
| Pancakes | with sugar and | Bannock |
| Canadian bacon | milk | Stewed apples and |
| Stewed prunes | Ry-Krisp | raisins |
| | Peanut butter and | |
| | jam | |

## Ninth Day

| *Breakfast* | *Lunch* | *Supper* |
|---|---|---|
| Orange juice | Lemonade or milk | Tea |
| Coffee or cocoa | Cold bannock or | "Instant" mashed |
| Omelet with bacon | biscuits | potatoes |
| Hot biscuits | Cold canned meat | Fried Canadian |
| | Dry raisins | bacon |
| | | Hot corn bread |
| | | Orange (blanc |
| | | mange) pudding |

## Tenth Day

| *Breakfast* | *Lunch* | *Supper* |
|---|---|---|
| Orange juice | Orangeade or milk | Tea |
| Coffee or cocoa | Grape-Nuts with | Scalloped potatoes |
| Oatmeal | milk and dry | with canned meat |
| Canadian bacon | raisins | Creamed onions |
| | Cold corn bread | Apple cobbler |
| | Butter and jam | |

This Ten-Day Menu may seem simple, but it is far more complicated than you are likely to use in actual wilderness travel. Three cooking pails, a frying pan, and a reflector oven are usually the outside limit of cooking utensils used on a wilderness trip. Where a menu calls for an additional vegetable, it will probably not be cooked. Variety is gained by alternating foods from meal to meal or day to day rather than in the variety of the individual meal. Fish and game, if procurable, usually upset any planned menu. While great simplicity is desirable, it is well to watch the balance in diet so that this is not sacrificed for the sake of convenience. Even woodsmen of long experience make the mistake of eating unbalanced meals simply because their appetites are good and because the most accessible food items are tasty and satisfying to them.

The noonday lunch has been a subject of endless discussion among experienced wilderness travelers, for almost always the time is short and you are anxious to start again on the trail. In consequence a number of novel items have been tried. I mentioned earlier a fruit cake heavily loaded with nuts, fruits, eggs, and complementary ingredients. This has proved a valuable adjunct to the daily menu, and when eaten alone at noon it has supplied a substantial and nourishing lunch. Moreover, it improves with age.

A candy bar makes a good quick lunch. You may also eat only part of the bar, but add a handful of nuts and a handful of raisins or other dried fruits, according to taste.

Mincemeat is another satisfactory item when a high percentage of animal meat and nuts is used in the mixture. It should be made heavier than for pies, and compressed into full ration cakes.

Your noon drink, since a fire is not usually built at this halt, will probably be water; but an envelope of citrus fruit powder, dry milk powder, or chocolate milk powder is easily mixed.

### WINTER FOOD ITEMS

Some mention has already been made of the preparation of food for winter trails. Winter camping calls for extra skills not required for camping in the milder seasons, and the proper preparation of food is one of them.

As you travel daily in subzero temperatures, you will not be able to prevent your food from freezing. Instead, you must take advantage of the cold to make life on the trail more pleasant. Forty- and fifty-below-zero temperatures do not permit casualness in the preparation of food. Fumbling to get a fire started where dry wood is scarce is hazardous. The secret is good planning. When breaking winter camp, save some of the dry kindling you have cut and store it in the tent stove, or tie it up and place it on the sled. This will assure you a quick, certain fire at the next camp and an early meal. The noonday meal can be supplied by hot foods and beverages from Thermos jugs and bottles.

All food for at least several days ahead should be cooked and frozen in meal-size rations, ready to be heated and served. When you are well fed and warm in your heated cabin or heated tent, then is the time to prepare for the next lap of your journey.

On long sledge trips convenience and simplicity can never be overemphasized. I have seen men making large quantities of doughnuts before they start out on the trail in order to simplify the problem of the "mug-up"—the stop for tea. In just the same way I have watched them prepare quantities of meat balls in advance. If you talked of variety to these men, you would only amuse them. They know the grim reality of the winter trail, its blizzards, fatigues, and hampering cold. A ready meal is a blessing, and repetition never diminishes their appetites.

In mild weather you may vary the "instant" potato diet with macaroni and rice. In winter travel you stick to "instant" potatoes combined with dry milk and salt; for all you have to do is to add hot water and serve. Cooking is at a minimum. The process is largely one of thawing and heating. Water is heated for tea, coffee, or cocoa, with enough to spare for the "instant" potatoes and the dishwashing.

Fresh meat can be carried on a winter trip, but it should be cut in advance, trimmed, boned, and frozen into meal-size portions, then wrapped in waxed paper. The paper will come off easily no matter how hard the portions are frozen. Steaks should be frozen flat so that they will not hump up in the frying pan. Steaks do not require thawing before frying, but they are cooked longer over a slower fire.

Meat to be boiled should be placed in boiling salted water. It can also be placed in a cooking pail with snow or ice and set over the fire. This method extracts more of the meat juices. You should drink the liquid that is left.

You can make water from melted snow; but when you do, keep pushing the snow to the bottom of the pail or the pail will scorch. The snow draws up the water by absorption and leaves the bottom dry. A bitter taste is imparted to tea and food when this happens.

Because a great deal of snow is required to make a small amount of water, to melt ice chipped from the lake or stream is quicker. If the ice is not too thick, a water hole can be cut. The water hole can be kept open by covering it with spruce boughs and snow; mark its location with an upright stick.

## SIMPLIFIED LIST OF WINTER FOODS AND THEIR ADVANCE PREPARATION

(A ten-day supply for three men)

|  | POUNDS |
|---|---|
| Fresh frozen meat in meal-size portions, boned, trimmed, wrapped in wax paper, then placed in food box. | 36 |
| Prepared stew made only of meat, baked in oven, completed with as little water as possible, frozen into meal-size portions, placed in plastic bags, then packed in food box. (See "Winter Trail Stew," page 217.) | 10 |
| Meat balls in gravy, prepared in oven, completed with as little water as possible, frozen into meal-size portions, wrapped in wax paper, then placed in plastic bags and packed in food box. (See "Meat Balls," pages 234 and 235.) | 10 |
| Baked beans with liberal amount of lean pork, baked in a flat pan, frozen into meal-size portions, wrapped in wax paper, then placed in plastic bags and packed in food box. (See "Beans Baked," page 222.) | 8 |

POUNDS

"Instant" potatoes: mix dry ingredients in advance of the trip. Two parts of "instant" potatoes, 1 part of dry whole milk, 1 level teaspoon of salt to each cup of mixed dry ingredients. At mealtime add only hot water, 4 parts to 1 part of dry potato mix. Carry this prepared mix in a plastic bag inserted in a paraffined cloth bag.     7

Apples: slice, cook in a flat pan in the oven, using just enough water to keep them moist. Freeze into meal-size bricks, wrap in wax paper, and place them in plastic bags. Or, substitute other fruits to taste, but apples are a good standby.     12

| | POUNDS |
|---|---|
| Citrus fruit powder | 1 |
| Coffee, regular (if "instant," then 1¼ pounds) | 5 |
| Tea | 2 |
| Cocoa | 1 |
| Dry whole milk | 4 |
| Doughnuts | 10 |
| Fruit cake | 8 |
| Bread | 8 |
| Sugar | 5 |
| Salt | 1 |
| Frying fat | 2 |
| Total | 130 |

Daily ration per man, 4⅓ pounds

This food list will vary greatly with the individual. For example, you may have difficulty with a straight meat diet. If you do, you should take enough complementary foods to give zest to your appetite. All of the citrus-powder ration should be taken in any event. You may balance the list to your own requirements, but emphasis should be on meat in cold weather. (See the reference to metabolism in the chapter on winter travel.)

There is always the possibility of a thaw. Note that the food bricks have been placed in plastic bags after being wrapped in wax paper to prevent possible leakage. Little, if any, thawing occurs if the food is allowed to freeze brick hard during subzero periods, and is closely packed and covered during thaws. No salt should be used in the preparation of such foods because salt has a thawing effect.

Add the salt when the food bricks are reheated. Food boxes carried on sleds or toboggans protect these frozen food items from animals outdoors. However, keep the sled dogs tied. They will chew through heavy wood boxes. Wolves and foxes will not come near a tent, nor are wolverines likely to bother your supplies when you are close by. This also applies to lynx and to mountain lions. Bears, except the polar species, are in hibernation. The polar bear is the boldest where humans are concerned. However, if empty cooking pails are hung over the food boxes, so that they will jangle when bumped, they will give warning of the incursion of any prowler.

## FOOD CACHE

At some place on an extended trip, if the return journey is to be along the same route, a food cache should be made. The simplest method is to build your cache high between two trees on a horizontal pole. It should be protected from rain. This may be done with birchbark, but it is best to provide a waterproof duffel bag, hanging the bag by the pucker rope, with at least two feet of wire between the bag and the pole. Fifty-pound tin lard cans with over-

Cache

lapping friction covers make excellent waterproof receptacles for a cache. They should be wired shut and hung between trees on a wire outside the reach of bears, and preferably in an undrained bog or swamp where the hazard of loss by forest fire is reduced. (See illustration.)

On winter trips, or when you are storing food through the winter, canned food items can be sunk in a lake to prevent their freezing. The depth of the water should be shallow enough so that you can retrieve them, but deep enough so that the thickest formation of ice will not reach them. Canned foods should be secured in heavy sacks or lard cans, and well ballasted to prevent drifting. In the North, one inch of ice for every degree of latitude is a fairly safe measure to determine the depth at which they should be placed. Mark the cans with wax crayon on the metal parts, or scratch them with a sharp instrument for identification, because the labels will wash off. Flour and potatoes in sacks can similarly be cached below the ice. Water will penetrate only a thin outer layer of the flour.

However, dry caches in winter are suitable for flour, potatoes, vegetables, and even eggs if they are kept frozen. Vegetables and eggs must be used immediately on thawing.

# 14

✳
✳ ✳
✳ ✳ ✳
✳ ✳ ✳ ✳

## Fishing for Food

A COMMON AND MISTAKEN BELIEF IS THAT ALL VIRGIN TERRITORY
contains an abundance of fish. In general, this is true, but occasionally you will encounter a famine of game and fish, especially
when you are forced to fish with a line rather than with a net.
When your provisions are reduced to mere complements to the
game and fish supply, this can create a very distressing situation.

On one such occasion I traveled for five days in a wilderness area
without seeing so much as a mouthful of fish or game, though I
fished every day and kept a close lookout for game. In the end I
took the mosquito netting from the tent and caught several pounds
of minnows, which I poured into a hot frying pan.

On a long journey, try to make arrangements with the Department of Game and Fish, to carry a section of gill net. Obviously,
on such a journey you will not be going to do commercial fishing,
and you will have no trouble with the authorities on this point.
Then, even if you catch fish with no difficulty with hook and line,
you will know that the net is there for emergency.

The rockbound lakes of the North Country do not offer fish the
kind of cover that lakes farther south provide where the bottoms
are of soil. Consequently, the method of trolling over weed beds in
soil-bottomed lakes will probably be unsuccessful in rockbound
lakes. Like game, fish want natural cover; furthermore, they must
eat. The combination of these two factors will give you an important cue to their habitat. Where you encounter waterfalls or
rapids, the problem of catching fish is as a rule not difficult. Back
eddies below a waterfall or rapid are usually productive. But here

247

a variation in the depth of the fishing can mean the difference between success and failure.

For example, the WALLEYE, commonly called "walleyed pike" in the Midwestern states, "pickerel" in Canada, and "pike perch" in the Eastern states, usually feeds at a low level. I have seen fishermen cast for an hour below a falls and catch only one or two fish. Then someone arrived who let his minnow "bump across the bottom," and results were immediate. However, allowing a minnow to "bump across the bottom" is not always easy, for snags can be plentiful. In such places you may find it wise to still-fish with minnows rather than to cast with a spinner and a minnow. Where minnows are not available, casting with a spinner and a pork rind will often be successful.

The walleye is found from southern Canada to the Gulf of Mexico. This is the fish of clean cold waters, and he loves to range widely. He is most at home in large lakes of several miles in area. He retires to deep water during the hotter months of the year, and this should be remembered when you are fishing for food. The walleye has been known to reach a length of over three feet, with weights up to seventeen and eighteen pounds; but such fish are not common, and the walleye usually does not exceed ten pounds.

The walleye spawns shortly after the ice melts. If you put your field thermometer in the water now and then, you will find that the spawning run starts when the water reaches a temperature of from 38 to 44 degrees. At that time they will move upstream in great numbers. The eggs are usually deposited in riffles, but many fish do not leave the lakes; they simply lay their eggs on gravel reefs in shallow waters. These are points to remember when fishing for food.

The NORTHERN PIKE is a great standby in northern waters. He is commonly called the "jackfish" in Canada. In some parts of the United States he is called a pickerel. Let us not belittle the eating qualities of the northern pike. In the South he is not the delectable food item that he is in the North. In the cold fast water of the North, he is the top eating fish for those who know. The meat is firm, white and, unlike the lake trout, relatively free from oil. In lakes where northern pike and trout abound, fish eaters prefer northern pike to lake trout. His one drawback, a negligible one, is the small *Y* bones in the meat; but this is not an objection when the fish is filleted or when it is large.

You are almost sure to find the northern pike at the foot of waterfalls or rapids. Often a very large one will take cover at the bottom of a small fall, and your first cast will have him on your tackle. Another good spot is where a stream empties into a lake. He is not easy to catch in an open lake where there are no entering stretches of fast water. However, if you will paddle along near the shore and make your casts at the trunks of fallen trees in the water (in rivers these are called "sweepers") or at any place where you think he might find concealment, you will get your fair share. If you live on such lakes or rivers, sink a number of trees at various points to create this cover; that is, do so if it is not against the law in your state.

The northern pike will strike at almost anything, but you may as well offer him his greatest delight as far as tackle goes. Because he apparently believes that everything that glitters is food, put on a shiny spoon, the so-called "hardware," either brass or nickel.

Like the walleye, northern pike spawn in the spring, right after the ice melts. They ascend small streams or move into the grassy marginal areas of lakes to deposit their eggs. The northern pike is a cannibal. When food is short he has no compunction in devouring his brother fish. Such cannibalism causes difficulties when he is propagated artificially. Shooting northerns during spawning periods as they lie in the shallows or at the edge of the spring-thawed ice is a sure source of food in early spring. In areas which prohibit this, it should be done only in an emergency.

Though the MUSKELLUNGE slightly resembles the northern pike, he differs in several respects. When muskellunges were reared in tanks, it was discovered that they would start slashing at one another if left without food for an hour. The muskellunge can be taken very much the same as a northern pike; but he is a fighter, and it is well to have your tackle ready and to be able to head for deep water when he strikes.

LAKE TROUT, the famous *Namaycush* of the North, is much sought after, but he is too oily for a steady diet. The lake trout is widely distributed throughout the Far North and has been found as far south as the Great Lakes. However, he is not as abundant in the northern lakes as commonly believed. Lake trout differ widely according to the color of the water, their location and for other reasons which become technical. Even the size of the lake trout varies according to the water he inhabits. He has been called a "landlocked salmon," but this is a misnomer. Lake trout love the cold deep-water lakes of the North, and are fairly abundant in Lake Superior, where they sometimes attain a size of one hundred pounds. In inland lakes, except in the larger bodies, lake trout usually do not exceed twenty pounds. For the best eating they should be about three to six pounds. (Lampreys now seriously threaten lake trout.)

Right after the spring breakup, lake trout can be taken with a fly or by trolling in shallow water. During the balance of the season they are caught by trolling in deep water. The depth of the water at which to troll is determined by the temperature of the water. In June the trolling depth should be in the neighborhood of thirty feet. Late in July, when the lakes have warmed up, it is well to go down to depths of from fifty to seventy feet. For fishing at this depth a metal trolling line is best.

Still-fishing for lake trout is not practiced very much as a rule, but I have had good results with this method in deep water when other ways have failed. Jigging a spinner with two minnows on the hook seems to bring better results than one minnow for some reason known only to the trout. They are not very active fighters, and are easily landed.

Lake trout spawn in the fall. At this time they are protected, but on expeditions where food is a matter of emergency they can be caught in shallow waters on such reefs as offer spawning ground. When you are trolling, either minnows or the tail and a small part of the body of a larger fish should be hooked onto the spoon. When you are permitted to use a net, a section of gill net will usually bring results if you place it in accordance with the water temperature and the season, as in line-fishing.

The three fish mentioned so far: the walleye, the northern pike, and the lake trout, are the three most commonly encountered in the wilderness lakes and rivers of the North. There are some others, however, which should be considered by the wilderness traveler. The STURGEON is one of these. FAST-WATER TROUT and SALMON are others.

The SUNFISH FAMILY—BASS, SUNFISH, and CRAPPIES—while abundant in southern lakes, are not to be found in the same abundance in northern lakes. Nevertheless, they should be mentioned in any list of food fish. Lakes where vegetation abounds give sanctuary to the sunfish family. The NORTHERN SMALLMOUTHED BASS is taken quite generally in lakes in the southern part of Canada, from Lake of the Woods to the East Coast, and of course south through the United States. The LARGEMOUTHED BASS has been taken in a few lakes near the border, but has its greatest distribution farther south. A sudden drop in temperature below normal can affect the propagation of largemouth bass, and they have little place in the Far North where northern pike, walleyes, arctic charr, and other trout enjoy life. Casting around lily pads, rushes, rocky projections or logs, will usually prove successful. Crappies and sunfish can be taken with flies and a small spinner, but worms for sunfish and minnows for crappies produce surer results.

BULLHEADS, which abound in southern waters, are taken with worms and liver. CATFISH, also a southern rather than a northern fish, are taken with minnows, but bite best on some foul-smelling, rotten concoction mixed with cotton batting. Because bullheads and catfish have no scales, the best way to skin them is to nail them through the head to a tree or wall, cut the skin loose around the head, and pull the skin off with pliers. They can also be filleted.

Occasionally in northern waters you will see a fish which measures six feet in length, and you will wonder if your partner has put a shot of liquor in your tea. This is the STURGEON. The sturgeon reaches two hundred pounds or better. Not often will you catch him on a hook and line, because he is a bottom feeder and lives on snails, crawfish, and insect larvae, algae and other vegetable matter. I mention the sturgeon because he is an important food supply for the Indians of the North; and he will be important to you too, if you are traveling in the interior along the Hudson Bay watershed. He is best caught in a pound net, but you will have to use a gill net because a pound net is too large to carry. A pound net is best described as a fish trap, where the fish are funneled into a compartment in the net from which they cannot escape. The funnels to the compartment are sometimes strung out for a mile.

The sturgeon likes shallow water, and is not too difficult to net. He swims upstream in the spring to spawn, which should be remembered by those who travel in the interior and must rely on every source for food. I do not mean to show disregard for game laws when I mention this: my advice is meant only for those who are thrown on the country for survival, and who must take game and fish as needed by the surest methods.

The sturgeon lends itself well to smoking, and if you catch some big ones I suggest that you hang them on a tripod and let the smoke from a fire surround them from day to day, in the meantime cutting from the surface such sticks of fish as you need. The thought of these amber, almost translucent pieces of fish makes my mouth water as I write. When you are netting sturgeon, keep a close eye on the net. One of the big ones can ruin it.

The fast-water trout and salmon are perhaps the most interesting of all the fish mentioned in this chapter, although they do not supply all-season food as readily as the common lake variety. The lake trout was mentioned earlier because of its general geographical position in northern travel. Here I shall briefly consider others in the salmon and trout family.

BLUEBACK and CHINOOK SALMON go a long way upstream to spawn, while the SILVER, HUMPBACK, and DOG SALMON spawn closer to the salt water in the lower streams and tributaries from Alaska to the Northwest United States coastal states.

Atlantic salmon are found from Labrador to the Northeast coastal states. Where the Pacific salmon die as a result of spawning, the Atlantic salmon survive two or three spawnings. They also ascend streams to spawn.

The LANDLOCKED SALMON, found from Labrador to Maine in lakes where smelts are a source of food, is sometimes confused with lake trout, perhaps because it is also called Sebago trout, lake salmon, and other names with confusing connotations. It ascends streams from the landlocked lakes to spawn.

The CUTTHROAT TROUT is found from Alaska to California in considerable variety, depending on the locality, elevation, and type of water it inhabits. The BROOK TROUT, owing to its wide introduction, has a distribution from the southeastern United States to British Columbia. The DOLLY VARDEN TROUT, also called WESTERN CHARR, has a distribution from Alaska through British Columbia and into Montana. The ARCTIC CHARR, a genus of trout, and the ARCTIC GRAYLING, have a distribution through Canada's northern territories and into Alaska. The AMERICAN GRAYLING is found in western

Montana. Trout have been introduced so widely, both in cold-water lakes and in streams, that endless discussion ensues because there seem to be so many hybrids and variations.

Trout and salmon usually respond to spinners and live bait as well as to flies. There are times, however, when trout will not rise to the fly or be interested in live bait. If hunger dogs your trail, block off a deep part of the stream so that you can drive the trout into a shoal, fenced in with rock. By using a stick and thrashing the water, you should be able to drive them into this trap without too much difficulty. Of course, you will not use this method in a settled area, or under any circumstances where other food is available. This would be a serious violation of the law as well as of the common sense of conservation. On the other hand, the stomach does not respect man's laws. An expedition, to succeed, is on occasion driven to unusual and even illegal measures. For survival such measures are necessary; and if objectors were compelled to suffer continued extreme exposure, and if they were deprived of food for days, but forced to complete a full day of hard travel no matter how they complained, they would soon understand the meaning of grim reality! Without food, human energy drains away so rapidly that the traveler cannot be active enough to keep warm. The equation is unyielding. One is not allowed the nicety of choice.

Before concluding this chapter, I must speak of the WHITEFISH, which swims under many names. True whitefish weigh less than four pounds, and are so uniform in size that all seem to have been cast in the same mold.

In the North the whitefish is dried in great quantities for dog food. It makes me envious to think of so delectable a fish swallowed almost whole by the dogs, without enjoyment of its excellent flavor. As dog food whitefish is sold in a "stick," meaning a number of fish, usually twelve.

The whitefish is not ordinary fare for the casual wilderness traveler because it feeds on planktonic crustacea, and thus is not often caught on hook and line. Here again the wilderness traveler will have to depend on the net for their capture; where weight is of importance, a small section of gill net should be used.

Whitefish spawn rather late in the fall, but usually start moving inshore earlier. This should be remembered by those planning on a supply of whitefish for the winter. Whitefish are wonderful to eat when smoked, and this method of preservation is widely used. For dog food, the fish is dried. Except in the spawning season, the whitefish must be caught at great depths, depending on the size and the temperature of the lake. The depths vary from one hundred to several hundred feet.

I should like to say a few words about fishing through the ice. Walleyes, northern pike, and lake trout can be taken through the ice with hook and line. Northern pike and arctic charr are commonly taken with a spear. Such methods will be quite inadequate to feed your dog team. You will either have to use a net or purchase the fish from the Indians or at a post.

The commercial fishermen of Lake Winnipeg have an ingenious device called a creeper for stringing a net under the ice. It consists of a 10-foot plank which has a ½ inch by 1 foot slot cut in the center on the flat side of the plank. A flat steel bar ¼ inch by 2 inches by 2 feet hangs in this slot, pivoted in such a fashion that 2 inches of the bar are above the plank, while the remainder of the bar hangs below. A steel rod, which runs through the plank edgewise and through the flat side of the bar, allows the bar to pivot. The small part of the bar which is above the plank is ratchet-toothed. The lower end of the bar has a hole drilled into it through which one end of a 100-foot rope is fastened.

To use this creeper device, a hole is cut in the ice with a chisel, and the creeper is then pushed under the ice. The plank, being buoyant, is forced up by the water against the underside of the ice. This brings the ratchet-toothed part of the bar up against the

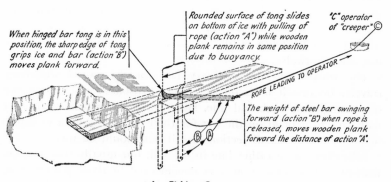

When hinged bar tong is in this position, the sharp edge of tong grips ice and bar (action "B") moves plank forward.

Rounded surface of tong slides on bottom of ice with pulling of rope (action "A") while wooden plank remains in same position due to buoyancy.

"C" operator of "creeper" ©

ROPE LEADING TO OPERATOR

The weight of steel bar swinging forward (action "B") when rope is released, moves wooden plank forward the distance of action "A".

**Ice-Fishing Creeper**

ice, the long end of the bar hanging below the plank in the water. One of two fishermen now pulls on the rope, then releases it. This pull brings the ratchet-toothed bar forward. On the release stroke the weight of the bar returns the bar to its vertical position. On the return stroke, the ratchet-toothed end of the bar bites into the underside of the ice, and this forces the plank forward a few inches. This pulling and releasing operation is then repeated over and over again. In this fashion the plank creeps along the underside of the ice. The sound of the ratchet-toothed bar clawing into the underside of the ice reveals the plank's position. As the second fisherman moves along, head cocked, listening for the sound of the moving plank, he reminds you of a robin on the alert for the sound of a worm. When the plank has crept far enough along for the first section of net to be inserted, a hole is cut in the ice at the position of the plank and the net is drawn down through the hole with the rope used to operate the ratchet bar. The entire process is then repeated until long sections of net have been strung. None of the Winnipeg fishermen seems to know who the brilliant inventor of this device was, except that the idea has been passed down for generations. Until recently, it seems to have been used nowhere but on Lake Winnipeg. (See above illustration.)

The wilderness traveler cannot, of course, carry such equipment as a creeper, and would construct such a device only if he were wintering in a cabin. If dog food must be acquired by fishing with a net in winter, the process will have to be carried on simply by cutting a number of holes in the ice at ten-foot intervals and by threading a net from one to the other with a long pole. Quite often, in the vicinity of fast-moving water, openings can be found for placing a net in winter.

In the Far North the ice is so thick that an ordinary short-handled ice chisel would not reach through the ice. The Hudson's Bay Company make an ice-chisel head with a large ferrule for receiving a long pole. The butt end of the pole is then placed in the ferrule so that the weight is at the chisel, the slender part of the pole being held by the hands. Another pole, to which a common minnow scoop is nailed, is used to scoop up the chipped ice.

The effect of weather upon fishing is always good for a lively discussion by a quorum of anglers. All kinds of weather have their advocates, but perhaps the liveliest discussion of all concerns whether varying air pressures as shown by a barometer can indicate good or bad fishing conditions. Many competent fishermen accept the possibility; others reject it. One prominent fishing camp in the Minnesota-Ontario region kept a three-year record of its catches under varying barometer readings and weather conditions. It was the opinion of this camp after the three-year average that the barometer was not a significant factor in the catching of fish. Though this record is extremely valuable, it is perhaps not comprehensive enough to give a scientifically sound conclusion; the application of the theory will have to be made over a far greater geographical area and over a much longer period of time to be conclusive.

While fish apparently are not concerned with barometric pressures, the effects of various kinds of weather on fishing is bound to be wide in scope. Walleyes seem to bite better in a lake when the water is rough. Water temperatures change the depths at which fish range, which naturally affects catches. These and many other conditions suggest the effects of weather on fishing.

In this chapter sea fishing has been omitted. However, if your expedition calls for coastal living and travel, you should investigate the problems and opportunities for your particular area if you wish to ensure an adequate food supply.

# 15

✳
✳ ✳
✳ ✳ ✳
✳ ✳ ✳ ✳

## *Hunting for Food*

WHEN I FIRST TRAVELED IN WILDERNESS AREAS, I CARRIED A .30/30
carbine, a single-shot .22 pistol, and on certain trips where geese
and ducks dominated the game choice, a 12-gauge shotgun. In course
of time I carried everything from a 6mm. Mannlicher to a .375
H.&H. Magnum.

Guns and ballistics have fascinated me since boyhood, and I hope
this elemental pleasure will endure, for it has offered me a great
deal of pleasure as well as kinship with others that only ballistics
and cozy campfires could possibly create. Such cartridges as the .270
Winchester, .300 H.&H. Magnum, .30/06, and even some of the
big-bore British favorites are as interesting to me as though magic
were contained in these combinations of figures.

I have shot the .270 and H.&H. Magnum loads on long-range
shots with a measure of success; but when I think of the great
majority of shots that were of short range, these so predominate
in the over-all picture that long range seems largely an armchair
novelty in ballistics discussion, and least important in current
hunting. Where the average shots were near, kills with the .270,
the H.&H. Magnum loads, and the .30/06 have so mutilated the
animals that I am convinced beyond a doubt that these cartridges
under these conditions overgun the hunter.

What has been the result? I have reached up to the gun rack
and taken down the .30/30 carbine by some process of natural
selection, not condoned perhaps by many experts but easily explained by those who spend long periods in the wilderness areas.
The .30/30 Winchester carbine is light, short, easily worked through

dense forest areas and, when carried over arduous trails, lends itself well to canoe, pack-horse, and dog-team travel. Also it is vested with the crowning glory—the open hammer and the lever action, which symbolize the outdoors as do the pattern of a snowshoe or a canoe.

The cardinal question is, "What about the killing power?" It has always seemed strange to me that during my earlier days in the wilderness, when the .30/30 had a striking energy of about 1,400 to 1,500 foot-pounds, we killed moose with it and did not question the certainty of the kill. Now that the factory cartridge is up to 1,800 or 1,900 foot-pounds of striking energy, it suddenly is labeled by certain ballistics experts as a varmint gun. Frankly, I do not shoot the factory cartridge on game bigger than deer, even though this cartridge has been very satisfactory; instead I have my cartridges loaded by a firm which gives me a cartridge driving a 180-grain bullet 2,300 feet per second. I understand they use Du Pont's 3031 powder in these reloads, which seems to be ideal for the job. If according to your opinion we have now moved out of the .30/30 class, you take it from there. Whatever you care to call these reloads, I still find the regular factory loads on deer and black bear better than the custom-loads. Completely shattered hams on uncertain running shots and other low salvage of meat animals is not conducive to hunting for food. Though I like guns, there does not exist in my nature a lust for killing. Perhaps it is this lack which makes it possible for me to place shots, free of the excessive emotional strain that most hunters experience with fairly simple animal targets. My wilderness trips have often been long, and living off the country has been routine. In a well-populated game area it has been good practice with me to simulate rifle shots by pressing the trigger on a down hammer or a "dead" cartridge to improve my aim. At one time I also carried a camera on a gunstock for this purpose, with a reticle over the film magazine simulating the running shots by a gun-trigger exposure of the film. This showed on the film where a bullet in using a gun might score a hit or a miss, the running animal being caught on the film in the reticle pattern.

I experienced no jumpy emotion while following these make-believe shots, and when the time came for an actual shot I felt no more than regret for having to make the kill. The careful and calm placing of .30/30 shots can give a better yield than is possible with a .300 H.&H. Magnum and scope in the hands of the occasional hunter whose heart is pounding with excitement and who hopes to maintain his high average with excessive loads.

As to small game, the combination over-and-under 410-.22 has been ample for me. The latest choice by the army in their survival-study methods has been to adopt the 410 M-6 Survival Rifle Shotgun. While it has limitations in wing shooting, it does not, as a rule, fail to provide small game; and the .22 Hornet, which forms the other half of the gun, is no idler if shots on big game become necessary and if the shots are well placed.

If you hunt specimens for a museum and if the expedition takes you primarily into mountainous country, you will very likely choose the .300 or .375 H.&H. Magnum, the .270, or possibly the highly accredited .30/06. If your travels demand extensive distances afoot, by canoe, dog team, or pack horse, the chances are that you will begin to lose interest in all but a short, light, highly adaptable carbine with which you will enjoy a new measure of success, the secret lying in the words "utility" and "mobility." I shifted to the .30/30 Winchester carbine about the same time that I gave up 95-pound canvas canoes in favor of aluminum canoes of equal size weighing 60 pounds. Accommodation is the word that should guide every choice of equipment for the wilderness, and unless that accommodation gives unrestricted movement the formula for living and traveling in the wilderness is a bad one. This is just as true with firearms as with canoes.

Much has been written about the shocking power of various bullets, and there is a great deal, no doubt, to be said about fast bullets of light weight. However, if you will observe ballistics charts, you will notice that while light, fast bullets maintain a flatter trajectory, they do not keep up the same sustained striking energy in foot-pounds as the heavy bullets do at long range. After all, it is the blow struck that counts. To depend on light bullets to maintain shocking power at great ranges is to defy physical law. After light, fast bullets lose their initial speed, they simply become expanding bullets of the slower type, and the shock principle is gone. Trajectory, moreover, is not a great factor, since sighting can compensate for it.

For example, the .300 H.&H. Magnum with a fast 180-grain bullet and flat trajectory leaves the muzzle at 3,060 feet per second, while the slower 220-grain bullet in the .300 H.&H. Magnum leaves the muzzle at only 2,730 feet per second. You would expect the lighter bullet driven at greater speed to hold up the striking energy at 300 yards better than the slower bullet. Now, at 300 yards the faster bullet has by comparison lost more striking energy than the slower bullet. As the yardage increases, the faster bullet loses striking energy rapidly, as compared to the slower, heavier bullet, so that at the far ranges the bullet which should be recorded as the long-range type is by comparison the shortest-range killing bullet.

It has been my experience, therefore, that the heaviest bullet your particular gun is chambered for is the best bullet to use for all ranges, despite its slower speed. In brush, heavier bullets stand up better, and at long ranges the longer bullet very likely will "keyhole" (upset) and kill better where mushrooming is at a minimum.

Game distribution covers too wide a range for this chapter, but I shall touch on a few of the small and the large game animals which the wilderness traveler is likely to find. The list is about as follows: bear, deer, moose, and caribou for the lake and timber region; mountain sheep, goat, elk, and antelope for the mountain and prairie region. The sea will offer others, such as seal and walrus. Duck, goose, ptarmigan, partridge, prairie chicken, pheasant, and rabbit will form the simplest list of small game. There are times when an emergency will call for the shooting of such animals as muskrat or beaver, but they should be listed apart from the general run of small game for food.

Because bear are found quite generally from the polar regions to the tropics, they have an important place in the food list. Bear meat has an advantage in that the taking of bear is usually not covered very strictly by conservation measures and laws, although perhaps it should be. A bear's diet is extremely varied. Berries of every kind, wild turnips, grasses, large animals, rodents, fish, ants, and carrion are only a small part of his seasonal fare. He is always hungry and never seems to get his fill. He is constantly on the prowl for food. During the blueberry season he moves into the most prolific patches and gorges himself on berries as long as they last. If the berry season has been good, and if he has fared well generally, he is usually quite fat by late fall. Then he starts looking for a place to hibernate. He is very timid in wild areas where there are no lumber-camp garbage dumps to enable him to become familiar with man. When he spots you he will be on his way in a hurry. When shot at and hit he sets up a howling cry very much like that of a man in agony. When he is skinned, he looks like a man. This may temper your appetite, but skip a few meals and your problem will be solved.

Very likely both the white-tailed and the mule deer will be a common item in your wilderness diet. They like to come out into open places, such as the fringe of a swamp, a burning, or other opening, early in the morning and at dusk. Their trails are usually well beaten, and a simple blind, with the wind in your favor, will often bring results.

Moose like marshy regions, although they spend much time in the uplands. In the summertime they put up a losing fight against the flies and mosquitoes which keep the moose in the water, usually where lily pads offer choice roots. Calling moose during the mating season, with a small trumpet made of birchbark, is a fairly certain method of getting food in a good moose country. He never fails to impress you as a spectacle as he heaves into sight from the nearby cover of the forest. His hearing is exceptionally keen; in fact, so keen that he will discern your call a long way off and be some time in reaching you. There is a liberal showing of brown on his head and legs, and some white on his belly, but these markings will be overshadowed by his imposing black bulk when you get your first glimpse of him. You are likely to see him standing half submerged in the water, feeding; or, since he is a very powerful swimmer, you may sight him swimming from one land mass to another. In winter, when the snow is deep, he yards up with more of his kind. He will, however, range through heavy snows to feed. It is quite a sight to see him craning his neck in an effort to reach his favorite food, the browse of the striped maple, and even more interesting to watch him straddle the smaller saplings to force them down within his reach. He is not built for grazing, but he will get down on his knees if certain grasses of his choice attract him.

In the far reaches of the North, perhaps the standard food item for the wilderness traveler is the caribou. Of the woodland caribou and the barren-ground caribou, the woodland animal is the larger, and inhabits the area as far north as trees grow. The barren-ground caribou inhabits treeless barren ground, although the term "barren" is certainly a misnomer. The moss which supplies him with a large part of his diet is a rich harvest of vegetation. The term "barren," of course, suggests the absence of trees.

An interesting feature of the caribou's body is his feet. His hoofs spread out on soft ground and snow, almost simulating a snowshoe, to keep him from sinking. In winter the "frog," or pad, on the hoof seems to shrink away, allowing the horny rims to keep him from slipping on ice. But it may also be that the horny rim has been worn off on the rocks and that the snow-covered ground permits the horny rim to grow back. He is also a natural swimmer. His broad feet move him along as forcefully as the stroke of a canoe paddle.

When the migration of the caribou takes place, in winter to the south, in spring to the north, he is easily shot. At other times the scattered small herds and lone animals will be harder to find and to stalk. Wolves and the botfly are his chief enemies. The young of the botfly develop under his hide, which must seem a diabolical manifestation of nature to the persecuted animal. August, when the coarse hairs of the caribou are shed, is the best time to kill him for clothing, the fur then being soft and adaptable to sleeping bags, parkas, and so on.

In winter the elk moves to the valleys where the snow generally does not lie so deep and where he can paw down to the grass for food. As the snow melts he gradually ascends to the higher levels. Caribou females have antlers; but only the male elk is so endowed. The elk is both a browser and a grazer. For some strange reason he does not always seek out the tender grasses and browse common to other members of the deer family, but is content to feed on coarse, weedy growths and heavier browse.

For many years I traveled with a packsack through the Canadian wilderness, carrying only such items of store food as would relieve a constant diet of meat. Because at that time in the forest belt there was abundance of partridge and rabbit, the risk of going hungry was not great. It was scarcely necessary to shoot big game for food. No type of travel seemed more independent, and none was so convenient and so sparing of wildlife. The chief trouble with a diet of rabbit and partridge is the shortage of fat. This item either has to be carried or a larger animal must be killed to supply it. A lean meat diet is one of slow starvation no matter how much you eat. And, ironically, eating only the choice parts of the animal also means starvation, in the form of diet deficiency. Nevertheless, living on a meat diet is satisfactory from a balanced-diet standpoint if all the edible parts of the animal are consumed. Some of the early explorers met a lingering death because they took the "best" parts of the animal and allowed only the "cheaper cuts" for the help. The more democratic and level-headed explorers who lived on a plane with their fellows generally managed to survive, and also learned the lesson of diet, which fortunately has been passed down to us. The results of a diet of the "best cuts" were diarrhea and increasing weakness complicated by extreme cold and fatigue, which eventually proved fatal.

Where it becomes necessary to live on partridge, rabbits, and other such animals, it is well to carry fat to supplement the lean diet. I carry mine in the form of butter because of its wide adaptability in cooking; but during warm weather oleo keeps better, and serves the same basic purpose. Almost any edible fat will supply the same lean-meat complement.

Perhaps one of the most interesting and noteworthy examples to illustrate the need for a fat complement on a rabbit diet occurred many years ago when during one winter the caribou deserted a region in the north central part of Canada. The Royal Canadian Mounted Police gave aid to a number of trappers who had lived on rabbits and who were in a state of malnutrition. One trapper who was called "Old Doughnuts" fared very well on rabbits, and no one could understand his apparent advantage over others. The secret, of course, lay in the doughnut. He always began his winter in earnest with a full day of doughnut making, storing immense quantities for the winter in his cache twenty feet above the ground. The combination of greasy doughnuts and lean rabbit meat allowed him to survive.

# 16

## Survival

POSSIBLY THE STRANGEST ASPECT OF SURVIVAL TRAINING OR INSTRUCTION is that the average individual feels, "It can't possibly happen to me." The various classes planned in large cities for survival in the event of enemy attack, hurricane, flood, fire, or earthquake have had only feeble attendance. The long history of storms catching sportsmen in the field, of trains or cars being stalled in snow-driven mountain passes, of planes grounded in the wilderness, is for the most part a sad commentary on the ability of the victims to sustain themselves.

Isolated cases of outstanding ability in survival must, of course, be noted, and these have developed and suggested ideas which are being thoroughly tested, especially by the military forces. Yet, even in military circles, one of the real problems is to create enthusiasm for this type of training. "It can't happen to me" is hard to translate into "It can happen to me." If all of us were forced into a predicament in which we had to face stark danger for a few minutes, and realize that "It is at this moment happening to me," we would be much more interested in survival training.

A few years ago several members of a Backs River biological expedition, for which I had planned a portion of the food budget and camping equipment, were in a Norseman plane heading home for Churchill. The expedition had been fairly successful, and arctic travel seemed relatively simple when well planned. Soon the returning party would be reaching Chesterfield Inlet; then Churchill and some easier living would be in store. Suddenly there was an oil splash on the windshield, and visibility became almost zero. The nearest surface of water was eagerly sought for a landing. Though the landing was in the water, on Kaminuriak Lake, reefs made short work of the plane. Doors were ripped from the plane by the survivors for a raft, and by using air mattresses all were able to reach shore.

Now, the Norseman plane is a good rugged unit in the rough travel of the North, and gives a feeling of security as great as a good modern car. For those in the accident, at one moment all the elements of modern living and mobility were at hand; but in less than a minute they were floundering on a reef in a state of desperation. I have gone into detail to bring out the sometimes forgotten fact that no matter where you are—in city or wilderness or quiet country suburb—you can at one moment be a well-dressed, well-fed individual with a promising future, and at the next, be fighting for your life. On Kaminuriak Lake the survivors by their skills managed to survive but to this day they will tell you that the terrifying transition from safety and comfort to hazard and suffering is not a special event that only happens to the other fellow.

The first idea to get rid of is that you are a comfort-loving animal, who must be rested, fed, nursed, and transported by all the means of modern invention. Sixty-five per cent of our people are overfed and overweight. Survival in its most serious application simply means saving enough of yourself as a functional being for rehabilitation once the means of rehabilitation are again at hand. Remember this: if you are the average well-fed or overfed individual that society accepts as normal, you already have enough food stored in your body to exist a surprisingly long time without eating. You can go a much longer time without food than you can without water. In short, you carry a food supply in your own body that will sustain you long enough, perhaps, to get you out of your predicament.

For this very reason you must be careful to go about the process of elimination just as though you were consuming a quantity of food every day. You will aid this elimination through the regular consumption of water, if it is available, which will in turn carry off the poisons that would otherwise accumulate in your body and bring about a breakdown. If you are stranded where ample fresh water is available, you have thus three factors working for your survival: a natural food supply in your body, water for elimination, and an element which is constantly building the system—oxygen.

With these three, your body for a while will not undergo severe punishment. The fact is that if you are the average individual you may even be improving your health for the first part of your survival period.

There are two other factors essential to success: the need to keep from panic and the will to live. There is no pat formula to prevent panic except to attempt a process of reasoning on the known premise that panic will seriously affect your chances for survival. Accept the fact that you will be afraid: fear is the natural reaction to any human predicament. Knowing this fact alone can help you retain your sense of mental balance.

Besides fear, you will experience another emotion: the feeling of loneliness and complete or partial frustration—the idea that you are in a situation where you are helpless. Unless you are seriously injured, you are not helpless; and you can and must do something about your plight. Fear, a hollow feeling of frustration, perhaps a weak feeling in your muscles—all three will grip you. Remember that they would grip anyone, especially a person without a full understanding or experience of what to do.

Don't for a single moment give up. If you do, it may lead to an emotional breakdown that will sap your reserve energy and may deepen into a lack of will to live. This feeling of hopelessness has brought more fatalities perhaps than any other cause, even the lack of food and water. The will to live is a powerful force in survival as well as in serious illness.

Most of us are familiar through newspaper accounts with the girl who was pinned under an automobile for nine days when it became wrecked in a California canyon. During that time she had neither food nor water. The accident would have no significance beyond the heroic qualities of the girl, were it not for the scientific light it shed on survival methods. Her suffering and imprisonment kept her in a state of immobility and part-time unconsciousness: this is the fact behind her survival. Had she been thrown from the car and injured, but still able to move about without food and water, she would probably have died. Movement would have reduced the moisture content in her body, and the food reserve stored in her tissues would have been used up. The girl also had an eager desire to live.

If you have ever had a feeling of claustrophobia (the dread of being shut in), you will now have the opposite feeling, agoraphobia (fear of crossing vast spaces, or of not having the protection of a shelter). Stranded without a tent, rain gear, or paraphernalia to ward off the elements, you will be confronted with the fear that you will die of exposure. This thought weighs heavily upon you in subzero regions. The fear that you may freeze to death if you fall asleep brings panic. You dare not go to sleep for fear that you will not wake up.

Actually, most of your danger is not in freezing to death but in your state of mind, and in the attrition that fear and lack of composure bring on. In short, you wear yourself out trying needlessly to stay awake. What actually happens when you fall asleep in subzero temperature is that you are soon awakened by the discomfort of cold. A few moments of activity to restore circulation allows you to sleep again. It is possible for you to die in falling asleep, but only if you fight sleep until utter exhaustion takes place and your body suffers a low functional depression. By trying to stay awake you simply augment the freezing process.

The basic concept that you are an animal, and not the well-fed product of a conventional world, should bear upon your whole plan of thought. Somewhere near you is an animal of some sort, perhaps a wolf, a mouse, a rabbit, depending upon where you are. At night that creature will travel or sleep, depending upon its nature. It is warm-blooded, like yourself. It will be exposed to drenching rains, storms, and cold. Yet it will remain healthy. Of course, its metabolism will depend upon its ability to hunt food. But there are famines among animals too, when lack of food causes them to become weak, lowering their resistance. Yet, almost always, they survive these periods of starvation, and reproduce their kind.

To compare yourself with such an animal may seem far-fetched. But, essentially, they are much the same as you are in bodily functions. You can lie outdoors in the driving rain and both you and the animal will suffer. But you will also survive, and that is what we are concerned about here.

Now we come to another stage in the survival equation. You must try to estimate the length of your working or traveling day, based on the physical resource you have left. This day will become shorter as the number of days increases. There will come a time, perhaps, when one hour per day, or less, will be the full measure of your physical effort. This, of course, is based on the assumption that you have no food.

If you have kept your mental stability, and traveled or worked on your survival program with a wise conservation of energy, the gradual shortening of each day to work or travel will have been prolonged much more than if you had panicked and tried to bolt your way out. This reserve may be just the slim margin you need to reach safety. Wisdom consists in a calm mind, rest, sleep, and resourcefulness.

We have tried to show that without food and shelter, but with water, much rest and sleep, the "human animal" is capable of existing for a long time. You now arrive at the point where, with only the reserve that you have in your body, with no shelter, but with water and some kind of food, your potential for survival has greatly increased.

If you are in a wooded area, your chances for water, food, and shelter are so great that if you keep your wits about you, survival is certain. It is almost impossible to remain in a wooded area long without seeing some form of living creature, small though it may be, which is edible and nourishing. Almost any warm-blooded animal is edible. So are snakes, turtles, lizards, and similar creatures. Mice, grasshoppers, ants, birds' eggs, frogs, and toads—depending on where you are—all come under the heading of food. If you are fortunate enough to have a gun with you, the list widens immeasurably.

Fish will be an important part of the diet if you can improvise a means to catch them. Nevertheless, many parties have found that, even with good tackle, it is sometimes difficult to catch enough fish to avoid starvation. I have already mentioned elsewhere the catching of minnows for food. This has always remained with me as one of the surest methods of getting food, and one that I think does not get sufficient consideration in survival literature. The use of a minnow net, mosquito netting from the tent, or even a shirt used as a net will provide food when all else fails. You can wade along most shores and scoop up a few pounds of minnows that can be fried or boiled into a very nourishing food ration. Such minnows are eaten in their entirety, head, intestines, and all; they are palatable, and there is no danger from eating both head and bones. In fact, minnows are a balanced emergency diet which needs more investigation. Analysis has shown that minnows eaten whole have a far greater balance of nutriments than dressed fish.

Along most shores a light shining into the water from a fire-brand, a torch, or flashlight will reveal crayfish and other edible water creatures. These are readily caught with the hand or with any simply contrived dip net made with a crotched stick and a bandanna handkerchief or a shirt.

The idea that an animal must have cloven feet to be edible is, of course, sheer superstitious nonsense. If you were traveling by dog team, and if you were starving, you would kill one dog at a time for food to survive. You might encounter other circumstances where game was scarce and where your choice narrowed itself down to such animals as muskrat, beaver, porcupine—whatever the country afforded. The porcupine can be killed with a stick. Actually, these animals are just as nourishing as any others, with some difference of opinion as to taste. But, since you will be converted to a raw-meat-eating savage after missing about twenty meals (and this on authority, no matter how nice and fastidious your appetite) don't worry about being able to eat such second-choice items. Your once jaded appetite will now not only tolerate but relish them.

In the North Country you will see growing on rocks a lichen of a dark, flat, scaly type, sometimes called "rock tripe," which when broken will show an interior white substance. This contains about 40 per cent starchy food and will, after a fashion, sustain life. This lichen must be boiled, dried, and powdered, and then boiled again to be edible. Or you can collect pieces of this rock tripe, build a fire, and so arrange the pieces near the heat that they will bake thoroughly. Err on the side of too much rather than of too little baking.

The root of the water lily can be cooked to supply nourishment, and so can the roots of many other plants. The safe plan is to cook a small part of any root, eat a very small portion, wait a couple of hours to note the effect, and then proceed cautiously until you find you can assimilate it without ill effect.

There is a great deal of concern about eating mushrooms and about the need to tell the edible kind from the poisonous varieties. You may well dispense with this item entirely as a possible source of food, because mushrooms are low in nearly all food values. Mushrooms contain no fat, no protein, and no carbohydrates. And the small amount of minerals and vitamins they have does not make them worth the bother.

Berries and nuts, of course, are edible. Among the common and generally familiar variety of wild berries are: blueberries, raspberries, cranberries, pincherries, and so on. In the North, only the baneberry is non-edible. The most common nuts are: acorns, hazelnuts, and pine nuts. The pine nut is a source of food often overlooked. Pine cones, broken open, will reveal these edible portions, which are very sustaining. Acorns should be ground with rocks to a flour if they are of the bitter kind; then water should be leached through the flour for several hours. Boil the flour into a mush; dry portions of it in the sun; and eat the hard bars as you travel.

In the North the aspen (popple) grows almost everywhere. The inner bark of this tree and the buds can be chewed, and considerable nourishment derived from them. However, the bark is best when cooked: better yet, for easier assimilation it should be cooked to a soft, gelatinous consistency.

Several roots in the arctic are edible, including the sweet vetch, or licorice root. The cooked root tastes like carrot and is very nourishing. Other roots are the woolly lousewort and the bistort, or snakewood. Because these plants resemble others, and because you may have need for them in an emergency at times other than at the flowering season when they may more easily be identified, they should be carefully studied on the ground, identified by natives in advance, or carefully observed in colored illustrations and in a botanical text.

The subject of animal snares, figure-four traps, deadfall and pit traps has been covered at such length in many volumes on trapping that I suggest that you refer to one of these volumes for a more comprehensive treatment than I could give in this chapter. Examine the cable snares for large animals as well as the rabbit wire snares. In such books look also for snares of natural fiber.

Consult trustworthy books dealing with the making of fire by friction, by flint and steel, by using a magnifying lens as a burning glass, by firing a shell from which the bullet has been removed, and for other emergency means of making fire. These should be an integral part of the survival program.

Smoke makes a good signal, and you should have this signal going at all times, if possible, so that a search party from the air can find your position. You can best decide, under your own circumstances, whether to remain where you are, and conserve your energy until a search party rescues you, or whether you should attempt to travel. If you are without food, cut down the amount of travel every succeeding day on the basis that best seems to sustain your energy.

Aspects of camping technique have been covered in the preceding chapters, from which survival material can be gleaned. Do not try to build the many lean-to shelters and other items mentioned in general survival if you are without food. To do so will use up your energy for travel. Huddle in the protection of whatever you can find during rain, or cut a large sheet of bark and suspend it or hold it over you.

If you have food, erect a shelter and live in keeping with your skill in woodcraft and equipment. Sheets of bark shingled on a sloping roof of poles will offer good shelter from the rain. Keep the shelter small, just large enough for protection. Start at the lower part of your roof poles and lap them uphill. If you are in a birch-bark area, cut these sheets as large as possible, but small enough to carry. Then, when breaking camp, stack one inside the other and carry them to the next camp as you would your tent. The labor of finding and cutting new sheets will under most circumstances be much greater than that of carrying your first supply. Other barks besides birch can be used, but such bark as aspen, while it affords good shelter, is too heavy to carry from one camp site to another.

One of the difficulties in traveling in some areas will be the crossing of rivers and lakes. The methodical construction of a raft without tools is not possible. (See Chapter 2, "Carrying the Pack Afoot.") It is unwise to attempt swimming such water obstacles, even if you have not been weakened by travel, unless they are very narrow. The solution is to move any fallen wood that will float, to the water's edge, tie the sections together as best you can with your clothes, then work yourself across with a long pole, riding as best you can by straddling the makeshift raft. You will, no doubt, ride partly submerged, but this contrivance is better than the risk of trying to swim.

For information regarding your direction of travel, see the chapter "Where Am I?"

If you have gone for some time without food, and then come into possession of some, or reach a settlement where there is food, eat very sparingly at first, and drink plenty of hot liquids, or you will find that food can be more punishing than starvation. Your stomach will not adjust to normal rations at once. Increase the amount as your body is able to assimilate it with comfort.

Thus, in learning to survive, you will learn how to live in austerity, a sound philosophy in camping or in living generally, where the effect of luxury too often is enervating. The success of camping and living is significantly summed up in the French phrase *Savoir faire—savoir vivre:* How to do—how to live.

# Index